TERRA ANTARCTICA

TERRA ANTARCTICA

Looking into the Emptiest Continent

WILLIAM L. FOX

SHOEMAKER & HOARD

Copyright © 2005 by William L. Fox

First Shoemaker & Hoard edition 2007

Library of Congress Cataloging in Publication Data
Fox, William L., 1949–
   Terra Antarctica : looking into the emptiest continent / William L. Fox.
     p. cm.
   Originally published: San Antonio, Tex. : Trinity University Press, 2005.

   Includes bibliographical references and index.

   ISBN-13 978-1-59376-148-6 (ALK. PAPER)
   ISBN-10 1-59376-148-1 (ALK. PAPER)
   1. Antarctica. I. Title.
   G860.F69   2007
   919.8'9—dc22   2007009574

Printed in the United States of America
Cover design by Gerilyn Attebery
Interior design by BookMatters, Berkeley, CA

Shoemaker Hoard
www.shoemakerhoard.com

9 8 7 6 5 4 3 2 1

for ice people

CONTENTS

Color plates follow page 128

ACKNOWLEDGMENTS

To thank those who made possible what resides between the covers of a book is to acknowledge that there is much that would not fit. To everyone who spent hours in patient conversation with me about the Antarctic, please know that even if your words do not appear here, they shaped the ones that are included.

The National Science Foundation (NSF) Antarctic Visiting Artists and Writers Program has long been administered by Guy Guthridge. The fact that the United States sees the continent as encompassed by both the sciences and the humanities is due in large part to his efforts. Thanks are also due to Robert Wharton, David Frisic, and Angel Gonzalez, the manager of the U.S. Antarctic Resource Center, which is run in conjunction with the United States Geological Survey.

Several organizations provided support during my research and writing. Charles Salas and Tom Crow at the Getty Research Institute invited me to participate as a visiting scholar in their "Frames of Viewing" project on art and cognition. Fellow scholars Charles Harrison, Larry Kruger, Jerry Moore, Dennis Sepper, and Terry Smith made helpful comments on the manuscript, and Sarah Warren gathered images. My gratitude to Sabine Schlosser, in whose regal hands everything from maps to expedition gear flowed from one life to another, is endless.

A 2002–2003 fellowship from the John Simon Guggenheim Memorial Foundation facilitated my finishing the first draft, as did an invitation from the Lannan Foundation to spend two months as a writer in residence at their facility in Marfa, Texas. The University of Nevada, Reno, provided a residency as a visiting scholar in the fall of 2003, during which I revised the manuscript. Bob Blesse, Mike Branch, Michael Cohen, Cheryll Glotfelty, Scott Slovic, and the Hilliard Fund were responsible for such a generous gift of time.

The UCLA Research Library, which holds the Mary Joe Goodwin Antarctic Collection within its Special Collections, was an invaluable resource. Goodwin (1920–1993) was an illustrator and writer who visited the Antarctic three times and gathered an extensive collection of Antarctic materials covering the period 1908–1991. My thanks to Paul Naiditch and Daniel Slive, who guided me to their copy of *Aurora Australis* and other primary materials. Raimond Goerler and Laura Kissel of the Ohio State University Archives and Lynn Lay, the librarian at the Byrd Polar Research Center, kindly walked me through their collections, in particular the papers and artworks of the painter David Paige. Jean and Jerry Parmer, of Parmer Books in San Diego, helped me assemble my personal research library, and one morning in early 1999 put into my hands for examination an exquisite watercolor by Edward Wilson.

Natalie Cadenhead at Antarctica New Zealand and Ruth Delaney at Creative New Zealand put me in touch with artists and writers from that country who have been to the ice. Felicity Milburn, curator of contemporary art at the Robert MacDougall Art Gallery in Christchurch, helped me establish context for the work of artists from that country.

Robert Stephenson, who maintains the online Antarctic Circle and Low Latitude Gazetteer, helped with research before the trip and now hosts my image chronology on his web site (www.antarctic-circle .org/fox.htm). My oldest New Zealand friend, Don Long, helped me get in touch with Creative New Zealand, and then patiently researched the voyages of Ui-te-Rangiora and Aru-Tanga-Nuku.

Matthew Coolidge, the director of the Center for Land Use Interpretation in Los Angeles sent a camera with me to the ice, and hosted an exhibition afterward about McMurdo, *Antarctic 1*. Also in Los Angeles, Mrs. Lucille Paige and David Paige, respectively the wife and son of the artist David Paige, graciously consented to an interview.

While I was in the Antarctic I was helped by many friends at home. David Abel, my closest literary colleague, administered my domestic affairs. Paul and Mary Jan Bancroft, Enrico Martignoni, Ric Hardman and Mickey Gustin, Verne and Carol Stanford, and Robert Beckmann were patrons. On the ice, numerous fellow grantees and representatives from both the NSF and Raytheon spent innumerable hours answering my questions, among them: Deborah Baldwin, Brennan Brunner, Ted Dettmar, Katy Jenson, Robbie Liben, Paul Mayewski, Mark Melcon, Ty Milford, Jeff Roberts, Stacey Rolland, Robbie Score, Jim Scott, Rae Spain, Bill Sutton, and John Wright. Jason Anthony shared with me his astonishing manuscript for *Albedo*, a book that juxtaposes his experiences on the ice with the literature of "white," then gave my own work a careful and much-appreciated reading. Former grantees Jennifer Dewey, Jody Forster, William Nisbet, Kim Stanley Robinson, David Rosenthal, and William Stout provided good advice in interviews. Several people who worked for Raytheon Polar Services, the contractor to the NSF that runs logistics for the United States Antarctic Program, deserve special thanks: Rhonda Rodriguez and Teri Fox at "Helo Ops" got me everywhere I needed to go; Kelly Brunt, the incomparable cartographer at McMurdo, fielded questions about polar geography and printed out maps on request; and Karen Joyce carved out an office space for me with the best view on the continent, kept my computer happy, and made sure I saw every piece of art at McMurdo.

It is my great fortune to have worked on this book with Barbara Ras, the director of Trinity University Press, as well as with the copyeditor Anne Canright. They brought an unruly mixture of musings about cognition, cartography, and the concurrent histories of science and art under some measure of control. At the same time, my agent,

Victoria Shoemaker, made sure that the business side received the same thoughtful attention.

Finally, my profound thanks go to Sarah Krall, who made possible an extraordinary week on Mt. Erebus, and to Melissa Iszard, senior assistant supervisor of Crary Laboratory at McMurdo, for putting my nose to the ground and showing me how life wants to live, even on the ice.

PREFACE

How the human mind transforms space into place, or land into landscape, is the line of inquiry that I have been following through several books. The process is most easily traced when watching the mind at work in large, unfamiliar, and relatively empty environments, where we often have difficulty understanding our personal scale in space and time, versus the temperate forests and savanna where we primarily evolved as a species, or in cities that we have constructed to fit our needs. Deserts are among the emptiest spaces on land encountered by humans, and the Antarctic is the largest and most extreme desert on Earth.

The trail of evidence I follow includes maps and paintings, collections of rocks and plants, the design of buildings, and works of fiction and poetry—artistic, cartographic, scientific, and utilitarian responses to these environments. Not only is the Antarctic a vast place where we become easily lost, but its cultural history, especially in comparison with other deserts, is very compact. Tracing the development of its images provides a rich yet comprehensible line of sight.

The first known artist to explore below the Antarctic Circle was William Hodges, who sailed with Captain James Cook during his legendary second exploration of the Pacific from 1772 to 1775. He has been followed by more than two hundred painters, photographers, sculptors, composers, poets, and novelists. Virtually all of the professional artists who have worked on the Antarctic continent have accompanied science expeditions sponsored by government agencies, most notably the United States Antarctic Program, which has been sending artists and writers to the ice since the 1960s. This book is, in part, a story about those artists, their journeys, and the works they have produced.

But this is also a book about that larger topic: how we use cultural means to augment our neurobiology in order to overcome the perceptual difficulties we experience when exploring large spaces. As such, it is a transdisciplinary look at the evolution of our vision and at the entwined histories of exploration, art, cartography, and science as they coincide in the Antarctic, a geographical supposition so remote that it was not even defined until Cook circumnavigated it. The continent itself was not confirmed until 1820, when Thaddeus von Bellingshausen and others first sighted it. Our understanding of it therefore coincides with the development of modern science and art. Because it has been for the most part kept free of commercial and military exploitation, it presents us with as clear a field of historical vision as its arid physical environment provides a literal view.

Why should we be interested in cognition and extreme landscapes? At the beginning of the twenty-first century, approximately one-fifth of the world's population lives in the deserts of the world or is dependent on their resources in some way, a figure that may rise to as high as fifty percent within decades. Partly this is because we are so numerous we have occupied all the more easily inhabited places and much of our population growth will be forced to settle in arid lands. It is also partly because we now have the technology to find and transport deep fossil water onto the deserts and to distribute petroleum-based fertilizer. We can now grow food in all but the most arid regions.

This situation results from our believing that once we have explored and mapped and visualized a space, thus turning it into a place, we now know and own it—that we can transform terrain into territory and then do with it as we please to fit our needs. Such representations and our consequent beliefs, which are rooted in the evolution and diaspora of our species, have less than desirable consequences, such as eventually causing the deserts themselves to grow as we deplete surface and ground waters, which in turn squeezes us into an increasingly tighter ecological corner of the planet.

The Antarctic is a relatively decipherable slate on which to examine these issues, issues that are presented in the vocabularies of both art and science, twin modes of intellectual inquiry possessed by humans. Some people consider the goals of art and science to be so allied that the methods of art and science ought to be described as two alphabets of the same language. Others, of course, disagree, framing the relationship between the two as antithetical, an argument that is also part of Antarctic history.

I present these overlapping narratives within the other story that this book recounts: of my journey to the ice during the Austral summer of 2001–2002 as a participant in the National Science Foundation's Antarctic Visiting Artists and Writers Program. My hope is that this contemporary travel narrative will be a trope for the human cognitive process that first turns land into landscape, then landscape into art. I am fortunate that this work allowed me to travel in the company of artists, scientists, and fieldworkers, and to experience Antarctica through their senses and thoughts as well as my own. This book, like my others, is based on the work of those people and their colleagues, whose works are listed and annotated at the end. I can only remind the reader that any mistakes contained in this book are solely my responsibility.

Antarctica is called "the continent of science," which means that most information about it comes in metric units. For the convenience of American readers, however, I have converted almost all measurements from the metric system, and temperatures are given in degrees Fahrenheit.

Many of the illustrations in *Terra Antarctica* will be unfamiliar to readers. The majority of historical images discussed are easily found in other publications about the Antarctic or in histories of art, cartography and science. I have therefore chosen to rely mostly on images by living artists, writers, and scientists to represent the continent.

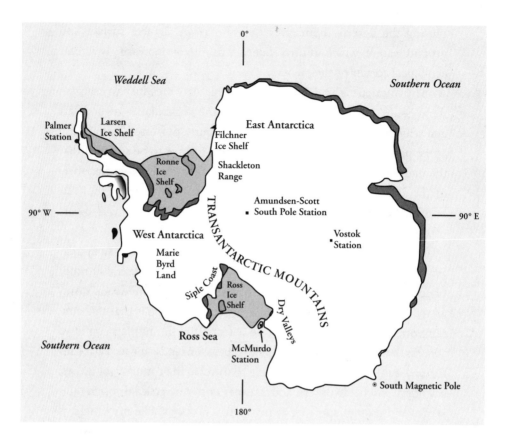

1 THE MIRROR
& THE EYE

IT IS SEVEN O'CLOCK on an early November evening, and five of us have gathered by the snowmobiles parked out on the sea ice below McMurdo, the largest American station in the Antarctic. It's already snowing, the temperature above zero degrees Fahrenheit for the first time in days, driven upward by moist air in a low pressure system rotating around from the south. After weeks of unrelenting Austral spring sunshine twenty-four hours a day, the streetlights have been turned on in town and it feels as if night has returned. The meteorology office has advised us to get back before midnight, when conditions are forecast to deteriorate into a whiteout, a condition in which the snow so perfectly disperses the dim light that it can be impossible to see your own feet, much less the person in front of you.

McMurdo is built on Ross Island, an ice-locked two-hundred-square-mile expanse of volcanic rock where both Robert Falcon Scott and Ernest Shackleton based their attempts to reach the South Pole. Still visible to us through the light snow is Scott's *Discovery* hut, which housed his first expedition a century ago in 1901–1904. The trip we're making tonight, a traditional pilgrimage for the residents of McMurdo, is out to the Cape Evans hut, a much larger building fourteen miles to the north that Scott erected when he reached the Antarctic aboard the *Terra Nova* in 1910. It was the starting point for his second and fatal expedition, the race against the Norwegian Roald Amundsen to the South

Pole the next year. As such, the hut is a mythical touchstone for everyone in the Antarctic.

Tonight we're going out with Ted Dettmar, the head of the mountaineering crew responsible for safety in the field as well as the local history guru. Bearded, slow to speak but with much to say, and wrinkled two decades beyond his thirty-six years, Ted looks like the kind of teamster who last century drove draft animals on the family farm—precisely the job for which he was apprenticing when he accepted a job as a general assistant at McMurdo in 1994. "GAs," as they're called, do everything from chip ice from underneath buildings to sort bolts in barrels, all of the less than romantic but absolutely essential tasks on station. Ted is a climber who for five winters ran the Harvard Mountaineering Club hut on Mt. Washington, the site of the highest recorded winds in the world, and by his second season on the ice he had earned a place on the backup search-and-rescue team.

Now, several years later, he's head of the Field Safety and Training Program, otherwise known as "F-Stop," and he runs us through the basics of snow machine operations. The Alpine II models we'll be riding are the workhorses of the ice fleet. Their top speed is only 45 mph, but they're reliable and easy to fix in the field if something goes wrong. And it always does. It's not that the machines are fragile—far from it—but that driving conditions on what is famously referred to as the "windiest, coldest, highest, and driest continent on Earth" are brutal on vehicles. By the time we get the survival bags loaded and prepare to pull out in single file onto the sea ice, it's quarter of eight and the visibility is beginning to close down.

The Antarctic is the size of the United States and Canada combined, but each Austral winter the sea around it freezes, almost doubling the size of the continent, then thaws out during spring, a cycle that's been called the largest seasonal event on the planet. This month the extent of the sea ice around McMurdo is greater than has ever been seen before, and it's ten to twelve feet thick, substantial enough for the nearby ice runway to accept fully loaded military C-141 cargo jets with ease. An iceberg the size of Delaware, labeled B-15, is parked off the island seventy-five miles to our north, both slowing down the circulation of ocean currents and injecting tons of freshwater into McMurdo Sound daily. It's the largest ever recorded of the five to ten thousand major icebergs that the Antarctic calves every year, and its presence means the ocean's salinity is diluted, so it is freezing more easily and the usual currents and wave action aren't breaking up the ice. Normally the frozen sea would be clearing out already, by the turn of the year making the American station the southernmost navigable port in the world.

The unusual thickness of the sea ice this year means we're not worried about running into cracks along our route tonight. The only concern on our minds is the storm. Weather reports in the Antarctic come in three flavors, all considered to be "severe" by the McMurdo meteorologists. Condition Three, the most benign, is what we're driving through: winds are less than 51 mph, wind chill is warmer than 75°F below zero, and visibility is a quarter mile or better. We are following flags—orange squares mounted on flexible bamboo poles—planted about a hundred feet apart, roughly ten to the quarter mile; as we leave fifteen are in sight. Under these conditions snowmobile travel is permitted as long as there are at least two in the party.

The next weather stage is Condition Two, which is defined as sustained winds of up to 66 mph, a wind chill between −75°F and −100°F, and visibility down to one hundred feet, or two flags. At this point snowmobile travel is not authorized. When wind chill drops below −100°F and visibility shrinks to less than a hundred feet, it's a Condition One lockdown. No one is allowed to leave the building they're in, much less travel in a vehicle. Such frigid whiteouts are usually caused by the local storms here referred to as "Herbies" (hurricane plus blizzard). That's the condition the weather office has said might develop sometime after midnight.

Ted rocks his machine to make sure its dual treads aren't frozen to the ice, guns the engine, and gives us a thumbs-up. I fall into line, then Andrea Donellan drops in behind me. A geomorphologist from the Jet Propulsion Laboratory in Pasadena, her multiyear project involves placing Global Positioning System (GPS) receivers out in the remote Marie

Byrd Land hundreds of miles to the northeast from here. She's attempting to measure the tectonic forces slowly driving apart the archipelago of islands that form the West Antarctic, where we are, from the East Antarctic, the high polar plateau to our south that sits behind the 1,370-mile-long Transantarctic Mountains. Normally during summertime along this route those mountains across the sound would be visible twenty-four hours a day, but tonight the entire world is shrouded in gray and white.

Following Andrea is Jeff Scaniello, a surveyor who works frequently out on the sea ice marking off the runways. Riding swing at the back, making sure we don't drop anything or anyone, is Charles Ray, or "Chas" as everyone calls him. A retired navy man who once worked at F-Stop, he guides on Denali in Alaska during the northern summers and is one of those lean quiet guys you'd happily follow anywhere. This season he's serving as Andrea's field safety person as she travels around placing her instruments on the peaks of mountains sticking up through the ice cap, which ranges from four thousand feet deep to over two miles thick. These "nunataks" (an Arctic Inuit word adopted for the Antarctic) provide the only stable platforms for the GPS units, which can detect as little as a millimeter of change in their position a year.

I'm a novice at Antarctic travel, but all five of us have been on snowmobiles in storms before; we're experienced enough to be wary but also enjoying the notion that we're heading out into something more than your average bus trip to the historic hut. We bounce across the transition ice—the ice within a few yards of shore where tidal action has rucked it up into small pressure mounds, almost like frozen ocean waves—and are soon on the smoother sea ice road leading north out of town.

The storm has thickened a bit already as we pass unseen Hut Point with Scott's modest bungalow. When Scott appeared on the scene leading the British National Antarctic Expedition in 1901–1904, he unloaded from the *Discovery* a prefabricated building modeled after an Australian outback homestead house, complete with deep verandas on all sides, a structure designed to shed heat instead of preserve it. It's no surprise that the 370-square-foot structure was the coldest of the three historic huts on the island. The modifications specified by Scott—double layers of tongue-and-groove Douglas fir insulated with wool felt—apparently were insufficient. Even today when you're inside the *Discovery* hut, with coal and seal blubber soot all over the walls and empty packing crates, and tattered woolen blankets hanging from the ceiling in an attempt to create smaller and more easily heated rooms, the hut is a miserable place.

We're riding along the margins of McMurdo Sound, that seasonal adjunct of the Ross Ice Shelf separating the island from the continent. Whereas ice in the sound usually breaks up and blows out by January of every year, the shelf is another matter entirely. For all intents and purposes, it is a permanent feature of the continent, a floating sheet of glacial ice that covers 190,000 square miles, an area the size of France. Ross Island sits on a corner of its northern edge, the shelf being 400 miles wide here and extending behind us more than 600 miles toward the South Pole. The shelf is nearly 1,000 feet thick at the ice front, or sea edge, and up to 2,300 feet thick at its southern root. It is the largest single piece of ice in the world.

The forty-five-minute trip goes quickly. Once well out from shore we're able to zip along at full speed, every couple of minutes turning around to check that the person behind us is still there and on course, a routine safety precaution. We sense rather than see the low profile of the Erebus Ice Tongue, a five-mile-long floating extension of a glacier that, when the sea ice clears out, calves icebergs into the sound. The dark volcanic Tent and Inaccessible Islands on our left side are equally invisible. Near the small islands we discover a dead Adélie penguin, stopping briefly to pay respects to the eighteen-inch-long bird and touch its feathers. This is probably the only time in my life I'll be able to approach a penguin so closely, as all wildlife here is strictly protected by the environmental protocols of the Antarctic Treaty. None of us know how or why the young bird got here, many miles from any open water, but it's not an uncommon sight this year. The slowing of the thaw caused by B-15 means the Adélies are having a hard time getting to open water and are slowly starving to death.

By the time we pull up in front of Scott's *Terra Nova* hut at Cape Evans, the winds are climbing past 25 mph, lowering the wind chill to minus forty-five. Visibility has slipped to eight of the orange flags. We park the snowmobiles fifty yards offshore; small pressure ridges and cracks have been multiplying here during the spring, and the walk to the hut is noticeably rougher than on my first visit a week ago. The wind is beginning to mewl around the corners of the hut with an ominous pitch.

When I was first here it was a clear and still evening, the Austral spring sun low over the mountains across the sound. I walked up to the highest point on the cape, only a hundred feet in elevation above the building, and scanned the view. The several square acres of Cape Evans ordered itself around the foursquare presence of the wooden hut. Behind me rose the smooth slopes of Mt. Erebus, a gently rising mass that is the southernmost active volcano in the world. From its summit floated a white plume of ash and steam. Erebus looked like a day hike, a common error in the Antarctic, fostered by the hyperarid air so clear things appear closer than they really are. In reality its 12,447-foot summit is more than a dozen miles distant, and snow camouflages the fact that its sides are scored by deep couloirs and heavily crevassed glaciers. The illusion helps creates a scene both as peaceful and as desolate as you can imagine. It's peaceful in part because, as in almost all of the Antarctic, there is little discernible noise apart from the wind and your heartbeat. It's desolate because there is only a single major human artifact in the landscape, the hut. Colors fall into three categories: dark brown volcanic earth, blue sky and ice, white clouds and snow. Nothing grows here that is visible to the naked eye. Nothing moves except for you and your companions.

Tonight is anything but peaceful, and it's with relief that we scrape off the snow on our boots and pass inside, leaving behind the wind and snow and concealing ourselves from a nature that seems to be measuring us. This is a primordial human response, personifying a storm as if it were a malevolent presence—a way of enfolding the impersonal nature of danger within a comprehensible emotion.

Scott's *Terra Nova* hut is the largest, best-insulated, and best-preserved of all the Heroic Age structures, a sturdy refuge fifty by twenty-five feet in size that was designed to hold twenty-five men. Historians broadly define the age as lasting from 1895—when the International Geographical Congress met in London and set off a wave of government-sponsored national expeditions—until 1922, the year Shackleton was buried on South Georgia Island while sailing into his third Antarctic adventure. Fourteen expeditions from eight countries transpired during the period, their stories still the primary source for more novels, nonfiction books, poems, films, and ephemera than any other facet of the continent.

Scott had first set foot on the ice in 1902 with Shackleton and the artist Edward "Bill" Wilson (1872–1912), who was officially serving as the expedition doctor. They landed at what is now known as Winter Quarters Bay, the location of present-day McMurdo, and erected their little outback building that they had bought in Australia, immediately complaining how drafty it was. When Scott returned in 1911 to the Ross Sea, he found McMurdo Sound still frozen and the *Discovery* hut inaccessible. Turning north, he cruised up to Cape Evans, the first logical anchoring point free of ice, and set up the custom-designed hut he'd had built the year before in England. Relatively spacious and insulated with layers of quilted seaweed, it had a ceiling that rose to sixteen feet at its apex and sleeping quarters for the officers partitioned from those of the seamen.

Despite the insulation improved over that of the *Discovery* hut, hoar frost lines the ceiling and the windows seem to steal the light from our flashlights rather than augment it. The cry of the wind stops at the door, and we hear nothing save our muffled footsteps, Ted's subdued commentary, and the occasional click of a camera. Studded boots hang motionless on the end of a bunk bed, cups dangle beneath a shelf in the kitchen area, and chemistry benches are landscaped with barren funnels and beakers. Tinned cocoa and mustard and bottles of ketchup sit on the shelves, reputedly still good to eat. I wouldn't bet my life on it, however, and consider this an urban legend that has been grafted onto the main trunk of the heroic myth embodied by the building (Plate 1).

At the far end of the hut is Herbert Ponting's darkroom, a six-by-eight-foot closet where he both slept and developed his seven-by-five-inch glass plates and movie films. Plates are stacked in boxes and fixing agents reside in their stoppered jars. Scott, understanding well the power of the photographic image for fundraising, had been keen to bring a professional with him. Ponting (1870–1935), who had worked previously in the mountains of Japan and the Swiss Alps, was equally ardent to join the expedition, although at times he found Antarctica a less than congenial place for his talents. Experienced in the telephotography necessary to magnify the mountain peaks in alpine scenery, for example—a convention left over from the nineteenth century's infatuation with exaggerated landscapes in quest of sublime images—he found that the severe temperature discontinuities over the sound between Cape Evans and the Transantarctics almost always dissolved such attempts into a meaningless blur.

Turning to my left from the darkroom door, I take two steps to the table that stands where Wilson painstakingly composed his watercolors. Its wooden top is occupied by the intact carcass of an emperor penguin, left hurriedly by a later expedition that had been commissioned to bring back the skins for stuffing. I stand where Wilson painted Antarctic landscapes and atmospheric phenomena, the last time a painter would accompany an Antarctic expedition as the person responsible for recording the topography (Plate 2). Although Ponting had trouble photographing the mountains across the sound, Wilson had sketched them on the previous expedition in a series of panoramic views that, even when scaled down in lithographs, still totaled more than one hundred feet long. Scott said that he could match the drawings to his maps with astonishing accuracy. Wilson died with Scott on the way back from the Pole, sketching the mountains almost to the end, but from this expedition onward it would be Ponting's successors, the ground and aerial photographers, who would do the job. And with that, a huge wedge would be driven between painters and scientists in the history of exploration.

The sleeping bags of the time, which are stretched out on the beds, were made of reindeer hides; they became so thoroughly frozen over the course of an expedition that men were reduced to inserting themselves one limb at a time to thaw them out and gain entrance. Looking at the tubular mass of hide, and having noted the pile of seal blubber that sits outside the door, we're grateful that the temperatures remain as low as they do. The olfactory assault would otherwise be intense, and many of the artifacts would self-destruct within weeks. Visitors often remark that the huts look as if the explorers had just stepped outside for a moment, but the artifacts are in fact decaying, if slowly. The humidity of our breath encourages the rust that's eating into the biscuit tins and the fungi that grow almost invisibly in the sleeping bags and hanging clothes.

While everyone else moves around taking their digital mementos, I pause at a mirror mounted on the wall outside Scott's bunk. Perhaps eighteen by twenty-four inches, a little larger than my torso, it hangs where it appears in a famous photograph of Scott and his men seated around the big table on his forty-third, and last, birthday. The silver has deleafed from the back, leaving a clear pane of glass behind which there are swatches of crumpled foil. The mirror line, that juncture where silver meets glass and your reflection is created, has been obliterated by cold. Your image falls into the glass and never comes back out, so perfect a metaphor for Scott's fate, and to some extent the Antarctic itself, that it's almost unfair to point it out.

Instead of gaining the fame and fortune that he thought a successful race to the Pole would bring him, Scott not only lost by a month to the Norwegian, but perished of cold and starvation along with Wilson and four other men on the return pull. His journey quickly became a touchstone in a world hungry for heroism, but to some extent it was a false picture constructed on death. Had Scott lived, he would have been a footnote to Amundsen. The empty mirror embodies for me both the fact that Scott never returned and the essential hollowness of his achievement.

And the Antarctic itself? Historian and natural history writer Stephen Pyne posits in his book *The Ice* that it is the least complicated of all the continents in terms of information. It hosts little in the way of a biotic community and has never been permanently occupied by people. Its geography is overwhelmed by ice, and it is the most unfamiliar landscape on Earth, more akin to the surface of Mars or the moons of Jupiter than to London, Los Angeles, or Lahore. He calls Antarctica "an information sink," a place where we expend far more energy and information than we receive in return, another mirror with no back.

By the time we get outside it's ten o'clock and the wind has graduated from making animal sounds to those found inside a wind tunnel. We can't even see the snowmobiles, less than two hundred feet away. I hope out loud that we will decide we have to hunker down, it now being a Condition Two, and suggest that we have an excuse to stay in the hut. Unfortunately, everyone else is sanguine about traveling in these worsening conditions, so off we go. Before leaving, however, Ted warns us that in a few minutes, as we round the point and come out of the lee of the Erebus Ice Tongue, the wind will become much worse.

We start out with three to four flags visible, our speed twenty-five miles per hour. It's easy to tell when we pass the invisible promontory of glacial ice fifteen minutes later, because the wind redoubles its force. Now we can see at best two flags, and we're in a marginal Condition One whiteout, following each other in a tight pack, eyes focused on the single red parka visible in front of us. My head is swathed in the thick coyote fur–trimmed hood of my parka, a bulky down-filled nylon garment that resembles a sleeping bag more than a jacket—and is meant to perform exactly that function in an emergency. My head is further covered by a pile hat, balaclava, neck gaiter, and neoprene face mask. Five snowmobiles chewing their way forward in a Herbie, the two-stroke engines straining against the wind, is not a quiet walk in the park—and yet I'm so muffled by the whiteout and government-issue extreme cold weather clothing that everything seems silent. Snowdrifts have formed across the track since we drove out an hour earlier, and I have the sensation not so much of moving forward as of floating up and down over snow drifts that I can't see, white on white on white.

Unexpectedly we break out into a circular clearing, the wind diminishes dramatically, and great masses of snow and cloud revolve around us. It's a small eye in the cyclonic disturbance that's blowing over Ross Island. A hundred feet overhead sunlight tinges the clouds yellow and orange as if the atmosphere were on fire, and the clouds smoke. It is glorious, magical, wild. I stand up on the snowmobile and let out a whoop of joy. J. M. W. Turner, the great English landscape painter, once had himself tied to the mast of a ship during a storm in order to paint the experience later. He would have loved this. Turner was Wilson's hero, and this is one of the reasons why: his love of the sublime, that which is simultaneously beautiful and terrifying.

I'd like to stop, but Ted picks up speed, hoping to minimize our exposure, and we plunge back into the clouds. The wind shifts from the east to the south and is even stronger. Visibility decreases to one flag, then less. Ted is relying now on how his machine reacts to the half-buried tracks as much as looking for each individual flag ahead, some of which have been ripped right off their poles.

Chas is ahead of me and for some reason is grasping the top of his windshield with one hand, which I know has to be chilling not only his arm but his entire body as the wind spills down his sleeve. Ten minutes later we pull off at a training hut still a mile and a half out of McMurdo, turn off the machines, and shout over the din. It turns out that one of the flanges attaching the windshield to the hood of Chas's snowmobile has fractured. If he hadn't been holding on to it, it would have flown off. Driving headlong into a Herbie without any wind protection is, we all agree, a bad idea, and we repair to the hut to decide what to do. Ted has seen this problem before, and thinks he can jury-rig a temporary solution with some of the electrical tape that he always carries.

Inside the prefab hut—nothing more than a shipping container that's been dragged onto the sea ice—Ted radios McMurdo Operations to let them know we may be a few minutes over our preset return time of midnight, a required protocol forestalling the launch of a search party. "MacOps" suggest we hunker down in the survival kits, a Condition One having been declared on base. Ted manages to keep an almost straight face while telling them it isn't that bad out here and he thinks we're just fine to finish the trip.

In the meantime, Andrea is pulling pieces of cake from her pack along with a single candle, which she solemnly places in the middle of one of the cakes. Earlier in the Cape Evans hut she'd been joking about lighting a candle, a strictly prohibited activity given how like tinder wooden structures become in the aridity here. It is not just that the conflagration of a venerated historical structure would cause an international diplomatic furor, but fire is the ultimate catastrophe that everyone in the Antarctic is taught to fear: lose your shelter and you lose your life. It turns out this is Chas's sixtieth birthday, and we present him with an almost melodic rendition of "Happy Birthday" with the wind as accompaniment.

Ted and Chas disappear outside to secure the windscreen, which they accomplish quickly, and we're off again. Now we lose sight for split seconds of even a single flag in the snow that's whipping across the ice, yet we have to find two turns, one of them ninety degrees, to bring us back to McMurdo. We make it by driving within a few feet of each other's machines and blinking as little as possible, Ted somehow able to keep us on track. Once back in the staging area below McMurdo, we line the machines up nose first into the wind and struggle to batten down the covers, then climb stiffly into the frigid box of a tracked Hagglunds vehicle that we drive back up the hill into town, a five-minute ride. It's just midnight and the town looks deserted, with everyone indoors waiting out the storm.

I climb into bed and try not to wake my roommate, a graduate student who in two weeks will start off on a two-month-long, 1,135-mile traverse across the ice in trailers, housing labs, and sleeping quarters, hauled by powerful tractors. The team will deploy crevasse-detecting radar as they visit sites to collect ice cores and atmospheric samples for climatological studies. It's the kind of mobile and multidimensional science project that you can envision being attempted on Mars. The contrast between modern travel in the Antarctic and the methods of the Heroic Age is instructive.

Tonight we made it back to town in what Ted called a "soft Condition One," on schedule with the plan he filed with MacOps before we left. It isn't cold or windy enough to qualify as a full-blown Herbie, although the windows of the dorm are booming and the lack of visibility is genuinely hazardous. I thought of how Wilson must have felt freezing and starving to death with Scott and the others, pinned down in a tent by a harsher storm less than ninety miles south of here and only eleven miles away from a food cache. The pendulum of history has been swinging this way and that over Scott, first declaring him a hero, then calling him a fool, not only for insisting on manhauling sleds, rather than using dogs, but also for taking a fifth and extra person with him to the Pole. With the recent publication of Susan Solomon's book *The Coldest March,* which points out that his party labored under colder than normal weather, historical opinion has moderated a little.

Tomorrow morning we'll have a good story to tell at breakfast, but we haven't performed any heroics, no matter how tempting it is to think of it that way. Tonight we were swaddled in synthetic clothes and traveling in mechanized security back to a warm bed. We're not explorers—we're not going where no one else has been before, in terms of either terrain or experience. The people with Scott and Shackleton, as well as our contemporaries who travel on foot and ski across the continent, such as Ann Bancroft or Reinhold Messner, have undergone tremendous hardships to do what they have done. Yet even they aren't explorers in the classic sense—they're only going where others have gone before. They are more accurately labeled adventurers, people driven to extend their knowledge more of themselves than of the world, and to map the ways in which we perceive and relate to that world.

The Antarctic is the same space as it was in the Heroic Age, but we've been living on the continent for almost fifty years and our perceptions of it are changing. We haven't tamed the winds or closed up the crevasses, but our constant imaging of its environment now leads us to accept the Antarctic as a place. By flagging routes on the ice, making sketch and topographical maps, taking aerial photographs, and representing the continent in paintings, poetry, novels, and music, we have defined the terrain and in the process circumscribed a territory with human activity and infused it with memories. How we have accomplished this arises from the nature of human vision.

2 THE EYE &
THE MIRROR

RESTING MY ELBOWS on a deep windowsill of the top floor of Crary Lab, I stare west at a 125-mile stretch of peaks and glaciers in the Transantarctic Mountains. The highest portion visible from here is the Royal Society Range, and at their northern end the entrances to the Dry Valleys are clearly visible fifty miles away. When I came to work at seven, the sun was traversing behind the hills above town and McMurdo Sound was flat white, as austere as a blank piece of paper. In the evenings when I work late, the sun tracks over the Transantarctics and transmutes the far glaciers and icefields into molten bronze.

Below the lab is the helicopter hanger and pad, and all morning the NSF's four helicopters have been taking off and landing, ferrying scientists and work crews to and from field camps within a 125-mile radius of the station. Downhill from the helo pad is the shoreline, where the sea ice starts; the snow machines are parked here, and a mechanic has been working at repairing the broken windshield from last night. Beyond that, an ice road runs out three miles to the sea-ice runway that is used until December, when the ice thins and operations are moved out onto a strip on the permanent ice shelf. Weather permitting, one or more of the drab green C-130s flown by the New York Air National Guard may lumber down from Christchurch, New Zealand, and land here every day until then. Past the airfield the sound stretches level and frozen across thirty miles to the shore of the continent.

To my left and at the farthest edge of the view southward is Minna Bluff. When clouds roll in over the low ridge it means you may have as little as forty-five minutes before a Herbie hits town and it's time to batten down anything loose. This afternoon, after the storm of last night, I can find no flaw in the blue bowl of sky, although there are a few inches of dry fresh snow on the ground, and a small drip of water pelting the windowsill next to me announces that the snow on the roof is melting off.

About 3,000 people will pass through McMurdo this season, but the population of McMurdo averages only around 1,200. This year nearly 130 of us are grantees of the NSF, and most of us work in Crary Laboratory when not out in the field. The lab is a 46,500-square-foot multilevel structure that is touted as a world-class, state-of-the-art research facility. Its first phase was opened in 1991–1992, and the building was supposedly finished in the 1995–1996 season. As I write this in November 2001, the contractor promises to finish the punch list of alterations and repairs next month, five years late, construction in the Antarctic never being a straightforward matter. They may or may not be able to fix the drip.

The lab is built on four floors staggered up the hillside on pilings, in theory to allow blowing snow the freedom to keep moving. Its bottom level holds an aquarium, the domain of Art deVries, who discovered and has been studying antifreeze in Antarctic fish at McMurdo for forty years. Six-foot-long *Mawsoni* cod, caught just offshore under the ice, swim sluggishly in circular tanks, the water kept at twenty-eight degrees Fahrenheit lest they expire from heat. The next two levels, reached by walking up long rubber-floored ramps, are filled with science and administrative offices, lab spaces, walk-in freezers, and stockrooms jammed with everything from glassware to microscopes, safety goggles to stationery. Posters, charts, and maps line the hallways, displaying the flow of ice streams, radar maps of the Dry Valleys, and the movement of B-15. On one floor a television monitor runs a real-time remote broadcast from the crater rim of Mt. Erebus, where one of the world's three persistent lava lakes occasionally tosses out molten bombs the size of minivans. I work in the library on the fourth floor, where the entire western exposure is lined with windows recessed into the foot-thick walls.

The Antarctic is a self-sustaining feedback loop of frigidity, the ice reflecting back into space 80 percent of the shortwave solar radiation falling upon it, as opposed to between 15 and 35 percent reflected back by ice-free ground elsewhere. This morning that fierce exchange manifests itself in thermal discontinuities—alternating layers of cooler and warmer air that turn the view into a mirage. Across the sound and at the foot of the mountains looms a glacial cliff that extends for twenty miles, scalloped battlements of ice that must be five hundred feet high to be visible from here, thirty miles away. As the morning wears on and the air stabilizes, however, the cliffs waver and shrink, only to reform the next day. This is the first time I've seen a "superior mirage," known famously to sailors worldwide as the Fata Morgana.

The thermal illusions most commonly seen in the American West, in the Mojave and Great Basin deserts where I grew up, are classified as inferior mirages. These arise when the ground surface and the few inches of air above it are many degrees hotter than the air immediately higher. The illusion of water shimmering on a highway in front of you is a common example, the thermal boundary between temperatures— yet another kind of mirror line—reflecting back the sky. The apparition can be so convincing that thirsty cattle will stampede for it, then drop to their knees dead of dehydration and heat exhaustion.

Superior mirages are caused by a reversal of the same discontinuity, this time the surface being much colder than the air above it—a temperature inversion—and reflecting not what is above, but instead magnifying what is below or behind it, in this case the far shoreline of the continent. The phenomenon was given the name Fata Morgana when Europeans observed the mirages over water and attributed them to Morgan le Fay, the enchantress half-sister of King Arthur who was believed to live in an undersea castle. Seamen claimed that she cast the image of her abode above the water as a false harbor, thus luring unwary navigators to their death. The Fata Morgana is a complicated mirage, often superimposing several images, and is thus prone to change radically as multiple layers of the atmosphere shift their temperatures even slightly. The "castles in the air" over Ross Sound constantly project upward and then deconstruct, the same optical morass in which the telephoto lens of Scott's photographer, Ponting, became mired.

The fable of Morgan le Fay sought to explain cognitive dissonance in an isotropic space: the brain, attempting to find and interpret visual cues in an environment that looks the same in all directions, interpreted the unfamiliar in terms of the familiar. Early Antarctic maps and reports are full of such misunderstandings, entire mountain ranges being proposed where none exist, images from hundreds of miles inland cast out to sea by inversions. Sight is our only long-distance sensing mechanism, and in a space of such vastness we rely primarily on it for orientation and a sense of self in relationship to what is around us.

Our perceptual wiring evolved over millions of year in more humid environments, first in Africa's arboreal forests, then in its woodlands and out on the open savanna. The noses of our primate ancestors shrunk, diminishing our ability to smell but allowing a greater field of vision as we moved into progressively larger landscapes. Put *Homo sapiens* on a frozen ocean in front of a mirage, and we cannot help but perceive it through inherited templates, some of them genetic, some cultural. I look out the window at Crary and think the Royal Society to be closer than it is, and translate both ice cliffs and their mirage into architecture, deploying an analog and creating a place I can inhabit imaginatively. A severe challenge in the Antarctic is trying to develop a sense of place where our ability to sense the space itself is so compromised.

Our visual sensory system, which includes the eyes, the optic nerve, and various portions of the brain, rigorously parses information through a series of steps meant to eliminate most of what we see, arriving at a small set of patterns such as lines, edges, and contrast. The rules of vision, which among other things force us to distinguish between figure and ground, are in force whether we're looking at a person in a field or a painting of a figure in a field. We codify the separation of objects and ground by mentally constructing continuous lines, or contours, which we assemble into approximately twenty-four basic geometric shapes. The easiest shapes for us to perceive are those that are closed, such as circles and squares. The more basic and symmetrical the closure, the faster we perceive it, circles being easiest, then squares, then rectangles, and so on. The more complicated the shape, the longer we have to look at it. The brain assembles these shapes into patterns that it subjects to an ongoing comparison with patterns it has stored previously, mostly in our long-term memory.

How critical basic contour recognition is to our survival shows up in the Antarctic during whiteout conditions, when we are subjected to a *Ganzfeld*, or visual field without contours. Stumbling around in a whiteout, where visible light is dispersed in a perfectly even manner, you start to lose your balance and coordination almost immediately, and within fifteen minutes may suffer a complete, though temporary, loss of vision. Remain deprived of contours in a *Ganzfeld* for very long, and hallucinations start, the brain making up something, anything, to see. To say that you are disoriented in a whiteout is to put it mildly.

Ranulph Fiennes and Mike Stroud, two British adventurers who made the first unsupported crossing of the Antarctic by manhauling sledges 1,500 miles in 1992–1993, reported problems with their vision caused by lack of the visual cues to which we are accustomed. As Fiennes reports in his account of the epic, *Mind Over Matter*, by the end of the expedition they had trouble focusing their vision. Fiennes went to see an ophthalmic surgeon on his return to England, who correctly diagnosed the condition as one similar to that suffered by long-range bomber pilots during World War II. Flying for many hours and peering through a windscreen with no discernible contours outside, the pilots would forget how to focus. The surgeon, pointing out to Fiennes that he had been similarly deprived by ninety-five days of travel on the ice, predicted that the condition would disappear within a few weeks as his mind retrained itself, and so it did.

Anne Dal Vera, who along with Ann Bancroft and two other women skied from the Ronne Ice Shelf to the South Pole that same season, a journey of 678 miles that took sixty-seven days, told me that they encountered a different set of problems. When the weather was fine, the women tended to focus on sastrugi as landmarks against which to maintain their bearings. The wind-shaped surface features, sometimes up to six feet in height, and subtle variations in the light and dark shades of snow occupied them endlessly, and, having no trouble finding things to look at on the polar plateau, they retaining their mental ability to visually process the world. An overcast day, however, meant that surface definition simply disappeared, and it took enormous concentration to stay on your feet, especially for the lead skier, unable to distinguish dips and rises under her skis. On those days, which Dal Vera considered claustrophobic compared with the sunny ones, she found it easier to ski with her eyes closed to avoid the vertigo.

Galen Rowell, an American mountaineer and renowned nature photographer who worked in both the Arctic and Antarctic, cautioned readers in *Poles Apart*, his photo book about the antipodes, that the paucity of familiar forms makes not just the ice itself, but even photographs of the ice difficult to see and engage with emotionally. In other words, not only does the Antarctic as a place present difficulties to our vision, but even our ability to read its representations is challenged.

The mind demands and receives three kinds of visual information: What an object is, where it is, and what it is doing. The first it receives as the perception of form through the construction and recognition of contours. The second it constructs through a variety of perspective perceptions, including those derived from our stereoscopic vision (particularly for close-up items), the elevation of our vision above the ground (for farther things), and through the breaking of contours by objects in front of each other. Motion is likewise constructed from a series of visual rules. The Antarctic with its monolithic expanses of flat white ice, flickering mirages, and lack of familiar geographical cues makes it the most difficult visual environment on the planet.

The longer you look at something, the more you assign it significance because you are cumulatively reinforcing physical pathways through your neurons while doing so. And if you're accustomed to a specific landscape, you look for the important features in it that you have burned deeply into your brain. If you grew up around foliage, your brain is used to looking to it and assigning it scale, which is to say its size relative to yours. In the Antarctic there are no familiar salient features in the landscape and your eye simply wanders, looking for something, anything, that your mind can recognize.

When we are confronted with something we didn't expect to see—a visual anomaly like Mt. Erebus, for example, the smoking volcano on Ross Island that's in the middle of what's supposed to be an icy continent—we experience *visual dissonance*. We have to stare at the unexpected sight for a long time in order to "believe our eyes." When we see something we don't understand, then act inappropriately in response, we are suffering from *cognitive dissonance*, which sometimes has fatal consequences. An example is attempting to cross a desert valley without carrying water because it looks small but is in fact very large, a fact apparent on the map we may have with us but choose to ignore because of the false visual perception. The cattle stampeding for the false promise of a mirage is another example, and the legend behind the name of Fata Morgana a cautionary one. Cognitive dissonance becomes a familiar state of mind in the Antarctic.

Our species evolved in a mixed terrain where primates moved down and out of trees and onto a grassland rich with the proteins that would support the growth and energy requirements of our cortex. These were places where hominids could measure themselves against the scale of trees, the height and distance of which they knew intimately. Not only were these trees they had climbed for millions of years, the structure of the limbs echoed in their own arms and legs—limbs of a different kind—but the tree branches were also refuge. You had to be able, at all times, to look around you and know how far away that refuge was, how long it would take you to get up it, and how far you could go. If you misjudged, you would be eaten by a predator that was higher up the food chain.

Our ancestors could place themselves in their immediate surroundings, but they also could look at the far mountains and, if unable to measure how far away they were in spatial distance, specify roughly how long a journey to them would take in time. Part of that ability arose from the fact that humidity in the air shifted the transparency of the atmosphere and the color of the landscape in a predictable manner, which their perceptual systems had evolved to understand. The outline of hills close by were sharper than those twenty miles off. The minuscule air droplets suspended in the air scattered the light so that what would be a brown and green mountainside nearby would appear to be bluish if far off, a cognitive strategy observed by Leonardo da Vinci and transplanted by him into landscape painting as "atmospheric perspective," a device used ever since by artists to indicate background distance.

What happens to us when we enter a place lacking the visual cues to which we have adapted ourselves, such as the Antarctic? We get lost. Without the visual clues to which we are accustomed, we misjudge distance, where to find paths across the terrain, and where refuge from threat may exist. We overcome this difficulty by constructing maps, which allow us to mechanically measure that which we cannot know instinctively. And it's not by coincidence that the earliest examples of cartography we have come from Mesopotamia and Egypt, two early desert societies.

During the last eight thousand years we have become accustomed to having our way with the surface of the earth, in part because maps have been highly successful cognitive aids, even when the environment is hostile. This means that it's not just the occasional vacationer who gets into trouble in the desert, however. It's entire civilizations. Mesopotamian civilization dried up, as has every other large-scale hydraulic desert society that assumed that, because they could overrule the land with maps, they could then rule over the land with irrigation and roads. Maps in their abstraction encourage us to think that one place is much the same as any other, that we can act in Nevada or Saudi Arabia the as we do in New Hampshire or Austria. Yet wherever we continue unchecked growth and overuse local resources, we're taking great risks. The Mesopotamians, for all their cleverness in urban planning and taxation (enabled in large part by their mapmaking skills), still took from the earth more than it could reasonably give and—in combination with a changing climate—put themselves out of business. So did the Mayans and the ancestral Pueblo Indians of the American Southwest. Egypt looks as if it will do the same. Cognitive dissonance isn't a matter just of individual perceptual mechanics but of social dynamics as well.

Cartography and art share a common and ancient visual framework that is especially important to understand when looking at the art produced during the exploration of unfamiliar environments, and most especially highly isotropic ones, whether the hot deserts of Egypt and the American West or the cold ones of the polar regions.

I've often speculated that the first visual gesture made on a two-dimensional surface might have occurred when one of our ancestors, having returned to the tribe from a hunting foray, tried to describe where he had been when he was unable to lead others there himself. Exploration would have been useless, after all, if you couldn't find your way back and bring others with you—or send them there. Perhaps after extending a digit in the direction to go, and having given what limited verbal instructions, if any, the language of the epoch could convey, our intrepid ancestor bent down and drew a path in the dirt, a sketch that said: "When you get beyond those trees we can see from here, go left around the first hill until you reach the stream, then follow it to the right and up into the next valley where there's a herd of gazelles." The first drawing may well have been a map, a way of getting us from "here" to "there."

The history of mapmaking is, among other things, a narrative about how we have applied geometry to the earth, taking one of the cognitive shapes we most easily perceive, the square, and wrapping it around the globe. Cartography was the cultural means we deployed to overcome our neurobiological limitations in new and extreme spaces, and it also provided the springboard from which was launched landscape art in the sixteenth and seventeenth centuries, a history with direct relevance to the early exploration of the Antarctic and every painting-of-place that's been done there, from William Hodges sailing with Captain James Cook in the 1770s to Edward Wilson sketching away with Scott on their way to the South Pole. Hodges spent much of his time on the voyage performing as a cartographic draftsman and sketching what were known as coastal profiles, drawings of shorelines used as navigational aids, a technique derived from Dutch and Flemish pilots of the sixteenth century. Wilson, seventy-odd years after the invention of photography, was still making coastal profiles and landscape panoramas.

Maps, however, come loaded with preconceptions that are necessary in order for us to use them, the most basic of which is that they attempt to represent a three-dimensional curved surface—the globe—with straight lines on a two-dimensional sheet of paper or computer screen. It's a convenient conceit when we're driving a car across town or taking a weeklong backpacking trip; the errors that accumulate from the translation don't matter at a small scale, most especially in the lower latitudes where the lines of longitude are farthest apart. But when you're surveying something the size of a state or country, the errors accumulate and you have to make little jogs to accommodate the map to the terrain. That's why, if you look at a map of Kansas or Nebraska, places where it's relatively flat and supposedly simple to grid off the territory, you'll find perfectly straight county roads suddenly taking a jig to one side, course corrections that bend the mapmakers' work to the curvature of the round globe. Things become, as you can imagine, much more difficult the closer you get to the South Pole, where the lines begin to converge toward a single point—not to mention where compasses begin to act more like an apparatus in a magician's act than a scientific instrument.

Of course, with satellite photos, Global Positioning System units, and laser surveying we can overcome almost all of those problems to within tolerances any farmer or politician would find more than acceptable. The problem that remains is the idea of the grid itself, a totalizing device adopted by the Mesopotamians in about 6,200 B.C. to ensure standardized (hence politically acceptable) taxation and subsequently used to reduce the world by formula to a common space.

When we grid a landscape, when we take a ruler and draw lines on it—when we over-rule it—we end up making the assumption that we rule over the land, and that a square of land in the desert is the same as a square of land in the grassland three states over. The fact is, what we're in charge of is a piece of paper, not the land, but we forget that. We confuse the representation for the reality, an intellectual dissonance that in the desert is related directly to our cognitive problems.

So we know that the square, even though based deep in our neurophysiology as a successful adaptation enabling us to see our way around in the world, can lead us into trouble with maps. Mapmaking and landscape art had started to split apart well before Edward Wilson picked up his first brush as a young man in the last decade of the nineteenth century. What do we find when we analyze representational landscape painting, the kind of art most often produced during the exploration of the Antarctic, along the same lines as maps? What kind of geometry exists there? What preconceptions does it contain, and what do they have to do with the natural world?

Look at the kinds of art that we prefer. Two Russian artists, Vitaly Komar and Alex Melamid, created an ongoing conceptual art piece to find out. They went to different countries around the world and surveyed people about what they would like to see in a painting and what they wouldn't. They then painted an example of each, adding them to a traveling exhibition. As it turns out, what we usually don't want to see is abstract art in bright colors. What we like to see most often, from country to country, is fairly predictable if we think about the evolutionary background of our vision: We like very traditional landscapes. We want trees in the foreground framing a view that opens to the middle distance where there is a water feature, such as a pond or lake or stream, and then a vista leading away into the distance. Usually we want figures placed in the paintings, preferably in the foreground or by the edge of the water. The results, from Kenya to Iceland, are remarkably consistent.

What we're describing is a woodland at the edge of a savanna with trees to scale, both in terms of measuring and offering refuge. We stand outside the picture frame, a square or rectangle of course, where it is safe and through which we can observe the landscape. When asked how such pictures make us feel, we're likely to respond that they are calming, a visible respite from the disorganized visual chaos surrounding us on our city streets and in our workplaces. In short, we want our deep ancestral home. We can find a related story when asking young children what kind of landscapes they prefer: it's much the same sort of territory we desire in our paintings. Their least favorite environment is the desert.

There is also, however, a corollary balancing act in our landscape preferences, be they in art or reality. If the children are older and have experienced other kinds of landscapes, have gotten to know a forest, the mountains, the desert, they may prefer the more exotic locales— even deserts. And if we ask adults who have spent some time contemplating a full range of art what kind of paintings they prefer, they, too, will sometimes prefer the less familiar, and respond that they like the mental challenges posed by the abstractions of Jackson Pollock, or the minimal geometries of Frank Stella, or other kinds of visual aesthetics all together, such as installation works. At some point in our experience of the world, we are often able to step beyond our comfort level and seek the unfamiliar, which is why some people collect contemporary abstract art rather than landscape paintings, and prefer living in McMurdo to Chicago.

The Antarctic is the world's largest desert. Its air is so dry and clear of particulate pollutants that atmospheric perspective barely comes into play before mountains disappear beyond the curvature of the earth. Its cartography doesn't have a true square on even a single map sheet—everything is bent into wedges as longitude lines converge toward the pole. What happens when our perceptual apparati are disordered by the most severe place on the planet? Can we learn something here about how we react to the environment at large? My assumption is that by looking through the art of place—primarily paintings and photographs that represent a specific locale—we can discern the shape of our mind about it, and thus why we treat it the way we do. Part of the reason is that landscape art is itself a mapping activity, a way of getting us from the familiar "here" to the unfamiliar "there."

Comparing the experiential reality of the Antarctic with our images of it, and assessing the kinds of dissonance we suffer in that environment, makes it possible also to understand how people construct stories about an extreme space in order to convert it into place. The images and the stories are inextricably linked, the art and cartography of the continent arising from, but also shaping, the historical and political narratives we use to govern it (Plate 3).

3 TRANSANTARCTICA I

TWENTY MILLION YEARS AGO Wright Valley was filled thousands of feet deep by ice flowing down from the ice sheet of the polar plateau and through the Transantarctic Mountains to the sea. But the range had been uplifting slowly for millions of years, and eventually it rose above the point where the ice could overtop the peaks—and the valley became ice free. Wright Valley is one of three parallel ice-free grooves in this part of the Transantarctics, the Dry Valleys. It has not rained here, the driest place on Earth, for more than 2 million years.

The wind blows steadily from my left. I keep my head down and parka hood pulled snug as I traverse up the lower flanks of the Asgard Range. The ground beneath my feet consists of a sandy soil thickly paved with ventifacts, or wind-shaped stones. The rocks are smaller than my palm, polished by the incessant grinding by grains of wind-blown sand and ice into gray and umber pyramids and polyhedra the likes of which I've never seen before. Their sharply faceted faces are oriented to the west, the direction of the prevailing summertime winds.

This is my first multiday excursion into the field. Almost all such forays available to visiting artists and writers are made in conjunction with science groups, which helps both to contain the logistical expenses and to provide a safety net. I've requested time in the Dry Valleys and have been assigned to accompany a group repairing seismological equipment. It's my first afternoon in Wright Valley, and I'm taking a solo hike, careful to stay within direct line-of-sight to the hut.

The Dry Valleys cover 1,370 square miles, a scenic and scientific anomaly the size of Delaware within the 5.4-million-square-mile continent that is 96.6 percent covered by ice. The geological record here is not buried under two miles of ice, and because the valleys are a pristine environment at the extreme end of the spectrum where life is possible, their ecology is more easily monitored than those in temperate regions, where the web of life is infinitely more complicated. Every effort is made to minimize human disturbances in the valleys, and back at Crary Lab a film is shown every day to newcomers on how to walk gently in the Dry Valleys.

The exposed valleys are also important to the study of aesthetics in the Antarctic. Precisely because they are predominantly ice free, they provide a place where human scale is more readily established than on the featureless ice sheet, and thus provide material more easily represented in art. Every artist who has visited the Antarctic since the valleys were discovered in the first decade of the twentieth century has made it a priority to come here. Eliot Porter, the first photographer sent to the Antarctic by the NSF, worked up and down this valley in 1975, when he was seventy-four years old. Porter was America's preeminent landscape photographer after Ansel Adams, and a pioneer in the use of color film outdoors. His book *Antarctica,* the first color coffee table book about the continent widely available in the United States, showed the public that the continent was more than a land of white snow. He photographed impossibly blue and green icebergs, red and orange lichens growing on rocks, and skies that ranged across the entire spectrum of hues. It was his photographs of the Dry Valleys that first interested me in coming to the Antarctic twenty-five years ago—not the white keep of the continental interior, but a dry labyrinth that produced an immediate and intense longing to walk this place for myself.

Ten percent of the Dry Valleys is exposed rock; the rest is covered with cold desert soils that lack topsoil, or almost any organic material. In Wright Valley, the soils are composed of coarse grains of sandstone, the gray granitic rock granodiorite, and dolerite, which is even harder than granite. The soils rest atop permafrost, frozen dirt and ice mixed together. Unlike the permafrost found in North America, which tends to stabilize at just under the freezing point, the underground layers in Wright Valley can become as cold as a single degree above zero. Some of the ground in isolated spots has been undisturbed for up to 15 million years and has turned yellowish and red from oxidation. The material under my feet, however, a stony pavement atop a fine sand the same color as the surface rocks, is much younger, perhaps dating from when the Ross Ice Sheet withdrew from McMurdo Sound during the termination of the Wisconsin glaciation, which ended around 10,000 years ago.

A braided stream, the Onyx River, flows for thirty miles inland during only six weeks at the height of summer, its origin the thin meltwaters from dozens of alpine glaciers that hang down from the mountains on either side, tongues of ice that end in abrupt vertical walls up to two hundred feet high. They've been there for 3.5 million years, managing to maintain position in face of the katabatic winds, formed when air is pulled by gravity from the higher plateau to the lower valleys, generating winds that grow progressively warmer as they fall, routinely exceeding 100 mph. The katabatics carry less than 10 percent humidity and simply sublimate glacial ice, taking frozen water straight into a gaseous state without its passing through a liquid phase. In other words, the glacier fronts evaporate in the wind. Just enough snow falls in the mountains to sustain the glaciers (Plate 4).

Wright Valley displays a classic interior basin-and-range topography that I recognize from Nevada, all its waters flowing inward. Steep mountain walls no more than three miles apart rise up more than six thousand feet on both sides. Across from me the Olympus Range is cut through by Bull Pass, which leads to the next valley north. Up the valley sits Lake Vanda, the permanently ice-covered terminus of the river. At the far head of the valley, thirty miles east, are the legendary thousand-foot-high, three-mile-wide Airdevronsix Icefalls, where the ice sheet still manages to breach the mountains. Like Niagara Falls, the ice is slowly retreating upstream, eating its way backward into the rock. Almost everywhere else around the circumference of the continent, that massive ice sheet succeeds in reaching the sea. Here, however, wind and sun abort the effort. The icefalls land on dry ground.

I've now hiked far enough up the side of the valley that I can see clearly the alternating yellow sandstone and dark gray dolerite bands of the Beacon Supergroup that run across a line of peaks, the last wall of rock before the polar plateau rises to the center of the continent. There's a "very low aerosol optical thickness" in the valleys, as an atmospheric scientist would put it, meaning there's no dust or moisture in the air to impede my view or shift the spectrum. It looks like another day hike, but the massive cliffs are thirty miles away.

The Transantarctics are composed of nearly horizontal layers of sedimentary rock, Devonian sandstone through which run sills of coal, shales, and most prominently dolerite, a dark lava similar to basalt. The rocks are related to those in southern Africa, India, South America, and Australia. Found within the sandstones are fossilized remains of *Lystrosaurus,* a semiaquatic herbivore that had a very limited swimming range—sort of a reptilian hippopotamus—that lived in New Zealand as well as those other regions. Both the rocks and fossils are proof that all these lands were once a part of the supercontinent Gondwanaland, which broke up during the Jurassic Period 135 to 180 million years ago. When the bodies of Scott and his companions were found, the rocks that Wilson had collected from the Beacon sandstones along the route of their descent down the Beardmore Glacier from the polar plateau were found with them. Wilson had insisted that they bring them back, as they contained fossil leaves of the extinct twelve-foot-tall woody fern *Glossopteris*—a fossil also found on those other southern continents. Continental drift wasn't yet a fully articulated theory, but he surmised correctly the fossils' importance.

The mountains began their uplift at the end of the Jurassic. Just as the Himalaya rose up to block waters draining south from Tibet into India, so the Transantarctics blocked most of the ice flowing from the polar plateau to the sea. In the Himalaya, the water cut channels through the uplifting chain, in one place creating the most profound gorge on Earth, the twenty-thousand-foot-deep Kali Gandaki Valley in between the peaks of Dhaulighiri and Annapurna. In Antarctica, the great outflow glaciers to the south of the Dry Valley, such as the Byrd and the Beardmore, have done much the same.

I stop my ascent when I come upon the mummified bodies of two crabeater seals resting on a thin layer of gravel. I'm almost forty miles from where the Dry Valleys meet the ocean, not to mention three hundred feet above and a mile uphill from the river. Some of the seal carcasses found in the valleys still have fur on the underside of their intact bodies, which in midsummer still ooze decaying flesh, while others have been dated to more than 3,500 years old. These two are so ancient that they've been almost sandblasted out of existence. Both seals and penguins regularly and for unknown reasons walk up into the Dry Valleys, the latter getting as far as fifty miles before succumbing to starvation.

Scott discovered the Dry Valleys by mistake when returning from a trip to the polar plateau during his first expedition. Descending the wrong glacier in a whiteout on the way back to McMurdo Sound, he found himself at one end of a frozen lake. At the other end was an arid valley he was unable to follow, sledging on snow being his only method of travel. He wrote in the *Discovery* expedition journal that it was a "wonderful place," but he stumbled across mummified seals then, too, and went on to exclaim that it was "a valley of the dead" where "even the great glacier which once pushed through it has withered away." Shackleton sent a team of three to investigate the eastern end of the valley in 1909, but it wasn't until the arrival of Griffith Taylor, the geomorphologist accompanying Scott in 1911, that the first valley was completely traversed. It was Taylor who figured out that glaciation carved the valleys out of the mountains more than 20 million years ago, and that there's been only minimal fluvial erosion during the last 15 million.

I head back down to the valley floor and the hut I am camped next to for a few days, a $1.5 million prefabricated refrigerator building twenty-five feet long, eleven feet wide, and more than ten feet high. It was pre-assembled, broken down into pieces light enough for helicopters to ferry over from McMurdo, then reassembled and tied down with twenty steel cables guyed to bedrock, anchors that can handle 200 mph winds. I pry open the heavy freezer door and enter an anteroom the size of a walk-in closet into which are crammed two diesel generators. Inside through another heavy door are racks of digital electronic gear, steel shelves holding twenty-four large batteries that store the solar power generated by panels mounted flat on the roof, and a large red tool chest from Sears that looks like it belongs in somebody's garage. There are also five guys inside, swaying and jiving to loud rock music playing on a laptop computer, their eyes fastened on a series of digital readouts. Apparently the work is going well.

The group inside is testing and performing maintenance on the equipment for the "Dry Valleys Seismograph Project," a complicated array of digital sensors and telemetry gear that records and forwards by radio data gathered here on earth movements. When I first read about the project, I thought it would be a straightforward science camp. NSF described the work being carried out here at Bull Pass as a joint venture with the New Zealand Antarctic Program "to record broadband, high-dynamic-range, digital seismic data from the remote Wright Valley, a site removed from the environmental and anthropogenic noise ubiquitous on Ross Island." The annual science summary mentioned that the site is ideal because it offers rare access to Antarctic bedrock, and that the data are digitized and telemetered to the Albuquerque Seismological Laboratory for public access. No mention was made of the underlying strategic mission.

Clay Himmelsback and his two sergeants, Arnold "A. J." Jones and Glen Breen, work for the Air Force Technical Applications Center (AFTAC), an obscure military unit that maintains nine seismic monitoring sites in the Southern Hemisphere. These sites provide data to the U.S. Atomic Energy Detection System, which is in turn part of the International Monitoring System for the Comprehensive Test Ban Treaty—forty countries hosting 321 stations that can detect nuclear explosions of a kiloton or less. The seismic, hydroacoustic, infrasound, and radionucleide stations detect, respectively, ground motion, sound waves in water, subaudible sound waves in the atmosphere, and the release of radioactivity from nuclear bomb tests. The network has done other work as well, for instance determining that the Russian submarine that sank in the Baltic Sea in 2000, the *Kursk*, suffered catastrophically not from being rammed by a ship but from internal explosions. The hydroacoustic units are part of a military remote-sensing technology used to detect troop movements across streams and rivers, equipment so sensitive that it can tell the difference between men and women by the resonance of their body cavities.

The other two men in the room, Doug MacDonald and Chris Badger, work for Northern Power, a Vermont company that builds power units for remote field stations. They specialize in wind and solar energy units for use off-grid, a desirable technology in the eyes of NSF, which is seeking to decrease its dependency on fossil fuels and consequent pollution in its field camps, particularly in the sensitive Dry Valleys.

The Bull Pass/Lake Vanda installation, established in 1985, is critical to the network because bedrock installations are difficult to find in the Southern Hemisphere, with its high ratio of ocean to land. Every winter for sixteen years, however, the station experienced power failures— until this last season, when Northern Power installed the new system, which worked very well. Now they're teaching the Air Force how to maintain it.

The AFTAC personnel aren't what either I or the Northern Power guys expected. For one thing, they're not wearing the olive-drab cold-weather gear that we're used to seeing on military personnel in the Antarctic. Instead they're authorized to purchase state-of-the-art mountaineering gear. In place of armored combat laptops they carry the latest and sleekest commercial models, machines capable of teleoperating the seismic sites from anywhere in the world. And loaded into those machines are thousands of vintage rock 'n' roll songs, as well as DVD players on which to watch any of the hundreds of recently released movies they've brought with them. The AFTAC gentleman are serious about their work and put in sixteen-hour days, but after hours they're some of the funniest and most recreationally adept people I've ever hung out with.

Antarctica is, by virtue of the multinational treaty governing it, a military-free zone at the philosophical level, but in reality the various national militaries opened up the continent, and the United States Navy remained the principal logistical organization until the late 1990s. Now logistics are contracted out to the international corporations that comprise the military-industrial complex, a business web within which the armed services are merely one element. No single entity can administer the logistics for an entire continent; it takes public funding channeled through corporations that act as private contractors to the military and governmental agencies to do the job. So the monitoring stations are military, but run in the interests of keeping peace, which is to the benefit of both individual citizens and multinational corporations. The collection of military intelligence (determining who's letting off bangs of what size where) is only one part of the underlying mission; another is occupying what is considered to be high ground, since both poles are potentially strategic routes for air traffic. All this is made manifest by the fact that three years ago Raytheon, the third largest defense contractor in America, won the bid for the NSF contract to administer operations on the ice.

It's nine o'clock before we're finished with our MREs—the "Meals Ready to Eat" that are ubiquitous to military camps—and ready to head up the nearest ridge of the Olympus Range, a prehistoric-looking spine of granodiorite that stands fifteen hundred feet above camp. An hour later we're clambering behind the two-hundred-foot-tall rock battlements, only to find that the boulders on the far side have been completely hollowed out by the wind into fantastic eggshell-thin shapes, enormous ventifacts weighing several tons. The geological disjunct between the two aspects of the ridge is the most severe I've ever seen, almost as if nature had constructed a false front to the scenery, which in a sense is how such cavernous weathering occurs. Silica is precipitated into microfractures on the outside of the rocks, hardening their shells, while windblown sand and ice abrade away the softer insides. The detritus from this cavernous weathering, which can reduce a granite boulder the size of a couch into sand within 100,000 years, runs down into Bull Pass in a series of steep dunes (Plate 5).

Eliot Porter photographed the boulders in the pass, framing them as if they were sculptures, and artists have compared them to artworks by Salvador Dalí and Henry Moore, evoking the spirit of surrealism with the former and modernist forms with the latter. The Antarctic is so extreme to our visual expectations that, once we attempt to move beyond measurement to describe it, analogies with other parts of nature fall short, and we resort to comparisons with cultural artifacts that push at the boundaries of our perceptions. Sometimes pieces of Antarctic nature are so odd to our senses that they actually reverse the flow of analogy and become cultural artifacts in their own right.

Robbie Score, the supervisor of Crary Laboratory and my official "point of contact" on the ice, went out with the geologist Scott Borg to collect a Bull Pass ventifact for the American Museum of Natural History, the curators of the Earth Sciences Hall wanting a dramatic sample to illustrate wind weathering. They found a tablelike affair up here where wind had gouged out the coarser grains and left four columnar legs of harder dolerite. Robbie thought it might weigh 200 pounds and thus be manageable on the stretcher they'd brought for transport to the helicopter. It turned out to be 700-plus pounds, but carry it they did. Borg later visited the piece at the museum and was quite surprised to find the boulder displayed upside down with its legs in the air, despite the photographs and careful installation notes he'd sent with the rock. When he asked the curators why the piece had been rotated out of true, he was told that it made for a more dramatic display. Even a science museum couldn't resist contextualizing these geological curiosities as visual artifacts.

We spend an hour climbing higher and higher until we reach the base of the main peak, where we stop to take pictures of our own. Doug jumps onto one of the dunes and makes an "angel" with his arms and legs, treating the sand as if it were snow. It's almost midnight and time to go down, so we run in great plunging steps down the dunes and into the pass, then circle back to camp. My tent is pitched next to a petite Stonehenge that Doug has erected with seismological cores. As I go to sleep, I imagine that the broken granite cores are miniature columns from an ancient temple, an anthropogenic version of the voids in the boulders, extracted positive shapes assembled to create a presence. Sculpture is commonly defined as a positive shape defining a negative space; the cores and the boulders are almost figure and shadow for each other. Doug's assemblage is a very direct way to turn land into landscape.

Having recuperated sufficiently from the hikes on Monday, I set off two mornings later in a blistering wind with a satellite photo in hand to find one of Mike Malin's rock ablation experiments. Malin, who earned a Ph.D. in planetary science and geology, has since 1990 been the president and chief scientist of Malin Space Science Systems, operator of the Mars Orbiter Camera that sends us many of the pictures of the planet we see in the news. In 1983–1984, while he was still teaching at Arizona State University, he led a team establishing eleven sites in the Dry Valleys with racks holding six thousand rock samples both above and below ground in order to study cold-environment weathering and erosion phenomena in Antarctica. NASA has used Wright Valley for years as an analog for the Martian environment, and Malin's experiments were meant to help him prepare for interpreting digital evidence of surface changes on the red planet. He returned five years later, and again at the ten-year mark, collecting the samples and measuring the weathering on rocks ranging from soft pyroclastic tuff to the much harder dolerite. Malin has since done field studies of ground movement caused by wind, water, and volcanic sources from Hawaii to Iceland, experiences that were invaluable when working with NASA on photogeological surveys of Mars, Venus, and the moons of Jupiter and Saturn. In 1987 he received a coveted MacArthur Foundation "genius" award, in part for his research in the Dry Valleys.

To help me in my quest, Kelly Brunt, the McMurdo cartographer, entered the GPS coordinates from Malin's website into her computer and matched them to a black-and-white photo from Landsat 4 with fifteen meters resolution, which I am carrying with me. I could use Glen's GPS unit to find the site, but he has it in his tent and is still asleep. So this is my own experiment, route-finding using a satellite image. It takes an hour and a half to get to where I should be, just opposite one of the glaciers dropping into the valley, and I'm pleased to find the Malin racks. Although samples remain on the racks at other sites, where it is presumed they will be recoverable for up to fifty years from their initial placement, these stand empty, their rocks already collected. I start taking photos of the site—or at least I hope I am. The film makes a crunching noise as it advances in the camera, leading me to believe it is so cold that the sprockets are tearing, which if true means I'm not taking any pictures at all. After fifteen minutes I head back, too cold to stand around.

What Malin's team discovered here was that two factors are significant in the ablation process: the small-scale topography surrounding the racks and the availability of loose debris small enough to be picked up by the wind and thrown against the samples. The lower the samples were on the racks, the greater the degree of abrasion, with even ice acting as a scouring agent. The other thing they determined was that the rates of erosion in Wright Valley were slow in comparison with other earth environments, presumably due to the lack of water—very much the sort of surface weathering you might expect on a now-dry Mars. This is a fine example of using visual evidence in the Antarctic as a platform from which to interpret images from an even more unfamiliar environment, that of another planet.

Returning to camp with the wind at my back, I'm able to keep my head up and can see well enough to direct myself to a large sandy dish surrounded by the darker and coarser desert pavement. Three battleship gray boulders of dolerite are clustered near the middle, smoothed into sails as if shaped and then placed precisely in a bed of prepared ground by a sculptor. In short, it is a Zen garden. I keep my footsteps to a minimum, stopping short of the cluster, as tempting as it is to touch them. I'm as concerned here about disturbing an aesthetic area as the scientists who work along the Onyx River are about disturbing its streambed, lest they inject unnatural amounts of dirt into the sediment flow they're trying to measure.

The surfaces of stony deserts are fragile and take eons to assemble themselves, stones slowly expressing up to ground level through the action of frost heaving, and the finer material in between each stone being blown away. Slowly the rocks are sorted by wind and weather into a desert pavement that in places will rival the intricate mosaics of ancient Islamic artists. Walking inevitably overturns the rocks, which are stained a lighter color by calcite on the bottom, and also exposes the sandy ground underneath. Footsteps in loose sand can be erased in hours, but it can take the wind centuries to reestablish desert pavement. There's nowhere I can walk without leaving a trace.

As I hike, I cross over lines in the soil. When first seen, they look like small watercourses bordered by rocks, lighter lines in the dirt that meander, branch, meet up with other lines. Stop for a moment to trace them and you realize they connect up in large polygons, usually with four or five sides and twenty to a hundred feet across. Such patterned ground is often found in polar deserts, the result of repeated freeze-thaw cycles that create ice wedges deep in the ground. Wherever there is perennially frozen ground or permafrost, often the remnants of a gla-cial period, vertical ice wedges will form, making cracks in the soil, which increasingly trap the windblown sediments. The wedging heaves up, rising as much as two inches per year, and thrusts material on the edges outward, within a few decades creating what are called unsorted polygons. Under the right conditions the action lifts up rocks on either side of the lines, eventually creating what look like rock-lined footpaths across the valley floor.

Strongly patterned ground is found in many parts of the Dry

Valleys. While the unsorted polygons can arise within decades, the rock-lined or sorted ones take much longer to grow and can be millions of years old. Twenty-six percent of lands on Earth have mean annual temperatures below freezing, and can thus support the severe frosts that produce patterned ground, and in 1999 Malin's Mars Orbital Camera satellite sent back pictures of polygons from the Martian South Pole. On Earth, Alaska hosts some of the larger terrestrial polygons, which can measure up to three hundred feet across; the ones on Mars imaged by Malin's satellite are two hundred times larger.

That evening I take off for another solo hike in the opposite direction, this time up the valley to Lake Vanda. Of the dozen or so Dry Valley lakes, Vanda has the most transparent ice with the smoothest surface, and it is the deepest and warmest body of water in the region. Depending on inflow from the Onyx River, the lake can be as deep as 230 feet. Its permanent ice cover, 12–13 feet thick, is constantly ablating at the top and freezing from the bottom, a process that aligns its ice crystals vertically into a giant lens that focuses the summer solar radiation into the waters below. Its quiet waters are dense with thermo- and chemoclines, delineated layers of varying temperature and chemical composition. The cold freshwater comes in through a narrow moat that thaws briefly in December but doesn't mix with the lower layer of brine, which after millennia of salt accumulation is denser than seawater, three times saltier, and never freezes. Water in the bottom layer can remain a comfortable 77°F year round, warmed by sunlight shining through the ice. Divers have told me that you can easily see the line demarcating the two layers, they are so sharply defined, and have been so for about 1,200 years.

The light transmitted downward allows algae to photosynthesize. Phytoplankton and microzooplankton swim and feed in the upper and mid layers of Vanda, the tiny plants and animals rising and falling in the water column according to temperature and chemical composition. The algae grow in thick mats on the bottom, pieces periodically detaching and floating up to the bottom of the ice, where they melt upward to the surface, then break up and blow away as freeze-dried scraps. Biologists describe the Dry Valley algae as being similar to the earliest life forms found in the history of the planet.

The hike to Vanda is disconcerting in that you're headed up the valley but walking downhill, a phenomenon common in the Great Basin and other desert regions of interior drainage. Humans are sometimes fooled by that anomalous topography; when lost, they adhere to the old Boy Scout doctrine: follow water downhill and you'll find your way back to civilization. In the Great Basin, that logic will take you out onto the middle of a dry lakebed and to death from dehydration. Here, it may be erroneous instincts in the errant seals and penguins that lead to their demise.

Just as my walking on the desert pavement in the morning worried me, now I fret about the dry streambed of the Onyx that meanders across my path and the increasingly moist soils I encounter. In streambeds where groundwater is present, a thin brine floating on the permafrost hosts microbial communities. And in the soils exists the simplest food chain known on Earth, with nematodes at the top of a tiny pyramid of three invertebrates that includes tardigrades and rotifers— microscopic land and aquatic animals that can lose 99 percent of their free water and become ametabolic for more than sixty years, then revive when conditions are favorable. Like the algal remains, they are dispersed by wind.

There are more than twelve thousand individual species of nematodes worldwide, including roundworms, hookworms, and the larvae that cause trichinosis. Mostly, however, nematodes are harmless to humans and critical to the survival of life on Earth. These microbivores eat each other as well as the smaller creatures, but they also break down rock into soils, which in turn help hold carbon in place. There are only five or six species of nematodes in the Antarctic; a single soil sample here might contain as few as three, whereas a comparable sample in the United States would contain more than a hundred. The most common nematode in the Dry Valleys is about a millimeter long and is basically a straight inline stomach with a mouth at one end and a rectum at the other. They are a transparent tube through which you can see what's ingested, the pinnacle of indigenous life in the valleys.

As is the case with much of the Antarctic, simplicity in the environment makes it valuable to science, which also makes it susceptible to damage by casual walking about. Anywhere else in the world it wouldn't matter as much to scientists that we might wipe out a few thousand microbial parasites. Here, life is so simplified that it's relatively easy to understand the linkages among all its forms, and the relationships to climate and geology. In turn, that makes Antarctic nematodes a valuable indicator species for environmental change. The lack of trees is useful to many of us working here to understand how the world works, making for less information clutter, less noise to signal. I take care not to loosen the banks of the streams when I cross, and wherever possible to use rocky outcroppings for my path.

The walk is three miles one way, about the length of my morning hike but with no wind, a rare occurrence that makes one listen all the harder for sounds that aren't there. The landscape is visually quiet as well, the light level blessedly lower. The sun has coursed horizontally behind the peaks of the Asgard Range, which it does every evening around eleven, and clouds further mute the light. This is as dark as it gets here at this time of year. When I reach the lake, its hyperclear shoreline ice glows with the unearthly blue it becomes when old and hard and dense enough to have squeezed out much of the air in it.

I stop at the edge of the ice and look into it. The surface is smooth and undulates in shallow dishes, every pebble on the lake bottom visible. When I step tentatively onto the surface and walk out a few yards, I am dumbstruck, surrounded by square acres of ice that is fractured in as intricate a geometry as the desert pavement is sorted into polygons. At this time of year the algae have not yet bloomed, and the frozen water is so clear you can see straight to the bottom of the lake until the water becomes so dark it's impenetrable; so clear, indeed, that my mind is saying I must be walking on just a few inches of ice, not several feet. It's like flying in a dream, and I have a hard time believing I won't fall.

As I shuffle carefully out from the shoreline, the uppermost layers of the ice begin to creak and crack. It's unnerving but safe; I turn around before I've gone a hundred yards, retreating to a boulder onshore to take notes and regain my composure before venturing out again. This time I get down on my hands and knees to listen to the cracking, which is loud and visible underneath me, like ice cubes popping when you twist the freezer tray to empty it. I take off my gloves. The surface doesn't feel cold; it is so smooth and hard that it isn't perceived by your skin as ice, but more as a dense unscratchable plastic (Plate 6).

I rise and continue across the lake, unable to look up from the intricate crystalline structures and elaborate bubble chains embedded in the ice. Inverted teardrops, assembled in ranks along the freezing front, arch into delicate plumes. Suspended columns of air like the arms of candelabra flare beneath me. Feeling as if I'm on the ceiling of a ballroom, I do a slow waltz on the incandescent ice, wishing for a partner.

When I get back to camp shortly after midnight, the sun still behind the mountains, everyone else is watching a movie on a laptop in the box. After checking in with them I go to bed, tired and overheated from the walk and visual stimulation, unable to sleep for hours. I neither think nor dream in the twilight of the tent, but trace polygons on the inside of my eyelids. Everywhere in Wright Valley I have struggled with its alien appearance. Humans rarely see a landscape that has not been altered by the flow of water, but almost everything on the surface of the Dry Valleys is entirely shaped by wind. The only way we can visually assimilate its rocks and frozen lakes is to compare them not so much to other rocks and bodies of water, but to cultural artifacts such as sculpture and architecture, products more of the imagination than of nature. And this is the easy part of the Antarctic to process visually from pure space into place.

4   FROM CHART TO ART

THE LIBRARY IN THE CRARY LAB contains only a few dozen shelves with less than a thousand titles, but among them are unexpected rarities. Today on an obscure bottom shelf I've found a set of Antarctic map folios produced from 1964 to 1971 by the American Geographical Society, now out of print. Melissa Iszard, a plant ecologist who works as a supervisor of the lab and oversees the library, hasn't had a chance yet to get to this particular shelf, and so she's joined me sitting on the floor with the folios fanned out around us.

The maps in the fifteen oversized folders, drawn at a variety of scales, display among other things the distribution of glaciers, animal life, plants, and fishes; the accumulation of snow; the thickness of the ice; and mean surface temperatures. Their survey data were compiled in the days before the GPS satellites were orbiting above and before airborne radar could penetrate the ice. Data were collected by surveys on foot, and cartographers worked outward from a benchmark still visible in the middle of McMurdo. Climatologists dug pits in the snow, and glaciologists measured the flow of glaciers by means of stakes stuck in the ice.

How our minds interact with a continent where most of its surface is perceptibly on the move is apparent in the cartographic history, and the folios are a major waypoint in the visualization of the Antarctic. One of the folios summarizes all the maps and surveys done on the ice from 1900 to 1964. From the beginning of the century until 1953, just prior to the International Geophysical Year, the multinational effort that established the first permanent bases at McMurdo and Pole, a total of 236 maps are listed. During the next decade, up until July 1964, the pace of mapmaking quickened and 116 maps from ten countries are listed. The list ends then because by 1965 the cartographic flow had become a torrent. By 1988 the governing body of the continent, the Scientific Committee on Antarctic Research (SCAR), had listed in its fifth map catalog 864 topographical maps and 88 composites made from Landsat photos and other satellite images. An e-mail from Sarah Birch at the Australian Antarctic Division, which coordinates such matters for SCAR, informs me that there are now 3,047 maps in the catalog.

Melissa and I sit cross-legged, surrounded by maps tracing the history of traverses with sledges hauled by men, dogs, and tractors; charts explicating the elevation contours of ice; and long tables showing how aerial photography started to accumulate with the Germans in 1938 but by 1964 covered more than 90 percent of the continent and was almost exclusively an American affair.

Maps not only plot the surface of the land but, seen in historical sequence, also show us how our attitudes have imposed changing conceptions of landscape on that same land. Sometimes those landscapes are more mental than physical—a national territorial claim is just a line on a piece of paper—but sometimes maps are prelude to and evidence of our actual manipulation of space into place as we carve roads, flood valleys with reservoirs, and sculpt hillsides into suburbs. Underlying all maps, however, is the presumption that we can impose a systematic geometry upon the planet, a belief founded on both the construction of the world itself and our own biology.

We are, in a sense, polar by nature. We have left and right hands, feet, eyes, and hemispheres of the brain. We have a top and a bottom, a back and a front. We are constructed the way the universe itself is because our biology obeys the laws of physics—and in turn, because we are a bilaterally symmetrical species, we conceive of the universe in terms of dualistic principles. Our senses extend physical symmetry outward from our bodies and into a worldview, an intimate framework around which we attempt to organize the otherwise chaotic dissonance of reality. As a result, we tend to oversimplify the world to some degree—classifying things as either right or wrong, black or white—but we also have a global view of our surroundings, a three-dimensional kinosphere. This is our sense of personal space, which changes shape and size according to circumstance and dictates how comfortable we are with other objects, especially other people, near us. Thus humans embody, literally, both dualistic and spherical geometries in (and of) the world—which is apparent in the history of cartography.

We use all of our senses to establish the kinosphere—for example, we unconsciously use our hearing to help determine the size of a room and our location in it, we smell the presence of other people, and we orient ourselves when we go outside by the touch of wind on our skin. But we use sight more than any other sense. We swivel our head from side to side and up and down, constantly appraising what is near to us and far, what is a resource we need to reach and a threat to avoid. We even project sight ahead of us to preempt our fear of the unknown, visualizing scenarios about what will happen when we cross an open space—such as a street—before we decide to start out.

We thus use vision to project ourselves forward in space and time, an ability that we apply to exploration and cartography as well as to walking around the house or driving to work. The Antarctic continent would not be sighted until January 1820, and not set foot upon until a year or so later by sealers—but its existence had been proposed for centuries, ever since the Greeks took the first sustained steps toward ordering the physical universe, creating a visual geometry that could be projected outward from the individual and then followed.

The earliest schema used by the Greeks to represent the Earth was a four-cornered parallelogram, that basic cognitive shape, a rectangle bifurcated by the east-west axis of the Mediterranean. But then came such astronomers and mathematicians as Thales of Miletus (c. 624–546

B.C.), his student Anaximander (c. 610–546 B.C.), and Pythagoras the supreme geometer (c. 580–500 B.C.), and the world gained shape and form, becoming first a circular plane and then that most perfect and harmonious shape, a sphere. Subsequently Parmenides (c. 515–450 B.C.) divided it into five parallel zones defined by climate, from a frigid north down through a temperate band, a torrid equatorial region, another temperate zone, and again a frigid south—and here we have the basis for a polar world. (*Klimata,* Greek for climate, means "slope of the sky," the angle at which sunlight strikes the earth, a foundational observation essential for development of the celestial navigation that would take us to the poles.) A final basic model for imagining the earth was proposed by Crates of Mellos, who envisioned a globe with four symmetrical continents, two in the Northern Hemisphere and two in the Southern, the Antipodes and the Antoikoi.

Greek geography was diverted by Socrates (469–399 B.C.), who declared that the proper study of man was mankind, not the universe, but the pendulum swung back in the fourth century with Eudoxus of Cnidus (c. 400–350 B.C.) and Aristotle (384–322 B.C.). Eudoxus agreed with Parmenides that the globe was divided into zones of climate, and argued as a philosopher that antipodal symmetry was the opposite side of the sphere from where you were standing. Aristotle, ever the empiricist, pointed out that the shadow thrown by the earth on the moon during an eclipse was curved, physical proof for the Pythagorean hypothesis of sphericity. Expanding on his colleagues' idea of climatic zones, he further postulated that a great southern landmass was needed to counterbalance the known lands in the northern hemisphere (Europe, Asia, and Africa). He named the northern polar region *Arktos,* Greek for bear and the name of the familiar northern constellation; the hypothetical south thus became the "opposite of Arktos," or *Antarktos.*

Understanding of the earth continued to evolve. Eratosthenes (c. 276–194 B.C.), head of the library in Alexandria, calculated in 240 B.C. that the earth's circumference was 25,000 miles (only 140 more than the actual measure from pole to pole to pole). He also came close to inventing the idea of latitude and longitude, which was ultimately arrived at some hundred years later by Hipparchus (c. 190–120 B.C.), the father of Greek astronomy. What had started out as lines used to delineate regions of the world thus became a way to fix location, an essential step in converting space into place.

In A.D. 150 Claudius Ptolemy, another scholar working at the library of Alexandria, proposed that the torrid zone was a barrier of fire occupied by monsters—a concept that would help discourage exploration southward for centuries to come. At the same time, he sought to rationalize cartographic practice by adopting the Hipparchian lines of latitude and longitude, setting forth his principles of mapmaking in his *Geographica*, which included coordinates for eight thousand places. Unfortunately, rather than using Eratosthenes' remarkably accurate measure for the circumference of the earth, Ptolemy turned to the Greek astronomer Poseidonius, whose calculation underestimated the globe's size by 25 percent. As a consequence, Ptolemy concluded that the Indian Ocean was enclosed to the south by a great landmass, which he labeled *Terra Incognita,* a mythical Ur-continent that would not be whittled down to size until the 1770s by James Cook.

The library at Alexandria, where so much energy was devoted to considering the world based on rational observation, had been in slow decline since A.D. 30; in 391 it was sacked by a Christian mob and converted into a church, putting an end to a remarkable era. Mathematics and astronomy were, however, only one way to address cognitive difficulties in conceiving of empty spaces and large distances; religion provided another, though the consequences were diametrically opposed. While the former assembled a consensual method that encouraged rational thinkers to look outward, the latter issued security by dictating that knowledge face inward toward the status quo, a strategy doomed to crash when it was eventually confronted with a flood of new geographical information.

During Europe's Middle Ages, world maps were religious artifacts rather than scientific ones and hung behind altars in cathedrals, their visual structure more allied to Crates than Ptolemy. Although numerous scholars continued to insist the world was spherical, the idea was dismissed by Christians as heretical; there being no biblical mention of a trip by the Apostles to the Antipodes, such a place could not exist, said Pope Zacharias in 741, who excommunicated an Irish priest for suggesting otherwise. Geometry still provided the organizing principle for the European worldview, but it was a flat versus a spherical one. The most prevalent cartographic representation of the world was based on the T-O scheme, so named because it divided the disk of the world into three continents: the upright separated Europe on the left and Africa on the right, while the crossbar set Asia apart on the top of the map. This placed east at the top, "orienting" the map. These *mappae mundi* served as allegorical devices as much as visual encyclopedias for a nonliterate constituency. Deploying illustration as well as cartography and text, blank places on the map were adorned with mythical creatures, the Christian mind abhorring the idea that any part of the world might be unknown to the church.

Not all the world was shrouded in darkness, however. The Arab cartographers, many of whom believed the world was spherical, translated Ptolemy's works in the ninth century; within a hundred years they were busy correcting his calculations, based on extensive trade voyages of their own and Chinese celestial charts they had obtained. Farther east, the Chinese, who had begun using magnetized needles to discern north from south in the third century A.D., were using compass bearings for navigation as early as the eleventh century.

By the end of the thirteenth century, Italian sailors had figured out how to mount a compass needle on a card and were using it to navigate around the Mediterranean—though forced to do so surreptitiously to avoid censure by the more pious among them, who considered the compass a trick of the devil. Maps soon followed. At first painting sixteen directions on the compass card, then further subdividing it into thirty-two directions, the Italians began to construct portolan charts (after *portolani,* or pilot books). Highly stylized, and now appreciated as much for their beauty as their historical significance, these maps focused in great detail on the Mediterranean and Black Sea coasts, which they displayed with relative accuracy. Portolans weren't navigational charts as such, however; more descriptive than mathematical, they used narrative and drawings to illustrate paths and destinations, the lines on them based on prevailing winds, not compass bearings. Nevertheless, in a sense they marked the dawning of quantification in Europe.

The earliest of the 130 *portolani* that still survive was drawn in either Pisa or Genoa in 1296, and portolan chartmakers would remain Western Europe's only cartographers until the mid–fifteenth century. The technique for making these charts was also transmitted to the Islamic world as early as the 1330s, and definitively by 1461. As part of this flourishing circulation of intellectual capital the Greek manuscript of Ptolemy's *Geographica,* which had been preserved in the libraries of Constantinople, was retrieved by a Florentine around 1400 and translated into Latin in 1407. The maps it contained, drawn according to Ptolemy's instructions, simultaneously revolutionized and twisted the West's worldview. Part of the reason its influence would be so pervasive, and how it would lead to an explorer navigating below the Antarctic Circle for the first time (Captain James Cook, in 1773), is that Ptolemy's misconceptions arrived just in time to be propagated through the printing press.

The first European printed map dates from 1472 and is a simple T-O *mappa mundi.* The 1486 Ulm edition of Ptolemy's world map, by contrast, is a marvel of sophistication and accuracy. Using a curved projection and numbered meridians and parallels, it indicates eight separate compass directions. Although this early version is nowhere near as accurate in its depiction of the Mediterranean region as were the *portolani,* that would soon be rectified, the firsthand observations of commercial navigators proving more constructive than the advice of an ancient Greek. And the Ptolemaic depiction of *Terra Incognita?* Africa shades off southward into an undifferentiated land engirdling most of the Southern Hemisphere. Voyages of exploration now showed that world to be far more interesting than Ptolemy ever imagined.

The rectilinear grid intended by Ptolemy to be inscribed over the earth was now a fixture of European imagination, both a creature of and a powerful propellant of what would become Western expansionism. Its major influence was to do something the *portolani* could not: predict what mariners would find beyond the known world. The *portolani* were projectionless, for one thing, and hand-copied for another. The grid, fixed through the medium of printer's ink and infinitely repeatable, made possible transoceanic and intercontinental discovery, that process by which you go out to explore and return with knowledge of how to get there again. Verifiable consistency in cartography was thus keeping pace with science, a methodology governed by observation, the projection of hypotheses, and the testing of them with repeated experiments that bore the same results. Cartography was now a system of visualization that could be projected forward, the cultural extension of a biological ability.

In the meantime, chartmaking and exploration advanced by leaps and bounds under the legacy of Prince Henry the Navigator, perhaps the single most important patron in the Age of Reconnaissance, who had established his Portuguese nautical college in 1419 and offered cash bonuses for sailors brave enough to sail off the edge of the map. His ambitions made it possible for Bartholomew Diaz to reach the Cape of Good Hope in 1488, and for Vasco da Gama to round it nine years later and cross the Indian Ocean, thus finally disproving that Africa and India were connected to *Terra Australis*. Henry's navigators also perfected the use of coastal profiles, topographical drawings that they could line up with the shape of the land in order to record the position of safe harbors and navigational hazards to avoid in the future. As we will see, these profiles play an important role in the creation of Antarctica.

Two controversial claims in the cartography of the Southern Hemisphere date from this period. One concerns a map fragment, the "Atlantic Chart" made by the great seaman and chartmaker Piri Re'is. Born in Gallipoli around 1470, he went to sea with his uncle when he was twelve, and rose from the status of pirate to admiral, commanding the Ottoman fleet in the Southeastern Seas of the Indian Ocean, Red Sea, and Persian Gulf. Before dying in 1554, he left behind both a comprehensive compendium of charts for the Mediterranean and a world map drawn in the portolan style, of which only a fragment is extant.

The Atlantic Chart, dated 1513 and apparently incorporating information from a chart made by Columbus that did not survive, was uncovered in 1926 when the Topkapi Museum in Istanbul was established. Its lower lefthand corner contains the coastline of a southern landmass that bears some resemblance to the corresponding shape of the Antarctic coast. Charles Hapgood asserted in his 1979 book *Maps of the Ancient Sea Kings: Evidence of Advanced Civilization in the Ice Age* that the map represents Antarctica before it was covered by ice. The fact that the continent has been covered by an ice sheet since the earliest Oligocene, about 34 million years ago, and currently bears up to 700,000 years' worth of accumulated ice is but one problem with this theory. Nevertheless, the fragment gives some people cause to speculate about the date when navigators may have first approached the southern continent.

The other controversy was created by Caspar Volpel, a mapmaker of Cologne, who claimed on his 1545 world map that *Terra Australis* had been sighted as early as 1499, which would fit within the timeline for Piri Re'is. Some cartographic experts argue, however, that the curvature of the supposed Antarctic coast on his map was caused simply by the shape of the hide on which it was drawn, a not uncommon practice of the time. Most historians agree that in both arguments, whether that of Volpel in the sixteenth century or Hapgood in the twentieth, it was more human imagination projecting the map than any physical exploration.

In 1520 Ferdinand Magellan sailed around South America, picking his way cautiously for a month through the strait south of Chile that would afterward bear his name. He and his crew were unsure if what they saw to the south was islands or part of the great southern continent. In 1531, states Alan Gurney in the first volume of his history of Antarctic discovery, *Below the Convergence,* a French map called it *Terra australis recenter invento sed nondum plene cognita,* or "the southern land newly discovered but not yet fully known." It was, in fact, the archipelago of Tierra del Fuego and not the Antarctic.

In any event, the outlining of the Pacific, an ocean that had not even existed on European maps before the sixteenth century, had now begun in earnest. So had the process of mapping where the Antarctic wasn't. The voyages of Balboa, Magellan, and others began to disprove the biblical notion that the earth was composed of six-tenths land, and to demonstrate that it was, instead, two-thirds water. This was a massive reordering of geophysical faith akin to moving from a geocentric view of the solar system to the heliocentric one Copernicus was formulating at the same time.

The next step forward in the application of geometry to the globe, and thus the positioning of the Antarctic, was made by Gerardus Mercator. Born in Flanders in 1512, Mercator was not only a gifted surveyor and mapmaker extraordinaire, but a talented engraver as well. In 1569 he published his world maps drawn on the method of projection that bears his name, the first one in which compass lines intersect meridians at a constant and given angle. Mercator's map could, therefore, be used by navigators to plot courses in a straight line, which was a major improvement to the merely rectilinear cartographic grid. His work also had two significant flaws. One, of course, was its distortion of high-latitude landmasses, an example being the extreme enlargement of Greenland. The other is that his map continued to show that great land to the south, *Terra Australis,* to be connected to the southern tips of Africa and Asia.

Mercator's graticule quickly became the standard mapmaking procedure. Not only did his projection have practical value in terms of navigation, but it also allowed people to predict mathematically where they would come to be in relationship to the rest of the world, a cartographic counterpart to the European art technique of projecting perspective onto the picture plane. Both were technological extensions of our neurophysiological ability to throw our vision forward into the distance. The cartographers were helping rationalize the world by sifting it through a neutral grid based on mathematics, versus the conventions of religious iconography.

This shift related intimately to that made earlier by artists, who in the early Renaissance had been moving from the patronage of the Church to that of commerce. In the process, artists also adjusted their working techniques. One major innovation—again paralleling cartography—was the use of the grid to achieve a perspective view. By applying a mathematical lattice to a visual field, an artist could now organize three-dimensional visual space onto a two-dimensional surface without awkward distortions, thereby placing both himself and the viewer firmly in control of the view. Art thus began to shift from portraying a finite world in which parallel lines never met, to representing an infinite space assimilated through vision. Both triangulation, as used in navigation, and perspective, as applied now to the depiction of the world in paintings, demonstrated the ongoing human need to organize unfamiliar space in a predictable fashion in order to transmit it visually from one person to another. If mapping the world was increasingly a necessity for the free flow of goods, then mapping the painting—establishing rules of perspective—was likewise necessary to create a common rational ground for the flow of knowledge and shared social conventions throughout a growing population.

In May 1570, the year after Mercator published his world maps, his friend and rival cartographer in Antwerp, Abraham Ortelius, published the first popular atlas. Consisting of seventy maps contributed by cartographers from various countries but engraved in a consistent format, his *Theatrum orbis terrarum* would go through more than forty editions until its last printing in 1612. Both the geographical knowledge and the cartography employed were state of the art, although inland cartography was still less resolved than its marine counterpart. Landmasses were illustrated graphically, with tiny hills and buildings representing mountain ranges and settlements, for example, while the coastlines tended to be exaggerated with immensely deep inlets and coves, in deference to the importance of the maps to navigators, who were still primarily coastal sailors.

The *mappa mundi* included in the atlas is recognizable to us today, the basic contours of the continents mapped out with reasonable fidelity to reality or, as in the case of North America, with inspired guesswork that nonetheless gets most of the world in the right place. The exception was the poles. The Arctic is displayed as four huge and frozen solid masses resting symmetrically above Asia, Europe, and North America. A northeast passage allows for navigation above the first two, while a northwest counterpart is delineated above the Americas, an aesthetic decision as much as a geographical supposition, and one that would drive Arctic exploration for centuries in search of northern trade routes.

And the Antarctic? *Terra australis nondum cognita* is still four times the size of its northern opposite. It has rivers and bays with fictitious names, and a shaded coastline. Terra del Fuego is shown as part of the continent, and it is separated from South America by the narrow Strait of Magellan. The only features on the interior of the empty continent are the converging meridians of longitude and the horizontal lines of latitude.

Ortelius's world map did at least show the Antarctic to be separated from Africa, and in 1578 that was confirmed as fact when Sir Francis Drake landed on Cape Horn. He lay down on the beach and, according to Gurney, spread out his arms and declared himself to be the southernmost man in the world. He had no way of knowing for sure, but he was probably correct. Cartographers, however, continued to show a massive *Terra Australis Incognita* covering almost all of the globe below fifty degrees south, an area five times greater than the actual Antarctic. And for all anyone knew, it could indeed have been populated by giants, gnomes, or gryphons.

At almost the same time that Mercator's map was being published in the Low Countries, the citizens there were beginning a revolution against their Spanish rulers, Catholics who had been cracking down harshly on the northern Protestants. It would take from 1566 until 1648 for the dust to settle, and for Spain to formally acknowledge their independence, but by then the Dutch burghers had absorbed the Iberian maritime expertise and transformed themselves into the greatest seagoing cartographers and merchants in the world.

Among the innovations the Dutch incorporated into their rutters, or pilots' sailing books, was topography—realistic drawings of the hills and indentations of the coast. By the 1600s, elongated and horizontal coastal profiles would be added routinely to charts and surveys, proving especially useful in navigating unfamiliar coasts or while sailing in poor visibility, a commonplace condition in the northern waters. It had been Ptolemy, in fact, who first insisted that geography provide an accurate pictorial representation of the world, and who had developed a style of illustration based on maps to reproduce identifiable features of specific places. This he called chorography, and in its pure form it was the domain of artists. As applied to mapmaking, it became known as topography.

In 1584 Lucas J. Waghenaer of Leiden published the first atlas of sea charts, which contained, in addition to portolan and depth charts, coastal profiles. Although at first it represented only the coasts of Western Europe, it eventually covered the entire known world. The English were not to publish their own sea atlas until 1689, but four years later, recognizing the importance that sketches made by seamen were having on navigation and exploration, a Drawing School was established at Christ's Hospital for the training of navy personnel in making coastal profiles and sea views.

Beginning in the sixteenth century, too, the Dutch, adopting the full panoply of perspective techniques developed in Italy during the preceding century, elaborated landscape painting as a distinct genre. In this, the coastal profile played a significant role, for it lent itself perfectly to representing the broad flats of the Dutch countryside. Whereas the Italians had cultivated a penchant for elevated landscape views by which to view and situate their towns, which were often built on hillsides, the Dutch adopted instead a lower and more panoramic viewpoint that included a generous view of the sky, an acknowledgment of how important weather was to navigation. Thus was the tradition of Dutch landscape painting shaped, a genre rooted in cartography and sustained, moreover, by private patronage from a middle class created by maritime commerce. Once voyagers begin to reach the southern continent, both these traditions—the coastal profile and Dutch landscape painting—came strongly into play as a means of understanding that strange land.

As cartography advanced, so did Europeans' firsthand knowledge of the globe, including the polar worlds. Partly for political reasons—the Spanish and Portuguese had locked up the trade routes around Africa and South America—it was left to the more northerly countries to search for commercially viable alternatives, which they hoped would be found in the Northeast and Northwest Passages, promised by the *mappae mundi* of Ortelius and others. By the mid-1800s, despite concerted efforts, it was clear that the Northwest Passage was not a commercially viable route. Meanwhile, the Russians finally forced the Northeast Passage (which can be kept open by icebreakers) in 1648, after several notable attempts, including those of the Englishmen Sir Hugh Willoughby and Richard Chancellor in 1553 and, proceeding in a westward direction, Sir Martin Frobisher, with three voyages from 1576 to 1578, and of the Dutchman Willem Barents, who also gave it three shots, from 1594 through 1597.

It took many attempts to discover that the Northwest Passage was not a commercially viable route. The quest evolved into a way to keep young British naval officers employed when no wars were raging, exploration being a time-honored strategy to maintain a standing maritime force. The displacement of military heroism into polar excursions is in no small way responsible for both the folly and fervor of nineteenth-century polar exploration. The disappearance of Sir John Franklin in 1845 during his Northwest Passage expedition spurred numerous unsuccessful rescue and recovery attempts, as well as an outpouring of romantic visual and literary imagery that continues to fuel new novels even today. The Northwest Passage wasn't completed under sail until the sturdy and meticulous Norwegian explorer Roald Amundsen, his boyhood fueled by visions of the Franklin expedition, traversed the Arctic in 1903–1906. This experience would serve him well as he led the first expedition to reach the South Pole several years later.

The Barents and Frobisher Arctic journeys presented us with the first visual images of the polar regions made on the scene, pictures that are also some of the earliest examples of exploration art. From the former we have a series of panels showing Barents's icebound ship and the subsequent efforts to build a cabin and survive. Among records of the latter are a painting by John White that shows Eskimos paddling kayaks in sea ice and four crude sketches of an iceberg made by Thomas Ellis, one of the sailors on Frobisher's third trip in 1578. His drawings depict an actual "Island of yce," four thumbnail sketches that give us a view-in-the-round of a hollow, somewhat architectonic iceberg. The die was thus cast early on in favor of art that demonstrated the navigational hazards of the polar regions.

As the Spanish and Portuguese empires declined and the Dutch merchants ascended, exploratory emphasis shifted slowly from the north to the south. In 1616 the Dutch found Tierra del Fuego to be an island, and by then had started to trace the shores of Australia. The next task was to begin comprehensive surveying of the southern extremities of the globe, to determine if it was land, ice, ocean, or ogres. The Dutch East Indies Company sent out Abel Tasman in 1642–1643, who discovered and then made extensive coastal profiles of Tasmania and New Zealand. Although Tasman never actually saw Australia, his two ships sailed entirely around the world's smallest continent, thus proving it was not connected to Antarctica. The farthest south they reached was latitude 49°4'S, where they were turned back by snow and cold.

The mid-1600s was a pivotal period in the incubation of an international scientific community. Rising literacy fueled the demand for printed books in all the national vernacular languages of the European continent. Latin was losing its grip as the sole language of the natural sciences, which made it imperative that universal weights and measures be adopted, such as the Fahrenheit scale for temperature. Concurrently, as explorers brought back entire new bodies of data about the world, it became increasingly untenable to support generalized worldviews that didn't square with the facts.

The perhaps inevitable result was the establishment of royal academies, intended to codify the role of science in society and to foster inquiry, the most significant being the Académie Royale des Sciences in Paris and the Royal Society of London. The Italian astronomer Giovanni Domenico Cassini (1625–1712) accepted an invitation to the Académie, arrived in Paris in 1669, and began the project of mapping France, creating the first topographical maps of a country to be based on triangulation, a massive incremental fieldwork that would be carried out by three generations of his offspring. The energetic cartographer made maps of the moon at the Paris Observatory in 1679, and prepared an enormous terrestrial *mappa mundi* on the observatory floor, refusing to include any positions on it not determined astronomically. At last Ptolemy's mistaken measurement of the Mediterranean was corrected, the revision appearing on a map Cassini published in 1696.

In 1682 the English astronomer Edmund Halley (1656–1742) dropped by to visit Cassini as he worked on the floor of the observatory. Halley was one of the most accomplished scientists during a time of remarkable polymaths, perhaps second only to Newton in the range of his interests and contributions. Although we mostly remember him in connection with the comet that bears his name, when he was twenty-one he spent a year on the island of St. Helena in the mid-Atlantic and compiled the first catalog of stars in the Southern Hemisphere, thus extending enormously the ability to navigate below the equator.

Halley went on to invent the meteorological chart in 1686, which mapped the prevailing trade winds in the lower latitudes, and in 1699 was awarded a temporary commission in the Royal Navy to undertake the first scientific sea voyage in history, sailing from 50°N to below 50°S in order to map the earth's magnetic field. On February 1, 1700, at latitude 52°24'S, his crew sighted three flat-topped white islands that the next day they determined to be made solely of ice. Halley sketched them into his logbook, the first pictures of Antarctic tabular icebergs.

Halley went on to become astronomer royal at Greenwich Observatory, upholding the formal links forged by Thales, Anaximander, Eratosthenes, and Hipparchus between astronomy and geography, as well as speculation about the great unknown southern continent. It was in this capacity that he set the stage for the greatest sea voyages south yet to be undertaken. As astronomer royal, he urged the government to send out expeditions to observe from at least two widely separated stations in southern waters the transits of Venus of June 1761 and June 1769. The measurement of Venus's progress across the disc of the sun was crucial in two respects: it would allow the distance of the sun from the earth to be established beyond question, and it would determine whether the shape of the earth was, as Newton had predicted, not a true sphere but, rather, an oblate spheroid, both of which facts had obvious significance for everything from theories of planetary formation to practical navigation.

Halley died at the age of eighty-five in 1742, but his word was heeded. The observations of 1761 by the 120 persons sent out by nine nations were frustrated by clouds, travel delays, warfare, and poor instruments; the Royal Society therefore put all its hopes into the voyages of 1769. Commanding the contingent to Tahiti was a forty-year-old marine surveyor who had been promoted for the task the previous year to the rank of second lieutenant. Along with his astronomical duties, the navy provided him with a sealed packet regarding what to do after obtaining the transit observation: go look for the southern continent. James Cook sailed off in 1768 on what would be the first of his three monumental voyages to the Pacific. He carried with him on his voyage to Tahiti a complement of natural historians, including Sir Joseph Banks; the young landscape painter Sydney Parkinson; the artist Alexander Buchon, noted for his sketches of native people; and the Finnish scientific illustrator Herman Sporing.

Cook returned three years later with solid observational data supporting Newton's theory, as well as maps and coastal profiles for five thousand miles of newly surveyed coastlines in New Zealand, the east coast of Australia, and various islands such as Tahiti. Cook had not just been separating the Antarctic from the other continents; he had cut away vigorously at the geographical myths attached to it by Aristotle, Crates, Ptolemy, and every other geographer since who had sought to balance the known world with a great unknown southern land.

In 1772 Cook was sent out again with a crew of scientists. Accompanying the voyage this time was the young William Hodges (1744–1797), a classically trained landscape artist. The officers themselves had been trained in art, but by another route and under the influence of another great painter, Alexander Cozens, the first major English artist to pursue landscape as a subject. Cozens had been hired to teach his more topographically oriented methods at the Royal Mathematical School of Christ's Hospital from 1750 to 1754. This style, rather than that of Claude Lorrain and other classicists, is what the officers demanded of Hodges— pragmatic coastal profiles and views, visual records of their discoveries that could be used by the navigators who would follow them.

His duty thus made clear, within three weeks of leaving port Hodges was producing topographical drawings and watercolors that elicited unanimous praise from the captain and his men. But Hodges brought something unique to this newly acquired style: the ability to inject the keen meteorological observations demanded of sailors into his paintings. Not only was he able to record the coastlines along which they sailed, but he also took into account the sky above them. This unique combination of skills allowed Hodges to represent faithfully both the lush tropical shores of Tahiti and the severe seascapes below the Antarctic Circle.

William Hodges produced a body of exploration art unlike any seen before, and he would go on to become the most widely traveled artist of his day. His paintings would influence those of J. M. W. Turner, whose work would be revered, in turn, by Thomas Moran in painting the exploration of the American West during the latter half of the nineteenth century. At the same time, a fledgling natural historian and amateur artist named Edward Wilson would be poring over Turner's work as well. Wilson would soon be asked by Scott to join him on the first of two voyages together to the Antarctic. The artist, making his landscape profiles and watercolors of the polar atmosphere, would become the hero-artist of the continent.

Hodges furthered significantly the topographical tradition in landscape art that had arisen out of cartography, which itself was founded on the ancient Greeks' reverence for geometry in the world. He helped establish a lineage of representational exploration art against which every artist sent to the ice would be measured. Furthermore, his coastal profiles and Cook's surveying techniques would remain state-of-the art cartography for the continent well into the twentieth century, becoming eclipsed only by the methods used to produce the map folios of the American Geographical Society.

5 THE PHYSICAL PLANT

I HAVE YET TO SEE anything growing in the Antarctic except algae, lichen, and bacteria, but Melissa—who is writing a natural history of Hut Point Peninsula—is determined to change that. We meet in the lab at seven on a Saturday morning for a hike to look for moss, but before we can get out the door her pager goes off. It's a seal scientist complaining that he can't access the station server, so he's unable to track where his telemetry-rigged subjects are swimming in the sound. Melissa rousts a couple of computer technicians by phone to see what can be done. As we're walking out we're stopped by a penguin researcher with the same problem. Backtrack to the office, more phone calls. We finally make our escape at 9:15, a cyber solution now in progress, and head up to the main street.

This dirt road, which runs from Scott's *Discovery* hut to Scott Base, the New Zealand station on the other side of Observation ("Ob") Hill, is, at 2.45 miles in length, the longest constructed street on land in the Antarctic. McMurdo adheres to its American urban roots and sprawls out along much of what residents wryly refer to as Antarctic 1, a collection of 104 buildings that range in color from the officially sanctioned brown-on-brown scheme to blue, green, and orange. Quonset huts abut corrugated metal shacks, and the huge prefab Crary Lab stands next to the NSF's wooden "chalet." The oldest standing structure is a modest navy building that dates from 1957, now completely rebuilt as the community center. What might be called the town plaza is a dirt lot bounded by dorms on one side and the galley on the other; it contains "Derelict Junction," the bus stop for shuttles to Scott Base and the runways out on the Ross Ice Shelf (Plate 7).

McMurdo overall looks like an Alaskan mining town. At the moment, huge fuel tanks are bermed on snowy hillsides above construction yards filled with material on the way to Pole, where they're building a new station to replace the venerable geodesic dome that's been almost completely subsumed by ice. Below the berms are dorms, laboratories, and support buildings where we eat, sleep, and work on overcranked schedules. The sun never dips below the horizon nor rises higher than thirty-five degrees during the Austral summer, so our hours are dictated mostly by when food is served and helicopters fly us into the field.

By my crude urban analogy, Hut Point is one of our two city parks, the one that in small towns inevitably contains a historic building. The other park is Ob Hill, the slightly wilder area at the edge of town where people go to hike. A steep trail leads to its summit more than 750 feet above town, where there's a wooden cross commemorating Scott's journey, as well as aerial views of McMurdo and Scott Bases and fine panoramas of Mt. Erebus, the Transantarctic Mountains, and the sound (Plate 8).

In the evenings a few people tend to promenade from town to the point, but this morning Melissa and I are alone as we set out toward Scott's hut, a ten-minute walk. The ground of the point has been bulldozed for years, as has much of the terrain surrounding the station, long vertical strips on the land like windrows marking where the volcanic material has been pushed downward as fill to create level ground for the town, which now covers about a hundred acres. The result is what geologists label thermokarst, hummocks, and hollow terrain, varieties of unstable ground surfaces resulting from repeated disturbances of the underlying permafrost. It will be many human lifetimes before weather and erosion can reestablish equilibrium here.

Winter Quarters Bay, an inlet only a few hundred yards across that separates the base's dorms from Scott's hut, has been equally if less visibly disturbed by McMurdo. Divers working inside the bay have found abandoned vehicles and fuel drums left thirty years ago by the U.S. Navy to fall through the ice, a practice long since discontinued. Only three hundred yards outside the sand bar that prevents the waters of the bay from mixing freely with the sound, however, hardly any traces of human activity are found. Likewise, once we turn the point and McMurdo is out of sight, the anthropogenic disruptions disappear. Here Melissa and I are in a world defined by sea ice, dark volcanic gullies, and the blue remnants of glaciers.

Although the nearest open water is seventy miles north, tides still act on the sea ice here, twice daily lifting it up and then dropping it, creating three-foot-high pressure ridges and deep cracks in the transition zone with the shore. A mere fifty yards out, the ice is strong enough to handle the fully loaded C-130 cargo planes that land almost daily. Next to the island the ice bears careful watching, and we stay on the shoreline wherever possible. Melissa, who lives in a cabin in Maine when not on the ice, is a cross-country runner and skier, and has been coming to the Antarctic on and off since 1993. She moves across the landscape with relative ease, careful to stay on snow when she can in order not to disturb the soils. I bumble about, planting my butt on icy patches and occasionally displacing dark rocks on the ground, the lighter ground underneath revealed until wind and weather can reshuffle the protective paving of stones back into place.

Her gaze focused downward, Melissa attempts to relocate the patches of moss she found last season. Although algae are relatively common in the Antarctic wherever there is standing water, and lichens are found on Ob Hill, moss is rare this far south. My new roommate, Andrew Klein, a scientist who has just arrived for a third year of sampling McMurdo soils and the sea bottom in the bay, is skeptical that we will find any moss growing here. Melissa, however, wrote her master's thesis on alpine plants and is accomplished at ferreting out miniature botanical treasures.

Algae are aquatic plants ranging in size and shape from unicellular plants only one-thousandth of a millimeter across to seaweeds the size of birch trees. Their terrestrial cousins grow in the Antarctic on moist soil, in snowbanks, and under translucent quartz rocks where they are protected from wind and ultraviolet radiation but still able to photosynthesize. They're found clear down to 86°29' S, more than five hundred miles south of us and less than three hundred miles from the Pole.

Algae are the photosynthetic partners that, in symbiosis with fungi, make up lichens, which are found even farther south, about 250 miles north of the South Pole. The four hundred species of Antarctic lichens recover very slowly after being frozen during the winter, taking weeks to recuperate and begin photosynthesis again, and grow very slowly, from one centimeter per century here at the coast to around a centimeter per thousand years in the Dry Valleys. Although some Antarctic varieties can convert sunlight into growth in temperatures down to −2°F, and seem to thrive in both rising temperatures and rising ultraviolet levels, they're sensitive to environmental pollutants, such as the pesticide DDT, which is found in lichens on the continent.

Like algae, lichens are relatively common in the stony areas of the Antarctic. Mosses are rare enough, however, that one particularly rich assemblage of them found at the northern end of the island is a restricted area you can enter only by permit. Mosses have leaves and stems but never roots, and may have been the first green land plants to evolve in the late Silurian or early Devonian (call it 410 million years ago or so). About a hundred species of the nonvascular bryophytes grow on the continent, plants that then evolved concurrently with early vascular plants later during the Devonian, such as grasses (which are the southernmost plants that have roots). Mosses are able to restart photosynthesis within hours after having been frozen, so like lichens they are quite hardy, though not as widely distributed.

As we walk, the wind pushes on the backs of our red parkas as if they were sails, unbalancing us. Once we round a second small point and start walking uphill out of the wind, Melissa scans the ground more intently. We pause at a series of tarns, the largest pond only twenty yards in diameter; its surface is a smaller version of Lake Vanda, a jigsaw geometry of stress fractures frozen into polygons several feet across. Scraps of algae are dried around its edges like thin scraps of recycled paper, but we find nothing growing. A tongue of old ice slowly erodes nearby into a layer cake dripping with icicles, and we skirt it as we continue up a gully.

When we do spot a fingernail-sized patch of moss a few minutes later, it's a solitary dense tuft of anomalous yellow-green nestled among the volcanic rocks. Through the magnifying glass we've borrowed from the lab it looks like a miniature forest; Antarctic mosses clump their stems closely together in order to minimize loss of water in the frigid aridity. The crown of the patch is bleached out, suggesting the genus to which the moss might belong, *Bryum*, which is often silvery in appearance on top from lack of chlorophyll in the upper leaf cells. Melissa expresses concern, though, that it might also be the result of UV damage. Diatoms in the Antarctic ocean seem to be adapting to the increased levels of radiation admitted by the annual ozone hole overhead at this time of year, but the effect on terrestrial flora appears to be headed the other way.

"Life wants to live," Melissa says, smiling, and it's so poignant to find it here that we hesitate to move lest we disturb other patches. Just as we're about to expand our search area, Melissa's pager goes off, discreetly muffled by her parka. It's the seal researcher again. We start back.

During the return hike we have a long gray view out across the sound to the mountains, the scale of the landscape even more indeterminate than usual. Human sensory perceptions tend to fail in the Antarctic as in other deserts, but the scale of the dislocation is so much larger here that it's constantly mythologized. We use superlatives for the continent such as emptiest, most isolated, coldest, windiest, highest, driest. All true, the harshness of the continent straining at the very limits of our language's ability to describe it. The heroic pedestals that we've erected underneath explorers such as Scott and Shackleton are another kind of cultural compensation for our difficulties in perceiving the continent, and their narratives place the ice in opposition to humans as a sterile space almost beyond comprehension. Both our choice of words and the historical elevation construct a framework through which we can begin to understand the Antarctic, but they also narrow our perception of it to fit a singular viewpoint, that of human size and history. Melissa, in contrast, is showing me that the Antarctic is a place where life works hard to flourish in every conceivable niche, and that the continent is a landscape we can understand better by climbing down from the pedestal and getting on our hands and knees, thereby expanding our sense of scale in both time and space.

The idea of finding plants in the Antarctic leads me by linguistic association to wonder about the "physical plant" of McMurdo itself, how it grows and organizes itself. People unfamiliar with contemporary Antarctica envision it as a place where we live in igloos or tents and get around with dogsleds. This is more of the myth that needs taking apart in order to construct a version of the landscape to which we can more accurately scale ourselves. Plants modify the environment in which they grow, and so does our built environment, both processes that by necessity respond in unique ways to the extreme conditions here.

In 1955, when the U.S. Navy was deciding where to put a base for our participation in the International Geophysical Year, the Ross Sea region attracted them for the same reasons that Scott and Shackleton had selected it for their operations: it provided the closest open water during the Austral summer to the South Pole. The Navy's first choice was Cape Evans, but when a thirty-ton bulldozer fell through the sea ice, taking the driver with it, they opted for a location deeper in the sound where the ice would be thicker. The tip of the seven-mile-long peninsula that runs out from Mt. Erebus and ends at Ob Hill offers a rare combination of attributes. First, the sea ice is stable enough to safely land large-wheeled aircraft during the first part of the summer, and later in the season the nearby Ross Ice Shelf runway can handle planes operating on either skis or wheels. The land is ice free for several square miles, and although it doesn't host any wildlife colonies to be disturbed, it is close to major ones for study. It's also within helo range of the Dry Valleys. Later, the island turned out to be on the edge of the fluctuating ozone hole as well, making it an ideal platform for studying a leading indicator of the planet's health.

American research facilities in the Antarctic have been administered by the NSF since 1971, but operation of the station didn't shift from the navy to civilian contractors hired by the NSF until the 1990s. Jim Scott, the Raytheon area manager, has volunteered to tour me through the station's infrastructure. He first came here in 1983 as the supervisor of the power plant, wintered over three times, took a lengthy break, then returned to the ice last year. Diane Nelson-Scott, an artist married to Jim, is also on station working in quality control for Raytheon, and is illustrating Melissa's natural history book. That kind of warp and weft in the social fabric is endemic within the network of people who work here. The place magnetizes people to it; no matter where they are, their emotions and thoughts remain oriented to the ice. They may stay away for a year or a decade, but the desire to return never ends.

A few days after the moss-hunting expedition, Jim and I drive one of the base's red pickup trucks up to the T-Site communications complex, located on a ridge behind town where the antennae farm stands. More than two dozen radio masts stand anchored by six miles of cable, forming a dense geometrical thicket through which transmissions are received and sent from around the continent and the outside world. During a Herbie it must keen up here like a symphony of demented violins.

Jim parks by the new T-Site building, a prefab blue box. The facility is clean, windowless, and crammed with electronic racks stacked with communication gear. It's noiseless, the readouts are digital, and the entire building is meant to be run remotely from town. It has less personality than the inside of a television set. Next door stands the original T-Site building, a weatherbeaten gray rectangle of corrugated metal that had its roof blown two-thirds off a few years ago. It was repaired, but the building will go cold in February and be dismantled next summer season. We enter the vestibule, then pass through a kitchen and into a lounge with a table and chairs, and small bedrooms off to one side. Windows look out over the sound, one of which is painted over with a vaguely Blakean mythical landscape of black ice.

The business end of the building contains heavy cables snaking down from the ceiling and plugged into the back of what looks like a giant old-fashioned telephone operator's switchboard. There's nothing digital here; each antenna configuration was once aimed by hand toward Pole or Christchurch while broadcasting. At the other end of the room is a pool table, a recreational analog for bouncing signals from one location to another. Making a circuit through the building, we double back and pass through a corridor filled with electronics featuring readouts in gauges and dials instead of the glowing digits next door.

"I think this stuff was brought here secondhand from a European-theater station in the Atlantic that was decommissioned in the early 1960s," says Jim. "We'll ship it back to the United States and put it up for auction. Ham radio operators will go crazy for it."

Walking out, it's hard not to feel romantic about one of the few facilities that was once staffed—both inside and out—throughout the fierce Antarctic winters. The duty must have been excruciatingly boring most of the time, enlivened when storms meant having to work outside in the frigid dark and wind to keep the antennae up and the comm links open, an existence at once banal and heroic all in one six-month shift.

There's a danger, though, in falling for the slow decay of industrial ruins. The heavy cables and manual switching equipment were much more risky to a sleepy technician than are the digital circuits next door, which are much easier to see, reach, and work on. Voltages are lower and better insulated. The unstaffed facility is a clean, well-lit workplace, and there's a basic humanity to that which should not be ignored.

On our slow descent back into town we detour to trace the fuel pipe that comes up through the saddle between McMurdo and Scott Base, and follow it down to the sea ice where the road transitions off the island and onto the ice shelf, heading out to Williams, or "Willy," Field, the airstrip that will open in a couple of weeks.

"This hose is six miles long," Jim explains. The tough plastic-impregnated fabric forms a tube thicker than my calf. "The one we run out to the field on the sea ice is three miles long, and that's how we determine where the runway will be each spring. We just run out the hose and draw a straight line at the end."

I ask about the road that the hose parallels, which has four separately flagged lanes.

"We have two open, and then a couple closed that we're always packing down the crust on for wheeled vehicles. And see how we mine snow here," he says, gesturing at a bay cut into the hillside snowbanks. "Gravel gets picked up by tires and thrown out onto the snow. It warms in the sun and creates meltpools . . ."

"Potholes," I interrupt.

"Exactly, so we're always spreading snow out on the roads to keep the gravel down." I find it typical Antarctic logic that road maintenance here would be the opposite of what it is at home, where we throw volcanic cinder out to sand the roads after snowstorms.

Going back into town we pass by the tank farm, which holds up to ten and a half million gallons of fuel for aviation, ground transportation, and generators, then turn into the storage yards that are stacked with approximately six million pounds of building materials. Some of it is waiting to be transferred out to Pole for the new station; some of it is being used here in town, or is slated for various science projects and field camps; and some of it has been sitting around so long no one knows what the hell it's for. In one area hundreds of spare tires are stacked up, ranging from beefy all-weather spares for the fifty-two pickups and vans on station to the massively treaded footwear of the big Caterpillar frontloaders. All together there are about 350 pieces of rolling stock at McMurdo, some of it running on metal treads, but much of it on rubber.

"UV eats tires here," Jim says. "We tried putting tarps on them, but the wind just beats the covers to pieces, so the tires tend to rot. We're going to cut a garage door into one of the old fuel storage tanks that we don't need and put them in there. Use what we have."

Behind us is an industrial-grade wood chipper, its circular maw raised high above the ground, ready to consume wooden pallets and construction debris. It spits out a steady stream of chips that move up a conveyor belt. Like the other three and a half million pounds of waste generated here annually, the chips go into containers that will be shipped out on the freighter that once a year both brings supplies and picks up the garbage, the *Greenwave*. Virtually all of the solid waste produced at American stations is sorted and then retrograded back to the States for recycling. The extensive waste management procedures were put into place partly in reaction to Greenpeace, the nonprofit environmental organization, which in 1986 established its World Park Base next to McMurdo and for five years publicized violations of the Antarctic Treaty's environmental regulations.

If you want to measure the American presence in the Antarctic, look at what comes in and goes out of McMurdo. The total cargo shipped in last year weighed in at 15,898,397 pounds, according to the NSF; the total sent out was 8,446,252 pounds. Do the arithmetic and you get 7.4 million pounds remaining on station. Some of that is consumed as food and fuel by the approximately three thousand people passing through, but much of it stays here, converted into buildings and other infrastructure. If you ask longtime NSF people what they're most proud of during their tenure, often their reply will be the reduction of the American impact on the Antarctic environment, even while our cumulative footprint has increased. No one pretends that fuel doesn't sometimes still escape the containment procedures, or that plastic scraps aren't blown out onto the sea ice, but the improvement has been applauded even by Greenpeace.

Our next stop is the VMF, or Vehicle Maintenance Facility, which contains a machine shop with lathes, drill presses, and band saws large enough to fabricate almost any other machine on base—as well as the occasional art piece. On the other side of the wall is a separate room where they reconstruct blown engines, stripped gearboxes, and other mangled equipment. Passing by a tool room that has an inventory of more than ten thousand items, we enter the kingdom of "Heavy." This is the garage where the monsters come to hulk in pain, where giant snow blowers are towed after they've thrown pieces through their radiators, and where the three Stretch-8 Cats built fifty years ago hobble in to be refurbished, a constant process.

There's romance here, too—in our veneration for things that have "lived" this long and worked this hard under such harsh conditions. But again, there's the reality that some of these are lumbering piles of rust that are unsafe, incredibly costly to maintain (with almost every replacement part having to be fabricated on site), and sometimes not able to do the work they are required to perform. Raytheon is aggressive about upgrading equipment on a fixed schedule, as it enables the company to fulfill its contractual responsibilities on budget, and it feels like an honor to be introduced to these machines before they're retired.

At the bottom of town is an area that's been flattened out for the sewage plant to be constructed next year, the first time the station will process human waste. This is part of the shoreline where the Navy used to dump its garbage, and there's a potent brew of heavy metals, PCBs, and other laboratory byproducts that make the divers working in the bay even more concerned about the integrity of their suits than elsewhere in the sound. The writer Barry Lopez, who has visited the Antarctic with NSF five times, calls this the most polluted bay on the planet, but he's careful to note that the sand bar stretching across its mouth, while preventing currents from diluting the mess, also keeps it from spreading. The surveys conducted by my roommate, Andrew, agree with his assessment. Since no one knows how to eliminate the contamination, the wisest course seems to be to let everything sediment over undisturbed. Like most anthropogenic pollution on the continent, it is intense but highly localized.

Occasionally—and humorously—the stories of environmental degradation shade into the bizarre. For example, when blasting was done at a spot just below our feet last year to recarve the topography in preparation for the sewage plant, a bit of inadvertent archeology occurred: piles of frozen sausages from the 1950s flew through the air, much to the delight of the local gulls, called skuas, and of Andrew, who found a readymade sampling site he would have been otherwise unable to reach.

On the manmade terrace above the sewage plant site, now unofficially dubbed "Sausage Point," sits Penguin Water and Power, the pumping twin hearts of the town run by Jordan Dickens, who is overseeing the modernization of the utilities. In one building squat six yellow sixteen-cylinder diesel engines the size of small trucks, two or three of which are always running. The maintenance log that Jordan shows me for one of the engines counts 94,000 hours of use; if it had been in a vehicle running at an average of forty-five miles per hour, it would have traveled 4.5 million miles. Each engine is serviced at every 20,000 hours, a job that takes a mechanic six weeks to perform.

The plant burns about 25,000 gallons of fuel a week, and these diesels, too, are slated to be replaced with new and more efficient models. But as I stand among them, listening to them work, it's hard not to anthropomorphize their strength and their steadfastness in doing an important job so well for so long. Machines on which we depend, and which we are in turn responsible for, become co-inhabitants of a place. Because the dependency here is so critical, it's easy to see how attachments could become deep, as they have between the drivers of the Stretch-8 Cats and their charges.

As well as these engines work, however, they convert only a third of each gallon into electricity. A third is lost out the exhaust stacks, and a third to water in the cooling jackets. In a brilliant bit of engineering, much of the latter's waste heat is captured in a heat exchanger, which not only preheats the seawater that's desalinated next door but also heats the glycol antifreeze that warms Crary, the dormitories, and the galley. This saves McMurdo one-half to three-quarters of a million gallons of fuel a year for heating, and decreases wear and tear on the power plant, where the radiators hardly have to run anymore, so efficiently is the heat extracted.

Next Jordan takes us to the desalinization plant, where again, modernization has taken place, the old Navy method of condensing steam through progressive refinements—which required immense amounts of power and was difficult to maintain—having given way to reverse osmosis filtration. The 29°F seawater is warmed to 36°, then passed through a four-stage multimedia filter to remove gross impurities, lest ice crystals or foreign matter under hundreds of pounds of pressure per square inch damage the more delicate osmosis membranes. Forty thousand gallons of potable water pop out the other end daily. Showers used to be limited to every other day, and shower monitors were checked rigorously to make sure that you turned off the water in between soaping up and rinsing off; now at times there's enough freshwater that some is dumped back into the bay.

As we walk out of the facility, I ask Jordan where else he could work and see so directly the fruits of his labors.

"Most of my life I've worked out of the country and in the Third World. You don't find many burgs in the States running plants this size — they're all getting their power from the grid that's generating it at huge fossil-fueled power plants located hundreds of miles away. Even in the Third World . . ." — his voices fades away momentarily as he gazes out over the sound. Then he resumes: "I've worked in Morocco, Israel, at the South Pole Station. There's a divorce of cause-and-effect in the States. You don't have to really learn a job thoroughly and take responsibility for it, because if you screw up, there's a lawyer to cover your ass."

That, I think is about as succinct a description of the attitude that binds people together here as I'm likely to hear.

Late that evening I walk around counting McMurdo's utility poles, which I number at roughly 145. Wood in and of itself is an utter anomaly here. The display area inside the main entryway to Crary displays not only part of a petrified tree trunk, but also fossil wood that's been, in essence, mummified. It hasn't turned to stone; it is simply so desiccated that it's preserved. The only forests in the Antarctic are the petrified ones found in solidified ash, where hundred-million-year-old trees are embedded upright in the cliffs — and then there's this forest, the one made out of utility poles. These "trees" look as if they've been clawed half to death, they've been climbed and restrung so many times.

In 1993 NSF sponsored a weeklong, on-site planning session for McMurdo conducted by visiting architects and students selected through a national competition. Their report recommended simplifying vehicular routes to save fuel and creating a town center with a reception building. They noted that the telephone poles could be used to define avenues in town as well as to create a sense of vertical scale, and suggested adding ceremonial poles to welcome new arrivals. The utility poles, however, are supposed to disappear within a couple of years, the power and phone lines to be buried in "Utilidors," or underground utility corridors. In the United States the aesthetics of almost any community would be improved by burying the lines, which are an unsightly interruption to what remains of our view of the "natural" world. Here they function in the opposite sense, providing strong vertical measurements of known size in the middleground of an incomprehensibly enormous landscape. They give us scale, which we use to pace ourselves as we walk through Antarctic 1. They also allow us to gauge the weather before venturing outside: my rule of thumb is that when I can't see the nearest pole, it's time to put on the down parka.

The environment that humans construct—the built environment— almost inevitably includes art, once habitation is established and basic needs are taken care of. These activities necessarily take place within a feedback loop, with the environment shaping the plant that shapes the environment, whether that "plant" is an organic moss or an inorganic building. Art is a critical part of this feedback loop, for not only does it influence how we see a place, but it is also a way in which we physically modify it.

The evening before my tour with Jim, my skeptical roommate, Andrew, and I had walked together up Ob Hill. He teaches geography at Texas A&M University, and we were mulling over how people in his field tend nowadays to focus more on social issues than on geophysical ones. It's always been my contention that physical landscape is intimately involved in the shaping of local culture, but Andrew pointed out that not everyone agrees with that analysis.

"You know," I said in between breaths as we climbed up the steep cinder path, "I've been looking at art done on station by people who

work here"—breathing break—"and they're using found materials."
Breathe, trudge upward a few steps. "And the materials are scrap metal
from machines here"—stop, admire the view—"that were designed
specifically to deal with the landscape." Another pause. "I mean, they're
pieces of steel from vehicles and buildings designed for the extreme
environment here. So there's this immediate circularity just in the
materials, much less in the contents, which are always playing with or
against what it's like to be here." Resume walking. Andrew is too out of
breath to argue.

The next day Melissa and I take two unofficial walking surveys
through town, the first led by Karen Joyce. She came to work here in
the 1980s as one of the first two hazardous materials persons—hired
while the Navy was still here and when there was no environmental
program in place whatsoever—and she remembers that the meltwater
rivulets now flowing down the street were once called "Buttermilk
Falls" in honor of the garbage-colored water they contained.

What Karen will show us is the ecology that we label "culture."
This doesn't mean tracking down a patch of moss or tracing a pipeline
as it wends its way through town, but rather ferreting out those visual
manifestations we call sculpture and painting. The first example is the
bridge the carpenters have constructed to get people over the six pipes
that run between Crary and the galley. A sturdy, unpainted wooden
affair about nine feet high by twenty-five feet long, it rises up eleven
steps, crosses the heavily insulated lines of glycol, fuel, water, and
sewage, then drops down again. On top are affixed rocks, small plastic
dinosaurs, phrases of poetry assembled from magnetic word strips, and
a metal cube that commands "Turn me over." On the other side it says
"Thank you." Karen and others have been enhancing the bridge daily
with objects, turning a utilitarian structure for pedestrian traffic into a
vehicle for pop culture and commentary as well.

A John Deere tractor pulls slowly uphill ahead of us, a large magnet
affixed to its undercarriage. It's picking up nails and other metallic
objects that have been buried until now under snow. Soon the annual
"daisy picking" will be held, a cleanup occasioned by the appearance of

construction debris when the snow melts. Melissa, however, picks up trash while it's still frozen into the ground, her pockets sometimes overflowing with string, plastic, screws, old military smoke bomb canisters, and other arcane detritus. The visual embellishment of a place, by definition, does not include haphazard litter.

We stop next at the string of hands that Risk Miller has cut out of a single long piece of scrap steel and mounted like a railing between yellow stanchions above the road across from the galley. Though large and obvious, it is unnoticed by almost everyone and thus mutely eloquent. Risk, who works in the metal shop, is also an artist with a bachelor of fine arts degree; his boss is a former Rhodes scholar. Such conjunctions of academia and more utilitarian schools of knowledge abound on the ice, which help define the aesthetic we're finding.

We continue up the "Goat Path," a short uphill pull to the next terrace in town where the carpentry shop, or "Carp," is located. The slippery track is lined with small faded Nepalese prayer flags, and a wind chime tinkles gently at the top, a traditional Himalayan flourish, making our walk feel like a minitrek. When we reach the top Melissa has to return to work, but Karen and I go into Carp where Karen skuas—or scavenges—a small nail for use later on our walk. Both the metal and carpentry shops feature wall drawings or small murals or sculptures assembled out of scrap, and next we go to visit the largest piece in town, a twenty-foot-long metal sculpture of an orca that was welded together out of found materials by Roy Eglund during his 1993 winterover. The rebar skeleton used to sit outside the Coffee House before an NSF official declared it object *non grata,* and the artist was obliged to transport it via forklift to the outskirts. The massive frame hints at both animal and machine power, and many people wish it were still in the middle of town.

As we return through the town center, Karen points out that Commander—a carpenter otherwise known as Mark Melcon—has been cleaning up "chickenheads," the fist-sized volcanic rocks that litter McMurdo, ones that you twist your ankle on after a couple of shots of Crown Royal downed after work in one of the three bars here. He's placed them, one by one on a daily basis, in a steadily growing pile around a utility pole guy wire—the taut strand yet another hazard for the unwary. In this manner he's effectively created a double negative, combining two dangers and so canceling both out. He's another person who constantly picks up remnants of work around town, often recycling it into folk art.

Crossing back over her bridge project between the lab and the galley, we stop so Karen can pound into it the nail she's appropriated from Carp, using it to affix to the handrail a small metal chain made for her by a friend out of scrap wire. We end this tour at a pile of rocks on the far side of Crary. The pile includes ventifacts from the Dry Valleys and specimens of sedimentary layers from the Transantarctics. Last year a guy fell in love with a woman who worked in the lab, and these are the tokens he brought her; as Karen says, "Just like any good penguin, he brought her stones every day to prove his devotion." The women, however, failed to be wooed by his charms or the rocks, and this season the rocks were removed from the lab and put at the bottom of the stairs. Karen's been picking them up and using them in her bridge project. To her dismay, most of the first two dozen she used were quickly appropriated by others. She knows it's a community "taking" of sorts, but still . . . now she glues them down.

The second tour of McMurdo's artistic side is led by Stacey Rolland, the assistant supervisor of the Mechanical Equipment Center, who also happens to be a performance artist and the curator of the annual McMurdo Alternative Art Gallery (MAAG) exhibition. Accompanying us are Melissa and Commander. His nickname, definitely not a title, is related somehow to the mix of military gear and Hawaiian shirts he favors. He wears his hair in a long braid, plays a wooden flute, and weaves zipper pulls from bright nylon cords, which many of us sport on our parkas. He also has most of a master's degree in mathematics. Stacey's been in the Antarctic for three summer seasons, and Commander has been in the Antarctic program for more than twenty years, eleven seasons of which he's been stationed at McMurdo.

This time we take a more thorough inventory of the major shops, finding dozens of found-art assemblages, among them a robot made out of old circuit boards and a Herc C-130 headdress a yard wide fashioned from cardboard. Paintings range from trompe l'oeil puns to Daliesque surreal landscapes; in F-Stop a slightly haunted-looking beauty gazes down on the room with an icebreaker in the background, the symbolism explicit. Everywhere we go we see bits and pieces of an ephemeral culture that have settled into the cracks. Sometimes they're lodged firmly in place for a decade or two, sometimes they're taken home at the end of the season—and sometimes the weather just picks them to pieces.

The method underlying most of the station's indigenous aesthetic is one familiar in extreme environments or circumstances, whether it's a polar terrain or the poverty of Depression-era America: the careful recycling of waste materials into value-added items. A traditional Inuit, for example, will take a bone that's had all or most of its caloric value removed and carve it into an item with spiritual or aesthetic value. He's thus adding value to it, whether it be as an object of veneration to fellow tribespeople, as a trinket for sale to a tourist, or as an artwork to be collected by a museum. Found art at McMurdo, whether done in the spirit of humor or serious cultural critique, or simply to beautify the industrial storage yards, relies on the availability of surplus material— though here, instead of walrus bone, the residents use leftover scrap metal and wood, circuit boards and paint. As always, human beings aren't content to leave anything alone. They're always weaving complexity out of—and into—the environment.

There's another important part of the physical plant to visit in the McMurdo area, and that's the greenhouse. Melissa and I excuse ourselves from Stacey and Commander and walk back into the thicket of storage units. She leads me through the double doors of a small, unassuming building with a tomato and a green pepper painted on it, and we're immediately enveloped in warm humid air and earthen smells. There's a darkened forecourt with thyme and basil growing in it, as well as flowers—in theory only edible ones such as nasturtiums and pansies, honoring the environmental protocols, which say you can't grow anything in the Antarctic that's of foreign origin unless it's for human consumption. The main room is a bright and shiny place. Banks of grow lights throw simulated daylight onto reflecting foil lining the walls, and classical music wafts out over double racks of lettuce and salad greens.

The ambience is such that you expect a disembodied computer voice to ask if there's anything it can do for you. Melissa plans to supersede that. We stretch out the two hammocks hanging on posts, and she unzips her parka to reveal a bottle of wine. While most of the station is at a raucous rock 'n' roll party in the helo hangar, we sit surrounded by spinach, operatic arias, and . . . rubber snakes. Never let it be said that the inhabitants of McMurdo let a chance for a visual pun go unheeded.

It's not as if NSF is unaware of the artistic subculture; to a certain extent it is in its best interests to aid and abet it. After all, while the occasional NSF rep may gripe about the graffiti around town, they've never taken a scrub brush to the place. Well aware that a balance between form and function is crucial to the mental stability of the workforce, this summer the agency has engaged the services of DMJM, the tenth largest architectural/engineering/construction firm in the United States, to analyze the built environment in terms of city planning. DMJM has designed and built everything from launch pads at Cape Canaveral to the Hyperion Sewage Treatment Plant in its hometown of Los Angeles, the largest such facility in the world. With seventeen offices abroad, the firm is involved in projects everywhere from Korea to Kuwait.

The firm has sent an ex-Israeli architect, Ralph Samach, whom I meet at the Coffee House bar one evening. His curly black hair is uncombed, and several days' growth of beard adds dash to a slightly wild-eyed expression. It's clear that he's radically short on sleep. Nor is he shy about describing his one-week inspection: "It's simple," he says. "The problems are so obvious: they brought the best of America here, and the worst. This is a mixture of *Blade Runner* and Stanley Kubrick—not my words, that's what people have been telling me, and they're right. It's incomprehensibly ugly, and it didn't have to be that way.

"The sprawl—it's inertia from the navy way of doing business. You have bedrooms—the dorms—and a kitchen—the galley—but you need a living room and a den and a study and a rec room. All that stuff is scattered around and needs to be consolidated. You also need to warehouse stuff and centralize it so you don't have the traffic. And because of the sprawl, this place runs on labor, as if you had all the labor in the world to expend, but this is some of the most expensive labor in the world.

"You have to create fire alleys—that's a real issue here, fire—but you don't have to spread out everything. And they've got to figure out how to paint the town. You can't try and hide the buildings. They're not really architecture, but industrial products like airplane bodies, which you identify with graphics. The buildings shouldn't be numbered— that's a holdover from the Cold War, when you didn't want the enemy to map your town. Some of the buildings have names, but they're hidden. The signs should be huge and on the front of the buildings. There are people who have been here for two months and they still can't find their way around. So the streets should be named."

I ask him what, if any, other architectural environments are models. "College campuses," he replies. "They have student centers and labs, dorms . . ." His voice trails off and he thinks for a minute.

"I did some early work in China—Shanghai," he continues. "It was an island of Western stuff in a sea of foreign. Two and a half million feet of mixed-use development: hotel, office space, residential, business, logistics. People there were expatriates, like here. And there's a 'Kurtz' factor in Asia that's similar to here, where if you go too far upriver you can't get back down again." He's referring to *Apocalypse Now,* the Francis Ford Coppola movie loosely based on the Joseph Conrad book *Heart of Darkness.* Samach has it right: ice people say that when you leave the Antarctic, part of you stays behind forever.

"I did the demographics here," he goes on, "and it's a high percentage of nonurban people. They're very concerned with civil disobedience, very worried about how the NSF perceives them. That should be a vision made large. I like the idea of people making murals on the sides of the buildings so people take ownership of them."

He shakes his head. "It's simple. It really is. People here know the solutions already. I've only had a week to do this; it's been so compressed. I wasn't all that into it at first, then right before I came down I started having these sleepless nights. What if I couldn't figure it out in a week? I've worked all over the place, but always in urban environments. I thought I'd just come down and do my thing, make a report. Now I want to come back and design the next building here. I want to make it functional and within budget, but make it a place good enough for the people."

Samach has put his finger on more than one good point. Stephen Pyne, the renowned historian of exploration who spent most of a year in the Antarctic and wrote one of the best books about it, *The Ice*, once figured out that it costs the NSF $10,000 per person per day to keep Antarctic operations going. He derived that figure simply by dividing the NSF Polar Programs budget for the continent and dividing it by the number of people present in a year, so it's a radically oversimplified story, but Antarctic labor is indeed the most expensive on the planet, exceeded only by the cost of putting astronauts in space.

Spending money on architecture and urban planning usually means you save money in the long run precisely because you can minimize the number of bodies needed and hours worked moving cargo from airplanes and the one cargo ship into town. You cut down on accidents, improve safety and morale, and so have a higher percentage of trained workers returning each year.

The issue of sprawl is perhaps more complicated than Samach thinks, though. Because of the way sunlight and wind hit the bay and surrounding hills, where supplies are stored, and even where excess snow is piled when plowing, involves careful decision-making—otherwise you end up with crates frozen into the ice. In the road system, numerous spacious turnarounds are critical, lest drivers, battling poor visibility because of the very clothes they wear—bulky parkas with hoods—bump into fuel and water lines as they back up. And the issue of fire (or any other catastrophe) is easy to underestimate. There are no second chances here if you're without shelter and essential services, which is why there are seven different generators around station as backups for medical and emergency services, specimen storage in Crary's walk-in freezer, and communications at T-Site.

All that takes space. Although everyone agrees that what exists could be better organized, minimizing the footprint of the station will take some careful thought, and the situation won't be unscrambled in a week.

After speaking with Samach, I interview the ultimate on-site authority, Dwight Fisher, the senior NSF representative on station. Dwight started coming here in 1982, when he was flying for the Navy. He ended up commanding the helicopter squadron that served the United States Antarctic Program, VXE-6 (or Airdevronsix, for which the icefalls are named). Out of the last twenty consecutive seasons, he's been here for fourteen or fifteen of them—he's lost track.

When I ask him what works by NSF artists and writers he likes best, he says the photographs first, followed by realistic paintings. "I don't mind abstract art," he explains, "but when it comes to this place, something I know so well, I think it's a distortion. If you show me a painting of sea ice that's just pattern and I have to sit there and figure it out . . ." He shakes his head. "So few of us get to come here, and we're really privileged. But for most people, who can't come here—not to show what it's really like, that's cheating them."

In other words, he's all for representation, but not for interpretation that veers too far from the common visual consensus, a not unusual attitude. His reasoning, though I disagree with it, is one of the clearest and most honest arguments for representational landscape art. It echoes the sentiments of astronaut Rusty Schweichart, as quoted by photographer Galen Rowell in *Poles Apart:* "It comes through to you so powerfully that you're the sensing element for humanity." There is therefore a reason that the architecture at McMurdo is as functional as the officially sponsored art: both reflect what the NSF and the scientific community understand to be a pragmatic and moral responsibility.

But as Samach pointed out, the residents here tend to think in ways distinctly counter to a corporate ethos, whether it's that of Raytheon or of government-sponsored science. Karen's bridge, the rebar orca, Risk Miller's balustrade of open hands—these are signs that art refuses simply to represent space, but rather insists on interpreting it, and in so doing creates place.

A few evenings later Melissa and I walk down the road from one of the Christmas parties being held this December weekend and stop by a pond created by residents of the dorm next to the chalet. Dirt has been scooped out to catch runoff diverted from a meltwater stream running down the side of the street; the result is a curvilinear basin in the shape of a duck, framed with a line of rocks. The "duck pond," in this case a whimsical water feature, is nonetheless descended from the English landscaping notion of an informal bit of nature placed near architecture.

We sit in the sun on one of the two park benches at the edge of the pond, our view extending out across the helo pad and the sea ice to the Royal Society Range, its glaciers pouring late molten light onto the sound. If we don't move, we preserve undisturbed a thin layer of air around our bodies and so can maintain the illusion that it's actually warm.

I think the pond was built, if not exactly out of irony, at least to point up the contrast between the familiar suburban American landscape of the station and the otherworldly one in front of us, and I suggest this aloud to Melissa. She, however, shakes her head in disagreement, tugging on an earring as she thinks, then says that it seems to her the purpose is more to make a homelike environment.

Perhaps it's both. Melissa and I are used to posing dualities for the sake of advancing a line of thought—whether it's because we're bilaterally symmetrical animals or because we were raised in a Western European scientific culture, or both—and we have to keep reminding ourselves that the world is complex enough to demand that we hold two contradictory thoughts in mind at the same time. Human beings are formed through both nature—our genetics—and nurture. Education and experience are built on, but then modify and channel, instinct.

We sit quietly in the sun, and I think about how the pond is a response not only to the physical scale of the view but also to its psychological scale. The human ego quails easily before the harshly reductive landscape of the ice, just as it does in the midst of any other desert or sea—any isotropic environment that minimalizes human presence. Religion sometimes acts as a shield against such voids, whether it is the strict fundamentalism of Islam in the arid Middle East, the equally stern quasi-Puritanism of early American whalers, or the ritual pieties of astronauts floating in space.

McMurdo's relationship to religion, however, is definitely skewed. The most noticeable totems of Christianity, crosses, aren't erected on Ross Island as much in memory of Christ as to memorialize people who have died here. The most famous example is the nine-foot-tall wooden cross on Ob Hill, the original of which was erected by members of Scott's last expedition in homage to the five men who died on their way back from the Pole. The cross must be replaced periodically as even the hard Australian jarrah wood is eaten away by the wind, yet each one has borne the same words, from Alfred Lord Tennyson's poem *Ulysses:* "To strive, to seek, to find, and not to yield."

Just southwest of the *Discovery* hut is another wooden cross, originally erected in 1902 in remembrance of George Vince. He slid off the icy slopes nearby and into the ocean during a Herbie, the first man to lose his life in McMurdo Sound. Just up the hill from the hut is the very peculiar monument formally known as the Our Lady of the Snows Shrine, but which everyone calls "Roll-Cage Mary" in reference to the four bent steel bars enclosing the statuette. Erected by navy personnel at McMurdo during Operation Deep Freeze in 1956, it honors Richard Williams, the Seabee equipment operator who went down with a Caterpillar D-8 tractor when it broke through the sea ice (Plate 9).

Also in 1956, volunteers built the first Chapel of the Snows, which has since burned down and been rebuilt twice. Situated just downhill from Derelict Junction and the three bars in town, it commands a fine view of the sound and the Royal Society Range. Its most notable interior feature, however, is not a depiction of Christ on a cross, but a stained glass window facing south. In addition to the conspicuous Christian imagery around its perimeter, the window depicts the Antarctic continent with a penguin standing guard over an open book, presumably the Bible (Plate 10).

The overarching theme of all these sites is the environment and our relationship to it, but the crosses seem to memorialize death more than celebrate life. Perhaps that's inevitable, given Christianity's emphasis on the afterlife rather than the here-and-now, not to mention the absence of much visible flora and fauna to contradict such a view. But I find myself, in my own relationship to the Antarctic, warming to the idea that we should be worshiping the life that's here, an energy that refuses to be quelled. I'm fascinated by the bacteria that have been found the last two years in the snow around the South Pole, psychrophilic enzymes that are synthesizing proteins in temperatures less than two degrees above zero and under the most intense solar radiation. And the Antarctic fish discovered by Art deVries that have antifreeze in their veins, which allows them to survive in subfreezing waters. James Raymond, a biochemist from the University of Nevada–Las Vegas, has been studying how unicellular phytoplankton survive in the ice. Unlike the fish, which use their body chemistry to keep from freezing, these extremophiles deploy proteins, "ice-active molecules," that allow them to freeze while minimizing the mechanical and osmotic damage that would otherwise disrupt their function or outright rupture them. The toughest one he's found so far has revived after being frozen in liquid nitrogen, which at sea level means it survives temperatures of −346°F.

Could it be, I wonder, that our sense of scale regarding the properties of life are as dissonant here as are our senses of time and space? We have for so long framed the Antarctic in the popular imagination as a place utterly inimical to life—part of the romantic extremities we invent in order to define the parameters of mainstream existence—that even after previewing most of the common literature on the Antarctic, tourists are surprised to find anything alive here beyond themselves and other visitors, such as breeding penguins and seals.

The ubiquity of microbes in the Antarctic does not square easily with our notions of a perfectly sterile space demanding heroic efforts to conquer it. The Antarctic is, as McMurdo ironists would have it, "a harsh continent" in which it is very difficult for life to exist—but exist it does. As is often the case, artists have already begun to break down the resulting cognitive dissonance in their work. While most of the images about the Antarctic made by visiting artists have emphasized the apparently empty landscape, the New Zealand multimedia sculptor Virginia King (b. 1946), who stayed at Scott Base in 1999 and visited the Dry Valleys, has been crafting six-foot-tall wooden sculptures based on photographs taken through an electron microscope of Antarctic diatoms found in the saline lakes of the valleys and underneath the sea ice (Plate 11). Enlarging the images of the invisible unicellular algae that are at the bottom of the food chain into three-dimensional objects, she suspends them from the ceiling in a darkened gallery, creating an environment scaled to the viewer. The sculptures are white under regular illumination, but when illuminated with ultraviolet light (a reference to the research at Scott Base and Crary that inspired her), they fluoresce in bright blues and oranges. Behind the slowly gyrating sculptures, King projects a video, which juxtaposes images she took at Cape Evans and Lake Vanda with the photomicroscopic images.

King is very deliberately establishing a visual dialogue with the historical conception of the Antarctic as a male-dominated heroic icescape by focusing on the biological instead of the geological, the microbial instead of the heroic. Her use of color is a foil to the black-and-white photographs and films of the Heroic Age. It's not that she would deny the value of earlier work by artists in the Antarctic, but this is a long way from the watercolor sketches made by William Hodges, the artist who accompanied Cook on his second voyage and who began the process of imaging the region directly.

6 NAVIGATING NATURE

JAMES COOK, ONE OF the greatest navigators in the history of exploration, did more to prepare geographers to accept the true nature and extent of the Antarctic continent than any of his predecessors. By taking William Hodges with him, he also helped transform the nature of landscape painting. How all this came to be is a story anchored, once again, in the entwined histories of cartography, science, and art.

Cook was born in Yorkshire in 1728 and went to sea when he was eighteen in the North Sea coal trade. Although considered a bit long in the tooth, when he was twenty-seven he joined the Royal Navy, and while serving in Canada during the summer of 1758 met a British Army surveyor who taught him how to triangulate positions on land using a plane table. The thirty-year-old's maturity would now become an asset as he disciplined himself to learn mathematics and astronomy. By that fall he had produced his first maritime chart, which brought him a commission to spend five years surveying the coast of Newfoundland, thus lifting him up from the ranks as a common man and setting him on a profound course of exploration.

By combining the marine survey practice of taking compass cross-bearings from his ship along the coastline—the practice known as a running traverse—and measuring off base lines on land with a chain, he was able to apply triangulation to both land and sea. Whenever possible

Cook confirmed his positions with astronomical sightings. As a result, his hybrid coastal profile and marine charts were far more accurate than other marine surveys and became the standard for the field. (Not coincidentally, this development in the measuring of sea- and landscapes paralleled the imaging of them in English landscape painting, which had its roots, via the Dutch School, in coastal profiles.)

Given his experience, Cook was a logical choice for the Admiralty to send south to Tahiti to observe the 1769 transit of Venus across the sun, a task at which he was successful, adding data to the worldwide effort that produced a fair estimate of the distance between the sun and the earth, which in turn led to more accurate measurements of the earth's dimensions and improved navigational standards. His observations concluded, Cook then proceeded about the second and secret order of business in his orders, searching for *Terra australis incognita*. He sailed south below the fortieth latitude and, failing to find a great southern continent where it had been theorized to exist, began to whittle down the remaining possibilities. In the process, he circumnavigated and charted New Zealand, thus proving it was not an Antarctic peninsula, and continued west to Australia, the east coast of which he charted and claimed for England. Returning home in 1771, he and his crew were lionized by the public for their discoveries, due in no small part to the visual record produced by artists accompanying him, whose works were reproduced as engravings in published accounts.

Thousands of artworks from the three Pacific voyages of Captain James Cook document an oceanic region that didn't even appear on world maps until the sixteenth century. The exploration accounts contain botanical and biological illustrations, hundreds of coastal profiles and charts, ethnographic sketches, and landscape paintings from places as varied as Tahiti, Hawaii, Tierra del Fuego, New Zealand, Easter Island, and Alaska. The efficacy of including artists to record the scientists' and navigators' work had been proven to the British Admiralty by Joseph Banks (1743–1820), who administered the natural history investigations of Cook's first voyage. Banks came from a family of wealthy antiquarians whose passion it was to travel and collect knowledge from ancient texts. Nominated to the Royal Society at the age of twenty-three, he was an enthusiastic archeologist and soon became England's most prominent patron of natural history. Banks journeyed to Newfoundland and Labrador in 1766 (during the period when Cook was mapping there), and upon his return he hired the foremost botanical artist of the day to illustrate the specimens he had collected.

James Cook was a surveyor firmly rooted in a northern European maritime tradition of imaging landscape as it was, and the scientific bent of Banks fit his style of exploration. But it wouldn't be Banks, or the artists that Banks himself chose, who would go with Cook on his second foray across the Pacific. Instead it would be William Hodges, trained in the southern European, specifically Italian, school of landscape painting, which specified that artists were to portray the world as it should be. The underlying conflict between imaging and imagining reality—between what we today tend to hold separate as scientific illustration and art—was very much an issue during the early stages of the voyage, and would return to haunt Hodges at the end of his life.

In the 1500s scholars and naturalists began to exchange knowledge at an increasing rate through both individual correspondence and books, which included original images painted directly from specimens of the natural world. This was a switch from the practice during the Middle Ages, when pictures of plants and animals were used only to embellish biblical paintings, manuscripts, and tapestries. As late as 1533 German herbalists refused to have illustrations competing with text in their books. Within a decade, however, the tide had turned irrevocably. The growing circulation of facts now demanded that the particulars of the world be clearly defined for comparison and cataloging, and even the most stubborn naturalists acknowledged that plants were more easily identified with pictures than with words.

Renaissance painters had likewise resisted accurate visual representation of the world. Landscape was merely scenery as a backdrop for historical action, entire mountain ranges often being implied by a single rocky outcrop. Even exploration artists up until the time of Hodges still used plants and animals familiar to home audiences when painting the New World and the Arctic, a cognitive strategy to bring the strange within comprehension. A 1768 British engraving showing the inhabitants of Hudson Bay, for example, has rushes and palm trees growing along the shores where an Inuit is paddling a kayak. The plants, although not indigenous to the British Isles, were accepted as conventional talismans for the exotic.

By the end of the sixteenth century, however, most naturalists had embraced pictures as accurate representations of real things, and the foundation for the rise of scientific illustration was secure. When Robert Hooke published his *Micrographia* in 1664, illustrations were essential; how else could a reader see what he saw through a microscope? Leonardo da Vinci and Albrecht Dürer were not only great artists of the age, but two of its finest scientific and cartographic illustrators. Da Vinci wrote in his notebooks: "The mind of the painter must resemble a mirror which permanently transforms itself into the color of its object and fills itself with as many images as there are things placed in front of it." And Dürer noted: "Nature is the original measure of art." Visual representation was no longer adjunct to understanding, but part of the process itself.

When Banks insisted on visual records of everything encountered during Cook's first voyage, he was following the lead of expeditions sponsored by other countries. The Spanish government had sent official artists to Mexico in the 1570s to record its natural history for Philip II; this in turn inspired the English geographer Richard Hakluyt to instruct explorers to include artists in their parties. Sir Francis Drake took an artist with him on his circumnavigation of the world in 1577–1580; and Frobisher, on his second Arctic voyage in 1577, had with him John White, a watercolorist experienced at painting in the field. Banks was particularly impressed by the Dutch military, who, while they held Brazil as a colony from 1630 to 1654, worked with artists to produce an immense natural and ethnographic encyclopedia of the territory, *Historia Naturalis Brasiliae,* which contained 533 woodcuts of exotic discoveries from swordfish to cannibalistic tribespeople.

The British Royal Society in its directives of 1665–1666 included language regarding the plotting and sketching of coastline in addition to its standing instructions concerning the collection of qualitative and quantitative data from around the world. The Admiralty institutionalized the directives in 1693 by establishing a Drawing School within the Royal Mathematical School at Christ's Hospital, where boys were trained for service in the navy. Drawing was subsequently placed on the curriculum of the Portsmouth Academy in 1733, and the Admiralty issued a directive that officers who could make topographical drawings should be employed in making coastal profiles whenever possible, particularly in foreign ports. The point wasn't to produce professional artists, but to ensure that the strategic skills of marine surveying and sketching were widely available as the English expanded and consolidated their sea power.

James Cook was himself a skilled draftsman, as were many of his seamen. Aboard the *Resolution* during the second voyage, for example, Henry Roberts, Joseph Gilbert, and Isaac Smith all drew coastal profiles and harbor views in their logs. But the most extraordinary landscape images made during any of Cook's three voyages were those by Hodges. Schooled in the neoclassical tradition of British landscape art as it existed at the time, he would soon master the techniques of exploration, which had its own vocabulary. Out of the two traditions he would forge a single visual style that would help J. M. W. Turner develop his own approach to painting, which in turn would profoundly shape the practice of landscape art to the present day.

Landscape painting is defined by the contemporary American geographer Yi-Fu Tuan as a depiction of natural and manmade features arranged in some kind of perspective order. The cultural critic W. J. T.

Mitchell posits such paintings to both present and represent a natural scene. Both are correct, but the geographer defines the term in a pragmatic way that the Dutch might find agreeable, while the art historian tips his hat toward the classicists of southern Europe. This split has its roots in the development of the genre as it arose out of the Middle Ages, a dichotomy based in the Greek argument over the purpose of philosophy: Aristotle's desire to examine the particulars of the world, versus Plato's search for the theoretical ideal reality.

As an explorer, James Cook needed landscape images based on the topographical practices of northern European artists, but Hodges had been schooled in the southern European tradition, epitomized by the artists of Italy. To some extent, the differences between the two art traditions stemmed from different regional geographies. The Italians were surrounded by the Mediterranean, a virtually landlocked body of water, and the known world was just that: known. Italian painting, as a result, didn't have to portray land that was new and strange; factual presentation was unnecessary to facilitate comprehension. Instead, the depiction of landscape tended to be highly idealized and metaphorical, revealing a stage on which historical events, religious beliefs, and the hierarchical value of property among nobles could be represented. Italian landscape paintings, which emerged slowly from within this tradition of history paintings, were static scenes framed by carefully arranged trees and other verticals in the foreground; their version of nature was not so much recorded as composed, a visual balance codified by Claude Lorrain (1600–1682).

Lorrain, a French painter who settled in Rome in 1627, was a talented outdoor sketcher, but he preferred to retreat to his studio where he organized his initial impressions of the land into landscapes with a dark foreground framed with trees, a sunlit second or middle ground—often suffused with the glow of a late Mediterranean afternoon or early evening sunset—and a background receding into the distance. It was as if our prehistoric predilection for the conceal-and-reveal landscape of the savanna had been tidied up and compressed into a stage set on which the glories of ancient Rome and the moralities of the Bible would be played.

British seamen, such as James Cook, and their predecessors the Dutch mariners—as well as the Portuguese navigators who gave them both coastal profiles—lived on oceans across which lay *terra incognita*. Their landscape art, as a result, was a pragmatic response to the need for mapping the world. The northern artists, moreover, although many of them traveled to Rome to learn the Italian style of painting, served a society that was thoroughly engaged with the world as it was, not as it might be. The Dutch painting tradition, in particular, was thus more about exploring, recording, and measuring reality, whether the subject matter was fruit on the kitchen table, a flotilla of ships in the harbor, or the jungles of Brazil.

A small but nevertheless ground-breaking work in the Dutch landscape tradition is worth mentioning here, because it provided a formula that English painters—including Hodges—would soon follow. The drawing, by Hendrik Goltzius (1558–1617), is called *Dune Landscape near Haarlem* (1603). It is remarkable in large part because, in contrast to the Italian tradition, which took a single strong point of view that idealized nature through generalized scenes, this work features no single viewpoint or line of perspective. Rather, a road leads the eye into the middle ground and then vanishes among a few sparse sandy features, while over it all is an immense sky, a unifying field filled with masses of marine moisture. No imaginary model, this was a panoramic survey of a specific piece of land, and it established what would become the dominant style of Dutch landscapes in the seventeenth century.

The development of topographical landscape art was part of an enormous shift in the visualization of the world during the eighteenth century. As Svetlana Alpers observes in her seminal book *The Art of Describing,* the scholastic tradition of reading and interpretation in the Renaissance was now evolving rapidly, thanks to an optical culture of lenses, into a method of inquiry that could see both very close up and very far into the distance. Science and art worked together to catalog the world by sending out expeditions, which brought back specimens that were inspected in museums and illustrated in the enormous encyclopedias of the time. William Hodges literally embodied the change in the course of his career.

English landscape art, which had developed as a distinct genre in the early 1700s, was shaped by both the southern and northern European traditions. By midcentury, Dutch artists were being commissioned by the English gentry to make both realistic landscape and marine paintings to document the growing affluence of England. For as had happened in the Netherlands, so in the British Isles: trade and exploration created so much new knowledge that it could be absorbed only through accurate visual representation and categorization. Comenius, the Dutch educational reformer, was brought to England to help transform the basis of its curriculum from rhetoric to the language of description; rather than simply reading a text about a subject, people now learned to rely on direct experience—"seeing is believing."

In 1755, William Shipley founded the Society for the Encouragement of Arts, Manufactures, and Commerce, an establishment promoting the use of drawing in art and science as a way of conveying information. Soon thereafter he took in a ten-year-old errand boy, a London blacksmith's son who had shown an aptitude for drawing. William Hodges, who would eventually become the most traveled artist of his time, was taught by Shipley himself until 1758, when Richard Wilson— Britain's first great landscape painter—noticing his talent, took him under his personal care as an apprentice. Hodges studied with Wilson for seven years, and adopted his master's style so successfully that museum curators in the twentieth century were still confusing works by the two men.

Hodges would have been relegated forever to the ranks of talented but forgotten students had he not taken a trip to Switzerland and Germany. Like Wilson, he was fully capable of executing topographical sketches, and on his return he produced four landscape paintings from his notebooks. Exhibited in 1771, they were seen by a member of the Admiralty Board, Lord Palmerston, who was reminded so vividly of his own trip through the Alps that he recommended Hodges to Cook for the second voyage.

Joseph Banks had been slated to accompany Cook, based on the success of their earlier collaboration. Indeed, the exotic illustrations of South Sea life produced during the first voyage and published in its accounts had so entranced the English public and Admiralty alike that a place for Banks, along with scientists and artists of his own choosing, seemed assured. Banks already had selected Johann Zoffany, a portrait and genre painter, as the artist for the expedition, as well as James Walker and John Frederick Miller, two natural history draftsmen, and the marine painter John Clevely. Banks's enthusiasm for including artists on expeditions was laudatory, but, combined with the ambitious number of scientists he insisted on including, plus two horn players, it meant raising and adding decks, as well as a roundhouse on top of the quarterdeck. The remodeled *Resolution* was so prone to capsizing during its passage down the Thames that the modifications were stripped away on orders of the Admiralty. Banks, his head swelled by the fame received after the initial voyage, huffed off with his artists, who that July accompanied him instead to Iceland.

With less than a month's notice prior to departure, Cook hired Hodges to replace Zoffany and the other artists and took on board two astronomers, William Blayly and William Wales. The latter, who would be one of Hodges's closest friends on the voyage, afterward became master at the Mathematical School of Christ's Hospital, where he taught, among others, the English writer Samuel Coleridge. Not only are there noticeable affinities between the images in Coleridge's 1798 poem "Rime of the Ancient Mariner" and descriptions of Antarctic sailing in Wales's notebooks, as noted by the preeminent historian of exploration in the South Pacific, Bernard Smith, but the paintings of icebergs that Hodges produced likewise were strongly echoed in the illustrations Gustave Doré supplied the poem eighty years later.

~

William Hodges, although the first artist to sail within the Antarctic Circle, never saw the continent itself. When Cook sailed to the South Pacific on his second voyage in 1772–1775, the world was still in the grip of the Little Ice Age, a period of record low temperatures that had begun in the 1500s and would last until 1850. Astronomers, peering through the newly invented telescope, had noted an absence of sunspots after 1645, the symptom of a reduction in solar radiation. It is estimated that the solar energy received by Earth during this period fell by as much as 1 percent—enough to shorten the growing season in Europe by three weeks. Glaciers advanced everywhere, from Alaska to the Andes; ice tongues descended from the Alps deep into Swiss valleys, the Rhône froze in its banks, and wolves roamed France.

The Canadian biologist David Campbell notes in *The Crystal Desert*, his book about working on the Antarctic Peninsula, that Cook's meteorological records for the voyage show only 3 percent of the first summer as having clear weather, and an abysmal 1 percent the following summer of 1773–1774. It seems likely that the Little Ice Age probably extended the pack ice surrounding the continent much farther out than its current limits. Campbell and other scientists point out that the annual cycle of ice in the Southern Ocean is the greatest seasonal event on the planet, with almost ten million square miles of pack ice freezing, melting, and reforming each year. Even today, at its winter peak the ice pack doubles the total Antarctic surface area until it equals that of South America. As a result, the exploration of the continent remained totally subject to the fluctuations of this cycle until the introduction of aviation and aerial photography in the mid–twentieth century. That Cook in wooden-hulled ships got to within eighty miles of the continent, much less during a cold cycle, was an extraordinary feat. Ships wouldn't even sail beneath the Antarctic Circle again until the Bellingshausen expedition in 1820.

Hodges was the first European to give us pictures of Antarctic ice, but the first person to make an image of an Antarctic iceberg may have been Ui-te-Rangiora, a legendary South Sea islander who possibly sailed into the pack ice during an earlier warm period. D. S. Long, a

New Zealand author and editor of Polynesian literature, first read about Ui-te-Rangiora in 1982 in L.B. Quartermain's book about the early history of the Ross Sea sector, *South to the Pole*. Quartermain mentions a handed-down account of Ui-te-Rangiora, who was said to have voyaged south to the place of bitter cold where the sea was covered in *pia*, the Polynesian word for arrowroot flour. *Pia* is a famine food that was taken along as a staple on huge oceangoing canoes; indeed, the discovery of how to leach the poisonous hydrogen cyanide out of it was one of the keys that opened up long-range Polynesian voyaging. According to Long, by using *pia* as an image, Ui was saying that he went where it was white and dangerous.

The oral history, which came from Rarotonga in the Cook Islands, was first translated by the nineteenth-century historian S. Percy Smith, who recounted the *whakapapa*, or family chant, in his book *Hawaiki*. The chant, a retelling of Ui's adventure by another seagoing chief, Te Aru-tanga-Nuku, put Ui forty-eight generations back before 1898 (when Smith heard it performed). Various authors date Ui's voyage at roughly A.D. 650; Te Aru sailed south 250 years after Ui, following his directions and in a similar vessel. The chant described in detail the great double-hulled voyaging canoe used by both men. (The adjective "great" does not begin to do these catamaranlike vessels justice. Some of them measured over a hundred feet in length, were powered by large sails on masts sixty-eight feet high, and carried cabins sitting on decks as large as twelve hundred square feet. Cook reported that the canoes were larger and faster than his own ship.) The chant then said that Ui saw "rocks that grow out of the sea in the space beyond Rapa; the monstrous seas; the female that dwells in those mountainous waves, whose tresses wave about in the waters and on the surface of the seas; and the frozen sea of pia, with the deceitful animal of that sea who dives to great depths—a foggy, misty, and dark place not seen by the sun. Other things are like [white] rocks, whose summits pierce the skies, they are completely bare and without any vegetation on them." Smith, believing that the descriptions were of icebergs, bull kelp, and sea lions, concluded that both men had in fact explored in Antarctic seas. If so, the two chiefs may have made roundtrip voyages with their crews in excess of 7,000 miles.

Although it has since been proven that it is indeed possible to travel huge distances in Polynesian canoes using traditional, full-body or "haptic" means of spatial orientation (in 2000, for example, master navigator Nainoa Thompson sailed from Molokai to Easter Island and back, an astonishing eight-month-long, 14,000-mile trip in which Thompson used only the stars and ocean currents to navigate), we will likely never know whether the story of Ui-te-Rangiora is the result of imaging or imagining the Antarctic. Nevertheless, the oral history reminds us that the earliest record of an Antarctic iceberg might be a literary one couched in visual terms, images of ice and rock turned into metaphor for the dangers of exploration in a distant land, a theme Coleridge would have recognized, and one that will be sounded throughout the art and literature of the continent.

Hodges had other predecessors in the histories and art produced by travelers to the Far North. Although the Antarctic and the Arctic resemble each other only superficially—the Arctic Basin is essentially an enormous river estuary filled with floating ice, whereas the Antarctic is a continent surrounded by an ocean—the visual template of a polar world was first cut to the pattern of the north during the Barents and Frobisher expeditions, with their paintings of men rowing in sea ice and crude sketches of icebergs. Hodges, however, would make a qualitative leap in the depiction of ice.

When the twenty-eight-year-old painter boarded the *Resolution,* he was entering into a very different contract from that held by the artists on Cook's first voyage, who had been chosen by and worked for Joseph Banks. Hodges was to work for Cook himself, and the captain invited him soon after sailing to paint out of the great multipaned stern window of the captain's cabin. The difference is important. The landscape painter Sydney Parkinson and his companions, responsible for artistic renderings on Cook's first voyage, were directed by an antiquarian who wanted to capture as much exotica as possible for the public as well as for science; as a consequence, they spent time meticulously recording everything from the facial tattoos of Maoris to picturesque views of river glades and seashore grottoes. Hodges, in contrast, once the voyage was under way, was promptly instructed by the officers as to the necessity for and techniques of coastal profiles and the recording of local meteorological conditions, information crucial to the seamen. In turn Hodges, who was a much more gifted and better trained landscape painter than Parkinson, gave lessons to Cook and others in the techniques of his trade. Instead of using the seamen's customary technique of delineating landforms with line drawing and hatching, he developed a technique of applying several shades of wash to provide contrast and contour, a much more painterly approach to topography.

The scientists on the second voyage also made an impression on Hodges. In addition to the two astronomers, the German father-and-son team of naturalists, John Reinhold Forster and George Forster, accompanied Cook. Both were trained to observe closely in the field, and they were fascinated by visual phenomena and the effects of light on land and water. All this interest in atmospheric conditions and appearances, combined with Hodges's willingness to set aside the mantle of classicism provided him by Wilson—plus the fact that watercolor pigments had been improved since the provisioning of Cook's first voyage in the 1760s—prompted him to lift his gaze and give weight to the architecture of the sky equal to that of the land and sea. The Dutch landscape artists of the previous century would have approved.

By the time the expedition arrived at Cape Town in late October 1772—where he painted a large oil of the Cape of Good Hope from the great cabin—Hodges was proficient in the topographical art of coastal profiles and harbor views, which he had been executing all down the west coast of the African continent. Already we can see that Hodges, while capturing accurately the scale and distances in the relationships between the harbor, the town, and the mountains, has simultaneously loosened his technique. If the composition retains some elements of a conventional order, the paint itself is handled with immediacy, almost impressionistically.

In March 1773 the *Resolution* and the *Adventure* were picking their way carefully through the icebergs at the edge of the ice pack, which stretched as far south as men could see from high in the rigging. George Forster, painting in gouache, an opaque watercolor that Hodges himself was not known to use (but easier for his student to apply, as mistakes can be painted over), made a definitive image of the Antarctic, *Ice Islands with Ice Blink* (Plate 12).

The two ships patrol in the middle ground of a rough sea, the horizon obscured by dark clouds on the left half of the picture, while on the right the "ice blink"—a reflection of sunlight off the pack ice—glows. In the left foreground the great gothic jaw of an old iceberg, hanging over one of the ships, is beaten by waves. The picture, though not painted as skillfully is Hodges might have managed, is a vivid representation of the specific conditions found in the polar environment. It is also, somewhat ironically for a picture made by a scientist, an utterly stilted and romantic composition that assumes an imaginary vantage point behind the jagged iceberg.

Hodges's *Taking in Ice for Water—The* Resolution *and* Adventure, *4 June 1773* is, by contrast, meticulous in its details. The draftsmanship indicates precisely how Cook has his ships rigged for the calm conditions. The essential method for securing freshwater is specified. And the cavernous iceberg in the background is scaled accurately to the masts of the *Adventure*. The India-ink wash and watercolor drawing is a handsome composition divided conventionally into thirds—details in the foreground, a scaled object in the midground, and the sky as background—but it is also a strategic document for the Admiralty.

Later that year the ships wintered in the South Pacific, where Hodges made numerous plein air paintings of Tahiti. Inspired by the warm, paradisiacal light after the chill of the Southern Ocean, Hodges took to painting views while facing directly into the sun, as difficult a technical problem for a painter of the time as it would be for photographers two centuries later. In these sketches Hodges accomplished a major breakthrough. Although he was still depicting the topography so faithfully that distances from the seashore to interior mountain peaks could be estimated with confidence by navigators, he wasn't content to let atmospheric perspective do its job in the background; instead he overrode convention and let yellow light, not the blue fade of distance, dissolve the landscape. This is not the sunset glow painted by Claude Lorrain and Richard Wilson, or the late-afternoon golden light to be sought eventually by color photographers; it was strong morning and midafternoon sun.

Cook and his crews returned to England on July 30, 1775, after sailing some sixty thousand miles over three years and eight days. A year later Cook sailed back to the Pacific, this time to search for a western entrance to the still hypothetical Northwest Passage. Weaving a series of great loops across the Pacific, he discovered the Hawaiian Islands, made the first detailed chart of the west coast of America, then sailed through the Bering Strait, demonstrating that Asia and North America were two separate continents. He crossed the Arctic Circle and came as close to the North Pole as he had to its antipode. Cook was killed on his return to the Hawaiian islands in 1779.

William Hodges continued to travel widely, becoming in 1780 the first professional artist to visit India. He crisscrossed the subcontinent in search of subjects for three years, concentrating on Hindu and Mughal sites. Although he professed to represent what he saw without imaginary enhancements, he reverted to his classical training, framing the exotic temples along the lines of Claude and Wilson rather than building on his innovations in the South Pacific. The works were handsome but relatively static, and within ten years he was struggling to make sales. In 1795, his career as an artist over, he became a banker, soon suffered bankruptcy, and died in 1797.

Hodges's six watercolor drawings made from close to or within the Antarctic Circle are, as historian Stephen Pyne notes, key images in the history of Antarctic art, demonstrating a range of human responses to the polar environment. He painted ships under full sail next to tabular icebergs, picking their way carefully through the edges of the pack ice, or stationary, framing sailors standing on the ice itself. And he was able to capture accurately the look of the Antarctic seas and skies with their complicated exchange of light, a technical challenge that required him to invent new painting techniques, ones that other artists would soon adopt.

The historical relationship between maps and landscape art, like the lands they represent, is an old and complex topography. Cartographic historians sometimes refer to an eight-thousand-year-old wall mural excavated during the 1960s at Catal Hayuk in southern Turkey as the first map; art historians have also called it the first piece of landscape art (Plate 13). The sixteen-and-a-half-foot-long mural was made when Catal Hayuk was a trading center of six thousand people, a terraced settlement built in 6500 B.C. that has been called the oldest known city in the world. The topographical painting shows the plan of the city as if seen from above; behind the rectangles representing the terraced houses are shown the twin cones of the actively erupting Hasan Dag, a volcano eight miles east of the town and still visible from the site.

This is a literal visual representation of place in plan and section, or profile—evidence that our visual organization of space follows very old mental templates. The town is laid out as if the viewer is looking down on it from above, the volcanoes are outlined or in profile, as if seen from the ground. Show this to architects, and they will tell you this is a drawing in elevation and plan, as if depicting a building. Show it to theater people, and they will say it's laid out as if it were a stage with a painted backdrop. Show it to Captain James Cook, and he would have told you it was a survey drawing. If you print out a copy of the mural and fold it horizontally in half, then peer at it from a view inches away, you have a view of the territory as if you were in an airplane. It is a graphic and cartographic image that we read immediately as territory even without being familiar with the terrain, and in its folded form bears uncanny resemblance to three-dimensional computer mapping and architectural graphics.

The prejudice against paintings realistically depicting the world—whether they be of landforms, botanical specimens, or geology—was widespread even in England when Hodges was at the height of his success. The work was considered utilitarian and serving other purposes than art (a correct assessment). Sir Joshua Reynolds (1723–1792), for example, a fervent supporter of the neoclassical principles of the Royal Academy, disparaged topographical landscapes as mechanical rather than creative art (precisely as the Italians of the sixteenth and seventeenth centuries had done), and held up Lorrain as the model to be followed. Henry Fuseli (1741–1825), one of the most popular English painters of his time and, like Reynolds, a professor at the Royal Academy, called landscape paintings "map-work." Indeed, it would take the genius of J. M. W. Turner to shift the tide of opinion. Even then, landscape painting has continued to be held in lower esteem than more symbolic or abstract representations, as the records of auction houses testify.

The last several decades have been marked by a current of critical revisionism, with a minor renascence of sorts in the genre occurring in America and elsewhere. At the same time, however, photography and digital media have extended the terms of the debate over the relative merits of representational and more emblematic forms of art, such as abstraction. Why, some people wonder, even attempt to depict the world in painting when the camera does a much better job? The point was perhaps first raised by Constantin Huygens, father of the Dutch astronomer Christian Huygens, who in 1622 brought a camera obscura back from England and declared painting to be dead—a somewhat premature pronouncement that has resurfaced regularly ever since, but never more vigorously than when the camera became a common instrument in the mid–nineteenth century. The photographic print, however, is limited to presenting in two dimensions only what the camera can capture in an instant, not what the mind constructs over time in three dimensions, a fact well known to both painters and photographers working in the Antarctic.

The real question may lie not in the narrow view of how we represent the world, but in an examination of the much larger visual culture that arose during the European Renaissance, in particular the lens-based culture of the Dutch and English, which has been the dominant technology for assembling, editing, and transferring information for several centuries. The purpose of topographical art (and by extension much of landscape painting), like that of maps, is to enable us to get from a place we could see to one we couldn't. Likewise, the culture of the microscope and telescope has everything to do with the assimilation of knowledge at scales in both space and time that we can't otherwise perceive—a related task. All of these technologies would be required to bring the Antarctic within our cognitive reach as we explored it.

7 POLE

THE LATE NOVEMBER SUN IS still behind the hills when I get up at 5:15 A.M. to catch a shuttle out to the planes on the sea ice. I have severe misgivings about a plane trying to maneuver on a runway as slick as wet glass, but the ancient LC-130 lumbers up and off to the south with ease. The "L" means that the plane is equipped with skis, which will be lowered for our landing at Pole. "Pole" is what ice people call the station, as opposed to "the Pole," a concept that remains curiously abstract even when standing there. Pole is a specific place, a territory where people live and work; the South Pole, although it's only a few hundred yards away and can be fixed by GPS, is more of an idea, a geo-physical ideal, as is the south magnetic pole.

I've been granted the opportunity to visit Pole for twenty-four hours, which was not something the NSF could guarantee beforehand, as the logistical pressure on air flights there is severe. Construction material for the new station has taken up almost all the space on every flight able to squeeze through the windows of good weather. We twelve passengers end up strapped in with ten thousand pounds of cargo, mostly science equipment. The scientists range from young postdocs to grizzled astrophysicists returning to Pole for their ump-teenth time. The first-timers, though trying to be very casual about it all, are obviously excited, and the senior scientists are laconic and suspicious of the new station. "Too many offices and meeting rooms," one grumbles. "That means more bureaucracy!"

The turboprop parallels the Transantarctics for an hour, flying 275 mph at 25,000 feet, the temperature outside sixty-eight below. Most of the flight I spend with my nose close to (but not pressed up against!) the window of a hatch watching the peaks and glaciers go by. We bank to the right to follow the Beardmore Glacier and gain the polar plateau, basically following Scott's route to the South Pole. The Beardmore, which gains more than a mile in elevation as it climbs for 124 miles from the sea ice to the interior, is one of the largest glaciers in the world—so big that only a satellite can photograph it in its entirety. Fourteen miles wide, it moves downhill about three feet a day. The glaciers that feed into it from every side, like so many creeks meeting a river, are larger than most alpine glaciers in Switzerland. It's all a matter of scale, though—as everywhere else in the Antarctic—because just across the East Antarctic Plateau is the largest glacier on the planet, the truly mammoth Lambert: 25 miles wide, 248 miles long, and draining an area the size of Egypt.

The race to reach the Pole during the first decade of the twentieth century wasn't just a rivalry between nations attempting to maintain a sense of destiny (England clinging to the notion of an empire on which the sun never set) or aspiring to a rung on the ladder of history (newly independent Norway seeking ways to cement its identity in the family of nations). Rather, it was rooted in that human desire expressed by the Greeks to know the size and shape of where we live, so that we might scale ourselves to the universe.

The Antarctic was the last place on Earth needed to complete the picture—although it loomed large in the collective imagination through exploration literature, early science fiction stories, and the cartographic imperative. It was the pivot at the bottom of the schoolroom globe, around which you spun your fantasies of travel and adventure. Cook had declared that, based on the icebergs he saw, the southernmost continent must be a land of ice for which no one could possibly have any use—but to the public it was still a place where anything could happen. Even at the end of the nineteenth century people thought it might be a tropical oasis filled with dinosaurs, a tunnel leading to the center of the earth, or more plausibly a keyhole through which the secrets of geomagnetism could be spied.

Scott, Edward Wilson, and Ernest Shackleton made the first foray toward the South Pole during the last two months of 1902. They left Hut Point on Ross Island on November 2 and on December 30 reached their farthest point south at 82°16'—while still on the floating Ross Ice Shelf. They never even made it onto terra firma. Wilson sketched a watercolor of the Transantarctic peaks in the distance through which they would have had to pass, a wistful picture with a red skyline beckoning them south as if a day were dawning.

Shackleton returned in 1908, now a rival of Scott's. Winter Quarters Bay and Hut Point were iced in and inaccessible, so he set up his base at Cape Royds further north on the island, from which his party of four sledded south. On November 26, 1908, they passed Scott's southernmost point and soon thereafter gained the Beardmore, a ferocious uphill maze riven with thousands of crevasses. At one point they lost their last pony, which disappeared into a crevasse without a trace; when the men peered in, all they saw was a "black, bottomless pit."

They reached the plateau only to run headfirst into blizzards that reduced their progress to four miles a day. On January 9, 1909, they reached 88°23' south latitude, where Shackleton determined that they should turn back. They were within ninety-seven miles of the pole, but risked starvation, scurvy, and terminal hypothermia if they continued. The same blizzards stalling their forward progress were now at their back, the weather pouring off the plateau and down the exit glaciers; they hoisted sails on the sledges and during one day made as much as twenty-nine miles, virtually flying down icefalls and literally over crevasses. When they finished their journey on March 5 and regained safety aboard the *Nimrod,* they had walked 1,700 miles in 128 days.

Roald Amundsen and Scott raced each other toward the Pole during late 1911. Amundsen established his base on the Ross Ice Shelf itself, giving him a ninety-mile advantage over Scott, who considered camping on the floating shelf too dangerous. Scott set up camp instead at Cape Evans, handicapped immediately not only by the greater distance, but also by his determination to repeat Shackleton's use of ponies for the first stages of his attempt, then manhauling for the remainder. Amundsen, having had previous experience in the Arctic, preferred dog teams for hauling. As a result, he made faster progress, didn't tire out his men as quickly, and was able to lay a larger number of food caches farther south than Scott.

The upshot is that Amundsen, traveling up the Axel Heiberg Glacier, arrived at the Pole on December 14, 1911, his well-planned and rigorously executed assault allowing him to achieve his goal in an almost prosaic fashion. Scott, who followed the Beardmore, found Amundsen's flag awaiting him. Already exhausted, cold, and hungry, the five-man team (one larger than originally planned) turned around dispiritedly to retrace their steps. They made it back down the Beardmore, dragging thirty-five pounds of rock specimens with them and Wilson continuing to make his topographical sketches. Edgar Evans and Titus Oates perished of cold and starvation on, respectively, February 17 and March 16. On March 21 the three remaining men— Scott, Wilson, and "Birdies" Bowers—finally bogged down in a blizzard out on the ice shelf. Scott's last journal entry was on the twenty-ninth; their bodies weren't found for another eight months. Today the name of the Amundsen-Scott South Pole Station acknowledges the dual achievement.

The LC-130 takes less than an hour to fly the length of the Beardmore. When we reach the plateau, everything below disappears in a painful light. It's so white you can't look at it for long, your brain having so little to process (Plate 14). When we spot the geometry of Pole, with its flagged runways, roads, buildings, and equipment dumps, it feels like a sanctuary for the mind as much as the body. The landing is as smooth as the takeoff, and we lurch off the plane dressed in as many layers of clothes as it's possible to wear. It's −35° with a 10 mph wind, making for a wind chill of about −65°—normal for this time of year. The average annual temperature at Pole is −56.7°, the record low −117°. The station sits at 9,300 feet, but because the atmosphere at the poles is thinner than at the temperate latitudes, the effect is that of being almost two thousand feet higher. The plateau to the north-northeast of us is even higher, and the wind is just the dense cold air sliding off the interior toward the coast via gravity, not the result of a pressure differential or storm system. The cold and the altitude and the sheer amazement of where we are conspire to take our breath away and not give it back.

We're met by Jerry Marty, the NSF representative at Pole and the person responsible for the construction of the new station. Jerry, a weatherbeaten, cheerful man who has been coming to the ice since 1969, leads us down the snow ramp that descends thirty feet to a dim tunnel that enters the most famous geodesic dome on Earth. We catch only a quick glimpse of the new station—a series of squared-off C-sections elevated on huge pylons—before we disappear into the sepulchral gloom of the legendary dome.

Everyone new to Pole expects to walk into a heated space, but the dome is only meant to be a wind shelter, and the continuation of the cold inside is startling. The dome itself is opaque, though with five of the panels at the top left open for ventilation, enough light seeps in to create an artificial twilight. Elaborate frost feathers grow downward from the ceiling, four-foot-long gothic embellishments that let loose every so often and float to the ground. The hoar crystals are formed by sublimation working in the opposite direction from that in the Dry Valleys—here, condensation phases directly from gaseous water vapor to ice—and the atmosphere is a cross between that of a cathedral and a sci-fi slum. The hexagonal polygons of the dome tile to one another with mathematical regularity, but are covered in dendritic flowers. It's like standing on the underside of the Lake Vanda ice looking upward (Plate 15).

Our first task is an inbriefing with Katy Jensen, the Raytheon station manager, to establish that we know enough to stay both warm and hydrated while at such a high and arid altitude. The humidity here averages only 2 percent, and dehydration quickly compounds the tendency of altitude to create pulmonary and cerebral edema. We promise to keep our faces covered and to drink fluids compulsively. Then it's time for lunch. The food at Pole is reputed to be the best on the continent and we're not disappointed; the walnut and blue cheese empanadas, a vegetarian alternative to the main course, are a magnitude of achievement beyond anything the galley in McMurdo could produce on a daily basis.

Before venturing outside, I'm given an quick orientation tour of the dome by Katy. In 1956 the newly established station consisted of a small row of arched wood-and-canvas Jamesway huts erected for the International Geophysical Year (IGY). The reinforced tents, still used widely in the Antarctic, were immediately and constantly being buried by snow. It snows only 2.5 to 3.2 inches yearly on this part of the plateau, but the gravity-driven winds cause relentless drifting. Enough snow accumulates against horizontal surfaces in a year to cover a single-story house; because there's no thawing, the elevation of the ice sheet itself at Pole rises eight inches per year.

The idea of using a dome at Pole was posed: strong and aerodynamic, it would avoid some of the drifting and be able to bear up under the weight of what snow did accumulate. Construction was started in 1970 on the aluminum shell, which shelters three two-story prefab orange buildings. It was finished in 1975, whereupon the old station was promptly abandoned. The structure consists of 1,129 beams and 952 panels, no individual part of which weighs more than fifty pounds. At 164 feet in diameter and 50 feet high, it took only five flights to bring in the pieces (versus 151 flights this year alone for new building materials in what will be a five-year project). A month after dedication of the dome, the Jamesways were already buried under twenty-five feet of snow.

In 1977, however, it was noticed that the dome was startling to settle, and by 1982 a two-foot tilt to one side was noticeable. In 1989 the tension ring at the bottom of the dome, which holds it together, snapped in two places from the strain as the foundation sagged and twisted from glacial movement and snow buildup. Under other conditions, the dome could have failed, but luckily the ice kept it frozen in place. The next year a crew came down with ten hand-jacks, lifted up and leveled the entire dome, and rebuilt the foundation—but NSF had already started to plan for a new station.

The dome was originally intended to house 18 science and support people during the winter and 33 in summer, but this season 220 people are living on station, most of them construction workers housed on the surface—in Jamesways, no less. The snow is now almost up to the top of the dome; only a deep moat surrounding it prevents it from being swallowed. The moat is a hazard to people walking on the surface, particularly during the Antarctic night, and the corrugated metal tunnels that radiate outward from the dome are threatened with failure from the weight of accumulated snow (Plate 16).

Two years from now the dome will be disassembled and the pieces shipped out. Original plans called for keeping the old dome intact, perhaps using it for storage, but when the Honolulu-based architectural firm of Ferraro Choi surveyed the station in 1991, they determined that that was economically unfeasible, given the constant strain of the snow loading, not to mention the science community's increasing need for more space to house increasing numbers of researchers at Pole. The panels will be disassembled, the frame blasted apart, and the aluminum recycled. Many people, myself included, aren't happy that the most important modernist statement in the history of exploration will become beer cans. The dome is one of the world's supreme architectural manifestations of a mathematical idea, the rare merging of the pragmatic with an ideal form, and it is uniquely situated at a place that is likewise a geographical expression of geometry.

The geodesic dome was invented in 1922 by a German engineer working at Zeiss Optical, Walter Bauersfield, who was seeking to design the screen for a planetarium projector. But it was Buckminster Fuller (1895–1983) who realized that the dome could be a solution to the world housing shortages that he projected in 1927 would occur by the end of the twentieth century. More than 300,000 of the domes, a cult among the online design community, now enclose more volume world-wide than buildings designed by any other architect.

The reason the dome reminds me of Lake Vanda and of all the other polygonal patterning in the Antarctic is not a coincidence. The root meaning of "geodesic" (Greek, of course, who else but the geometry-obsessed Greeks?) is "earth dividing." Take a sphere and draw the longest possible line around it: that's a great circle, which corresponds to a longitude line on the globe. Using triangles, the simplest polygon, you can symmetrically divide the globe into a vectorial design of great circles. A geodesic is also the shortest line between any two points on the surface of a sphere.

Starting in the late 1920s, Fuller began deciphering the synergies (a word he subsequently popularized) between geometry and nature and applying them to engineering problems. He realized that a sphere is the most efficient geometrical structure that exists, insofar as it encloses maximum space with the least amount of surface through which to lose heat or suffer wind damage. The self-bracing triangles of a geodesic dome use the least amount of material needed to construct a sphere or any portion thereof, making the structures stronger, lighter, and cheaper to build than comparable conventional buildings. The larger they are, the proportionally stronger, lighter, and cheaper they become. And the domes, if warmed on the inside to a temperature greater than that outside, actually experience lift, making them even more durable.

The polymath Fuller used the same geometry to develop a method of projecting the continents on a flat surface with minimal distortion. In the last few years it's been discovered that his polygonal geometry exists in nature as the complex spheroidal carbon molecules known as Buckyballs (and in their elongated state, Fullerenes). The geometry he applied to architecture thus functions in cartography and at scales in nature other than the human.

Fuller proposed that Islamic and Chinese navigators, negotiating the isotropic environments of deserts and seas using celestial computation, were the first to develop trigonometry—the study of triangles, that most stable of polygons. Throughout his life he stressed that the synergies among geometry, nature, and engineering would be critical to understanding how we will survive on the planet. He considered nature to be the most economical of all engineers by necessity, and the dome at the South Pole has for decades been the epitome of that philosophy by virtue of withstanding the most extreme weather on the planet. Simultaneously, it represents the pole around which the planet revolves and the end point of human planetary navigation.

Geodesic domes are practical structures used around the Antarctic to house critical facilities, such as satellite communications; they are also the architectural epitome of 2,500 years of Western geophysical imagination, as well as a visual surface resonating strongly with Antarctic geomorphology. "Beer cans," I think disgustedly as Katy leads me back up the ramp (Plate 17).

As our eyes readjust to the vehement sunlight of the plateau, I realize that Pole resembles nothing so much as a construction site. Graders rumble by constantly, as do forklifts loaded with steel beams and building materials. A particular goal of mine is to visit the tunneling project run by the hard-rock miner John Wright. He's on the surface at the moment, using a large portable drilling rig to sink a ventilation hole twenty-five feet down to meet a six-by-ten-foot rectangular tunnel beneath us, part of the updated infrastructure necessary to accommodate the new building. As I stand there watching, ice accumulating on my neck gaiter as my breath condenses and freezes, he adds sections of auger with his bare hands. He warms his fingers in his pockets every few seconds, gets the bit reset in the hole, and lowers it to resume drilling.

When he's finished punching through the ventilation hole, he takes me down into the tunnel itself for a tour of the 2,000-foot long excavation. This is a utility tunnel that will carry water and sewage lines from the new station out to the wells and waste "bulbs." Water for the station is derived by inserting a heating element—which looks like a brass plumb bob 12 feet in diameter—150 feet into the ice and then pumping out the meltwater. After a sphere has been hollowed out over several years, creating a bulb that bottoms out 500 feet below the surface, they move to a new area, using the old bulb to store up to a million gallons of sewage, which freezes in place—sort of. The catch is, the ice cap is moving northward toward the coast (and Rio de Janeiro) at a rate of about an inch a day, or 33 feet per year. That movement means that the tunnels are steadily compressing; as a result, they have to be reamed out every few years to maintain room for the insulated water and sewage pipes. Because each sewage bulb fills up in five to six years, they're hoping—based on the length of the tunnel and the number of bulbs they can create off it (perhaps seven or eight)—this project will have a forty-year lifespan. Ultimately, in about the year A.D. 102,000, the whole mess should drop into the ocean.

At the tunnel face, a machine eats away at the snow with chisels mounted on a rotating drum. Twenty-five feet down the snow is almost as dense and hard as Douglas fir, well on its way to becoming ice. Excavated into a rectangular cross section here, it's strong enough to support the weight of a large Cat passing directly overhead on the surface. Although the machine looks like it's merely flailing at the wall, it carves out a four-inch-thick bite in less than two minutes. In essence, this is hard-rock mining. Ice began to accumulate here during the Miocene, 25 million years ago; by 15 million years ago the continent was covered. Scientists estimate that there's about 700,000 years' worth of accumulated ice on the plateau, and that the ice sheet puts one ton per square inch of pressure on the bedrock more than two miles beneath us, which helps explain why the continent is depressed, up to 1,400 feet below sea level in places.

I walk down to the end of the tunnel with one of the drilling crew, the ambient temperature where the air is undisturbed a brutal −50°F. It feels far colder than being outside in the wind, and we quickly become "cold-soaked" by the native geological stratum of the Antarctic, the raw material from which it is assembled as a continent and out of which we construct passageways, shelters while camping on the surface, and sculptural decorations for parties. To have cold permeate you as if it were a physical liquid—which is why they call this kind of deep chill getting "cold-soaked"—is a condition that you can't overcome with your internal heat. You have to find an external source, and once at the end of the tunnel we turn around quickly and head back toward the tunneling machine, where there's a cramped plywood box with a small stove in it for warming up. I stay there for five minutes, then return to the surface and scurry inside the dome to find Jerry, who has volunteered to lead an infrastructure tour that will complement the McMurdo one.

The first place Jerry takes me is one of the most anomalous: the greenhouse. Up on the roof of one of the orange prefab buildings, our footsteps muffled by old mattresses so we don't wake those sleeping below, we enter the six-by-twenty-foot space that started out as a kind of do-it-yourself home improvement project. Unlike the larger, newer facility at McMurdo, this greenhouse feels more like a leftover closet than a planned space.

The first season after seeding plants here, Polies found out that they could grow one to two salads per person per week—and by accident they also discovered that the room had therapeutic benefits: it is a private sanctuary in a station with almost no place to retreat from other people. As at McMurdo, the greenhouse has grow lights, thriving vegetation that smells positively earthy, and classical music is played for the health of the plants. People would find excuses to come hang out here, a fact noticed by the station doctor, who started prescribing time in the greenhouse to offset the effects of the long winter night. NASA paid attention because of the relevance to off-planet exploration, and so it became a cooperative project with official protocols—but it's nice to know that science can still start out as a simple building project. The greenery is also a counterpoint to the plastic plants in the galley, which showed up earlier in the season for a party and proved so popular that no one will take them down.

The rest of the tour is spent comparing the old with the new. First we wander through the arched tunnels to examine the fuel storage facility. The fuel of choice in the Antarctic is highly refined light jet aviation fuel, which stays liquid and burns reliably at low temperatures. Metal tanks containing 450,000 gallons of the highly volatile liquid, more than a year's supply, have replaced relatively fragile neoprene bladders. (There's an entire off-site power plant and fuel storage facility for a backup, should this one suffer a catastrophe.) Next we hit the old garage, which, though large by domestic standards, is so small that they couldn't drive in the larger vehicles to work on them but would have to disassemble them outside in eighty below temperatures and bring in the pieces. In the new garage, by contrast, an entire crane is being serviced.

Jerry then takes me down into the dome's original "utilidor," which serves the same function as the new tunnel John Wright is excavating. Water, sewage, and electrical conduits run in parallel through a curved corrugated metal passage fifteen feet underground. You can smell faint sewage even in the cold, and in the past the tunnel has flooded. Mixing water and electricity under a station that's tinder dry from the aridity of the air is potentially a nightmare scenario. They caught the leak in time, but it could have destroyed the station. And if that were ever to happen, whether in summer or winter, it would be catastrophic. It doesn't take long to freeze to death when it's thirty-five below or colder and you're without shelter.

The last facility we visit is the new station. The senior scientists on the plane were correct: the new facility will have more meeting rooms. But there will also be more privacy in the sleeping quarters than in the dome, where many of the bathrooms are unisex and the walls are so thin you can hear what's going on four doors down.

The first phase and a half of the two-story steel outer shell has already been completed, sitting fourteen feet above the ice on thirty-six pylons that will allow the wind to scour out snow from underneath it. The columns are footed onto a grid of horizontal steel beams that distribute the load of the 120,000-square-foot building onto wooden platforms resting on compacted snow, a foundation with the density and strength of construction-grade timber. The station is more like a raft floating on a very slow moving sea of ice two miles deep than a traditional building footed on the ground. The simulations run by Ferraro Choi in Honolulu demonstrated that this design should accommodate both the drifting snow and the inevitable settling of the building for about fifteen years, at which point the station can be jacked up. The complex is designed to be raised twice the full height of a story during its twenty-five-year lifespan.

The problem with all this is that the design is based on models that simply cannot predict with any accuracy what will happen. Because drifting snow is the primary reason the dome can't be saved, Ferraro Choi put some effort into studying that problem. They placed a model of the new station in an aquarium, where sand was used as an analog for snow, and watched the dynamics of accumulation. Sand, however, does not behave the same way that snow does, and I have seen for myself how the Ferraro Choi designs at McMurdo have failed to cope with drifts. They also put a large tabletop model outside at Pole for several years to study how snow accumulated, and subjected a model to wind tunnel studies. None of this can do more than provide educated guesses, and if those are as faulty as the assumptions underlying the sinking rate of the station, the drifts will be a problem.

Indeed, sinking into the ice is already an issue. Based on compression studies of the snow at Pole down to twenty-five feet deep, the station pylons were supposed to distribute the building's approximately forty thousand tons evenly enough over its footprint that it would sink up to perhaps a maximum of thirty-six inches over a fifty-year period. A manual hydraulic system can be used to raise the station on the pylons an additional twelve feet in ten-inch increments. Already, however, the pylons are sinking at a rate of up to five inches a year, and doing so unevenly. The station will have to be raised and leveled every year, and at this point it seems doubtful that its lifespan will be as long as originally planned. I don't take these to be design failures so much as simple reminders that we don't know much about building on snow, much less fully comprehend the physics of the East Antarctic ice cap.

Inside the new station, the initial framing of dorm rooms, kitchen, and galley are complete, and they will be occupied this winter, the first meal to be served in the galley a beef Wellington. The sleeping quarters are dormlike, as at McMurdo, but the majority are for single occupancy, privacy being a critical requirement for people working in such an environmentally confined and isolated place for long periods of time. The efficiency that's being achieved is obvious: the new space is only 28 percent larger than the current facility, but will hold almost five times as many people indoors.

Just as the pieces of the dome had to be kept within tight size and weight limits, so with the materials for the new building. All of its pieces must fit inside the cargo holds of planes—a space only eight by eight by thirty-eight feet. The hope was that construction would be finished in 2006, but every year the number of flights canceled due to weather and mechanical problems exceeds the contingency factors that Jerry and others build in to the schedule. Four million pounds were scheduled to be flown in this summer, but weather and equipment delays will trim that by at least a million pounds. That's a year's worth of delay.

Polies figure that the longer it takes to complete the new station, the longer the dome might stay up, so some people have ambivalent feelings about the schedule. Unlike the dome, this building will perch on the surface, an architecture alien and in opposition to the Antarctic landscape. And yet . . . the steel framing and raw plywood sheets outline a structure that will feel grand at times, its right angles and verticality a defiant statement of human endeavor. And the galley's wall of windows will admit an elevated view of the plateau otherwise not easily available to everyone for contemplation. When the sun dips and the rings and arcs of ice high in the atmosphere surround it, it will be like sitting on a frozen planet at the outer edge of the solar system.

Jerry sends me off to sleep on the surface in a Hypertat, a kind of plastic Jamesway. I fear that staying asleep will be difficult not because it's cold, but because bulldozers scrape by outside every hour, constantly pushing back the drifting snow; cranes lift steel beams into place; fork-lifts shuttle building materials. The building season at Pole is only 110 days long, and people move about in that restless three-shift rhythm that only a twenty-four-hour-a-day operation, whether a casino or a construction project, can provide. It doesn't help that the dorms have thin walls and the doors are only accordions of plastic, or that light seeps in at all hours. Nevertheless, I manage to enjoy a deep and satis-fying sleep with vivid dreams—often the experience of visitors to Pole, as if the blankness of the land outside opens up the ability of, and per-haps even a necessity for, the mind to imagine a more intense interior.

The next morning, and after touring the infrastructure of the sta-tion the day before, I'm ready to take a look at the point of it all: the sci-ence being done at Pole. Midmorning finds me walking with Julie Palais, the NSF science officer, into the "Dark Sector." One of the odd things about Pole is that you can't just wander around here unescorted, despite the fact that you're in the middle of the largest open continen-tal space on the planet. Most of the ice around Pole is off-limits so as to prevent stray light, sound, vibration, or atmospheric pollutants from interfering with the very precise measurements that science is able to make only in this most pure environment on Earth. Not only is the air cleaner here than anywhere else, but the rotation of the earth pushes the atmosphere into a bulge at the equator, which thins it overhead at the Pole. The earth's magnetic field also bends the flow of charged par-ticles flowing through space toward the poles, making them more available to inspection.

The Dark Sector is a quadrant devoted to the largest and most expensive science projects in the Antarctic, and its headquarters is a dark green two-story building with tinted bubble windows, an astro-physics observatory that looks as if it was designed by Jules Verne. Propped up next to it are two large cones with their wide ends aimed at the sky. I climb into one with John Carlstrom, an astrophysicist from the University of Chicago who is the head of CARA, the Center for Astrophysical Research in Antarctica, which has installed several major instruments here that track down various aspects of cosmic microwave background radiation (CMBR). We're standing in the middle of a mirrored exclosure about thirty feet in diameter, its reflective panels mounted on steeply angled pieces of plywood, one of which lets down as a kind of trapdoor for egress. In the middle is mounted DASI (pronounced "Daisy"), or the Degree Angular Scale Interferometer. Its thirteen stubby silver tubes are mounted into the front of a white box the size of a dining room table. Carlstrom pats it, obviously a proud parent.

Interferometers are instruments that have an array of multiple elements, or apertures, through which they gather light or other kinds of electromagnetic radiation. Because each element receives information at a slightly different angle, by combining and comparing the data from various combinations of the elements you can assemble much better images than with an instrument that has only one aperture, even if it is a much larger one. Interferometers require powerful computers to be used to full advantage, and as a result have come into their own for astrophysical research only during the last two decades. The world's largest optical telescopes can collect photons from about halfway back to the 13.5-billion-year-old Big Bang, but an interferometer such as DASI—working in wavelengths other than visible light—can peer back to within 380,000 years of the beginning of the universe.

As Carlstrom explains it, the CMBR is a relic of the rapid expansion of the universe after the Big Bang. Three hundred and eighty thousand years afterward the expanding universe became cool enough (about half as hot as the surface of the sun) for its particles to settle down and photons—particles of light—could begin to travel unimpeded for long distances. At first the photons were energetic enough that they were in the invisible range of the electromagnetic spectrum, but over billions of years their energy diminished and they slipped into the longer and cooler wavelengths of light.

Microwave radiation is susceptible to distortion by water in the atmosphere, and the severe aridity of Pole helps observers, as does its low temperatures. The temperature we call absolute zero, where no wavelength activity whatsoever occurs, is just under −459°F. The CMBR, those ancient photons, propagate at about −454°, which is why

DASI is at the South Pole, where the average daily temperature runs –56°. The telescopes are further cooled to within a few degrees or even millidegrees of absolute zero, and are housed within mirrored structures (the cones) to exclude radiation not only from the station but from the surrounding horizon as well. What is left to be picked up by these conical exclosures is about four hundred photons per cubic centimeter, traveling through space at microwave frequencies at the speed of light. Scan enough of the sky and you can, in essence, create a map of the CMBR, and thus of the early universe.

Since its discovery in 1965, the CMBR had been observed to be very isotropic; that is, everywhere we looked we found the same level of radiation. But cosmological theories from the 1940s onward predicted this shouldn't be so, and finally, in 1992, ripples in the radiation were discovered by satellite observation. If the CMBR had been found to be perfectly even, it would have been hard to explain how those clumps of matter we know as galaxies were formed, an awkward shortcoming for contemporary physics. The ideal realm of mathematics would have found itself very much at odds with the particulars of the universe.

DASI produces images of much finer resolution than those captured by the satellite, and in 2000 Carlstrom and his colleagues announced that the perturbations it detected appeared to be energy fluctuations at the quantum scale, and that they existed when the universe was about the size of a human fist. (By comparison, only one second after the Big Bang the universe was already several light years across.) Among other things, this helps confirm that the universe may exist primarily in a flat plane, rather than having a spherical shape. This made many astrophysicists happy, as it agreed with existing mathematical predictions for the "inflation" model of the universe: how the universe could have pushed explosively outward from that singularity, propagating harmonic sound waves as it went.

Carlstrom pauses in his explanation, then acknowledges that the CMBR observations also reaffirm a chasm of ignorance about the stuff of which the universe is made. Only 5 percent of the universe, he points out, consists of ordinary matter; 35 percent consists of what is predicted to be "dark matter," and an astonishing 60 percent is something else entirely, what Carlstrom and others call "dark energy." It has been known since the mid–twentieth century that the universe is expanding. Our understanding of gravity predicts that the rate of expansion should slow over time, yet instead it appears to be accelerating. The research into dark matter and energy at Pole is critical to understanding why this might be so.

As I'm transcribing all this, Carlstrom stops, looks at me, his head cocked to one side, and asks: "So, what does this have to do with your history of images of the Antarctic?"

I grin. "And you're telling me that you come to the largest flat cold place on the planet to look at the largest cold flat place there is in the universe, and map it?" He laughs. The connections, though, are even more numerous, starting with how the Greeks predicted the spherical shape of the world based on their observation of the rotating night sky, and then proposed the existence of a great southern continent to balance the landmasses of the northern hemisphere. They made a model of the world, and then explorers went out to see if the facts confirmed or denied it—the same method of inquiry that Carlstrom and his colleagues are using (versus the scientific methodology of Cook's time, which was to collect facts first and then theorize about them). The astrophysicists are still calculating the shape of the world around us, still seeking ways to establish the scale of what it means to be human in the universe, and using a rhetoric of geometry to do so. And they are doing it in the Antarctic precisely because they can see more with their extensions of human perceptual abilities in an extreme and isotropic place.

Julie Palais continues our tour of the CARA facility, showing me several of the other instruments looking at the CMBR at different scales. Viper, for instance, is an optical telescope that scans enormous areas of the sky in rapid movements akin to human saccades, and has mapped fine-scale structures otherwise invisible. It hosted a polarization experiment last year that went further back in time than even the DASI array. Viper, using instruments cooled to within a millidegree of absolute zero, was able to characterize temperature fluctuations that occurred within a fraction of a second after the Big Bang. A very small fraction: try a decimal point followed by 32 zeros and a one.

The instruments here seek to record minute temperature fluctuations in the background radiation that will eventually tell us the structure of the young universe, and help predict whether it will expand forever, collapse, or find some kind of everlasting balance. While DASI and Viper are looking as far out into space and as far back in time as is currently possible, other instruments are looking at the magnetic fields and gasses within our own galaxy to see how they, too, coalesced to form stars. They do so not by taking pictures as such, but by compiling maps that can overlap and compare different kinds of information with each other. Wilfred Walsh, a young astronomer from Harvard who will be wintering over to mind one of the instruments, points out, "There's a change in the language used by astronomers from 'mapping' to 'imaging' as the technology changes. Telescopes do much more than make a two-dimensional map; they make multidimensional images of comparative brightness, color, temperature, density, polarization, and chemical composition. The information landscape we can explore is much more complicated, much richer" than that accessible by older optical telescopes.

All of these variables, when displayed, are assigned colors so we can distinguish both change and difference—increasingly bright reds, say, to represent increasing temperature, and deepening blues for density. If you broaden the definition of art to include the application of aesthetics in all the visible representations of the world that we construct, then you are dealing with a larger body of knowledge called visual culture. It's within this larger arena that the differences between art and science begin to diminish and the similarities between the two modes of inquiry become more prominent.

If astrophysics is the most expensive science conducted in the Antarctic, the search for the missing dark matter and energy is certainly its single largest budget item. Consider the problem of neutrino detection.

Neutrinos, according to Frederick Reines, who shared a Nobel Prize with Clyde Cowan in 1957 for first detecting them, are the tiniest bit of reality a human can imagine. Of infinitesimal mass and carrying no electrical charge, they travel through the universe unhindered by magnetic fields or intervening matter. They are also much more numerous than even the commonplace protons; trillions of them stream through every square yard of our planet every second—yet another kind of background radiation from an earlier time in the universe.

They are, therefore, candidates for providing us with intelligence about the nature of the cosmos. Among other things, they may make up a significant portion of the dark matter we haven't yet seen. But because they don't react eagerly with anything else, they are hard to detect. Occasionally, however, they smash into a proton or neutron, and the resulting debris includes a muon, which, if it's created in water, leaves behind a blue glow, the Cherenkov light familiar from pictures of nuclear reactors. You have to have a huge instrument deep below the surface of the earth—therefore shielded from interference by cosmic rays, which also create muons—in order to see even this indirect evidence of neutrinos.

Physicists said that the detector necessary to detect neutrinos created by distant galactic events would have to be buried a mile deep and be more than six hundred feet in diameter—a footprint larger than that occupied by the Eiffel Tower. Digging the requisite hole in the ground would have been hideously expensive. Melting a hole in ice, which at that depth is perfectly dark and almost completely free of radioactivity, was more reasonable. As Julie and I leave the astrophysics center, we walk over AMANDA, the Antarctic Muon and Neutrino Detector Array—though I'm not even aware of it until Julie tells me later. Constructed at Pole during the 1990s, AMANDA deploys 679 photodetectors, suspended on nineteen strings down 6,500-foot holes like so many Christmas tree lights dropped into the optically pure ice.

The history of neutrino detection goes back a couple of decades, however. In the late 1980s, the Japanese, who had taken on neutrino detection as a matter of national pride, installed the Kamiokande neutrino detector—a tank containing three thousand tons of pure water, which they lined with one thousand photomultiplier tubes—inside a mine deep in the Japanese Alps. Buoyed by their subsequent success in detecting neutrinos from a supernova explosion outside our galaxy, in 1996 we installed AMANDA and the Japanese built Super-Kamiokande. The latter was designed to detect neutrinos generated even farther away, and deployed a tank that contained fifty-five thousand tons of water and thirteen thousand tubes. Before it was filled, it looked like the multifaceted eye of an enormous insect turned inside out. Once operational, "Super-K" confirmed that neutrinos sometimes have mass, a major success.

Two days before I flew to Pole, word arrived on the Internet that a photomultiplier inside Super-K had exploded, causing an inexplicable chain reaction that destroyed virtually all of the other tubes, rendering the instrument useless for years. This gives an extra push for the construction of "Ice Cube," an immense project that calls for suspending five thousand modules in a cubic kilometer of ice, each of which will hold a photomultiplier tube housed in a glass pressure vessel. As with particle accelerators, this is science where size counts: the larger the detectors, the more likely you are to capture light from the interactions. Ice Cube, which will supersede to some extent the other detectors, will cost at least $250 million to build—and make John Wright's tunneling job look like small potatoes. Such a huge-ticket item, however, threatens to displace the science budgets of every other project on the ice and strain the construction and infrastructure of Pole beyond its capabilities. The National Science Board, the governing body of NSF, had approved Ice Cube in concept but, cognizant of the logistical nightmare, was moving ahead slowly. In late 2001 Congress, under pressure from elected officials whose districts include the powerful University of Wisconsin–Madison, the lead research institution affiliated with Ice Cube, went ahead and forced an appropriation on NSF to start moving forward.

This development means individual scientists are now chewing their nails, knowing that NSF will have to push back their projects to accommodate Ice Cube, and Raytheon managers are ready to pull out their hair. Not to mention that the majority of the scientific establishment is upset that a rational planning process and the sanctity of the NSF peer review process, which determines funding priorities, has been threatened. It sounds familiar, for it is very similar to how public funding for Cook and Scott and Byrd came about—never exactly on the most rational footing, but squirreled through a corkscrew political process.

The current runways at McMurdo and Pole can handle between 200 and 250 flights per construction season. At least twice as many would be needed for Ice Cube. To alleviate that bottleneck, not only will new runways have to be installed, but NSF is now considering an overland supply route across the Ross Ice Shelf and up one of the outflow glaciers to the plateau and on to Pole. The idea sounds outrageous—cargo tractor trains on the ice—but it would actually be a safer and cleaner way to transport the enormous amounts of fuel needed. Similarly, the data pipeline is already clogged up by the available satellite coverage, which touches Pole only for a few hours every day and is far too small to handle the flow of information that will be generated by Ice Cube. The expensive solution would be to launch a series of geosynchronous satellites to orbit the Antarctic. As an alternative, NSF is considering the feasibility of laying a fiber optic cable from McMurdo to Pole.

These are all engineering feats akin to those required to explore another planet, and the only explanation I have for why politicians should spend taxpayer money on such innovations is that the human need to know the shape of the world and our place in it remains undiminished. Very little of the work done at Pole has to do with matters of an immediate practical nature, or even with life on Earth—but it has everything to do with how our minds interact with the largest environment of which we can conceive.

All day while Julie and I are walking around, a prismatic halo has encircled the sun, its lower edge touching and seeming to go flat with the

PLATE 1: Interior of Scott's *Terra Nova* hut, Cape Evans. Photo by William Sutton, 2002. The de-silvered mirror is on the wall to the left.

PLATE 2: Dr. Wilson working up a sketch, British Antarctic Expedition, 1910–1913. Photo by Herbert Ponting. Courtesy of Scott Polar Research Institute.

PLATE 3: Panorama at South Pole. Photo by Stuart Klipper, 1989. The barely visible objects anchoring the horizon are black markers on the runway.

PLATE 4: David Rosenthal, *Upper Wright Valley*, 1995. Oil on linen, 29" × 30". The ice of the East Antarctic Plateau breaches the Transantarctic Mountains and flows into Wright Valley; these frozen rivers form the legendary Airdevronsix Icefalls, one of the most painted and photographed scenic climaxes on the continent.

PLATE 5: Alan Campbell, *Ramparts-Bull Pass,* 1993. Watercolor, 15" × 22". Cavernously weathered boulders are strewn everywhere across the slopes above Lake Vanda.

PLATE 6: Lake ice in the Dry Valleys. Photo by Ty Milford, 1999. Milford, a photographer and mountain guide, worked for several years with McMurdo's Field and Safety Team.

PLATE 7: McMurdo Station from ice runway. Photo by William Sutton, 2001. Crary Laboratory is visible as the sprawling building behind the blue-green structures.

PLATE 8: McMurdo from Observation Hill. Photo by Ty Milford, 1999.

PLATE 9: Roll-Cage Mary, McMurdo Station. Photo by William Sutton, 2002. Observation Hill is to the right of the sculpture.

PLATE 10: Stained glass window in Our Lady of the Snows. Photo by Ty Milford, 2000.

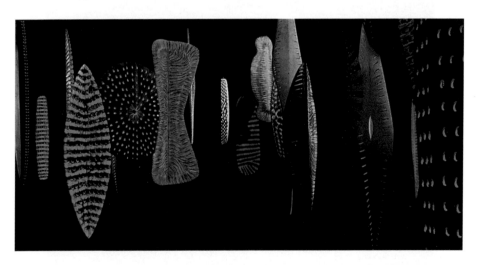

PLATE 11: Virginia King, *Antarctic Heart*. Mixed media installation. Photo by Haru Sameshima, 2001.

PLATE 12: George Forster, *Ice Islands with Ice Blink,* 1773. Gouache, 13¾" × 21½". Courtesy of State Library of New South Wales, Sydney.

PLATE 13: Reconstruction of wall mural at Catal Hayuk, Turkey (detail). Red monochrome painting, original approximately 16 feet long, 6200 B.C. Courtesy of Ankara Museum of Civilization.

PLATE 14: Stuart Klipper, *Panoramic View from Cockpit of LC-130*.
Color photograph, 1999.

PLATE 16: Skylab panorama. Photo by Robert Stokstad, 2001. Stokstad, a
scientist who has worked on both AMANDA and IceCube, took this digital
panorama of Pole from one of the science buildings. Notice the deep snow moat
surrounding the dome. The new station building is in the right background, its
construction camp on the left.

PLATE 15: Inside the Dome. Photo by Kim Stanley Robinson, 1995. The photographer, better known as a best-selling novelist, was an NSF visiting writer and set part of his novel *Antarctica* at the Amundsen-Scott Station.

PLATE 17: Polygonal patterning and geodesic communication domes on Black Island. Photo by Ty Milford, 2000.

PLATE 18: The Martin A. Pomerantz Observatory (MAPO). Photo by Stephanie Rowatt. The building, named for an early Antarctic astronomer, is the head-quarters of the Center for Astrophysical Research (CARA). On the left is the DASI ground shield in its open position; to the right is the Viper telescope.

PLATE 19: Campbell Stokes Sunshine Recorders, South Pole. Photo by Katy Jensen, 2001.

PLATE 20: Stuart Klipper, *Ferrar Glacier, Asgard and Olympus Ranges, Transantarctic Mountains, Victorialand, Antarctica.* Color photograph, 1992.

PLATE 21: Stuart Klipper, *Ross Ice Shelf, East of Cape Crozier, Ross Island, Ross Sea, Southern Ocean, Antarctica.* Color photograph, 1992.

PLATE 22: David Rosenthal, *Summer View of Taylor Valley*, 1995. Oil on linen, 28" × 30". Seen from the Lake Bonney side, the Seuss Glacier falls out of the Asgard Range, crosses the narrow Taylor Valley, and leaves only a small gap, the Defile (out of sight to the right), through which to walk. On the left is a narrow moat of open water at the edge of an otherwise permanently frozen pond. Noteworthy is Rosenthal's ability to capture water and ice in various phases while maintaining visible brushwork—a style that not only makes clear that this is a painting and not a photograph but also leads to a sense of detail that a camera would fail to capture.

PLATE 23: Mummified fur seal and Seuss Glacier, Taylor Valley. Photo by William Sutton, 2002. In a view looking back upvalley toward the Defile (hidden on the left), a seal carcass perhaps several centuries old rests among faceted ventifacts.

PLATE 24: Canada Glacier and Lake Hoare, Taylor Valley. Photo by William Sutton, 2002. Evening light shines on the face of the glacier. The "beach" is the sandy area directly under the ice in the background.

PLATE 25: Mt. Erebus erupting beyond Big Razorback Island. Photo by William Sutton, 2002.

PLATE 26: J. E. Davis, *Beaufort Island and Mount Erebus, Discovered 28 January 1841*. Watercolor. Courtesy of National Maritime Museum, London.

PLATE 27: Ted Dettmar at the crater rim. Photo by Ty Milford, 2002.

PLATE 28: Landsat image of Mt. Erebus, 1985.

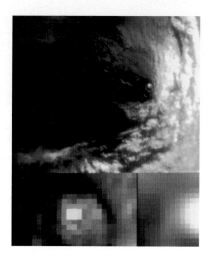

PLATE 29: Jody Forster, *Ice Garden, Barne Glacier.* Color photograph, 1996.

PLATE 30: Anne Noble, *William's Field #3* (from the series *Whiteout, Under Erebus, 2002*). Pigment print.

PLATE 31: Daniel Lang, *Mt. Erebus,* 1975. Oil on canvas, 28" × 72". Collection of the artist.

PLATE 32: Peter Nisbet, *VXE-6 Icefalls,* 1996. Oil on canvas, 12" × 24".

PLATE 33: Jody Forster, *VXE-6 Icefalls*. Black-and-white photograph, 1996. Nisbet and Forster made these views of the icefalls from the same vantage point. Compare with David Rosenthal's view (Plate 4).

PLATE 34: Nel Law, *Imaginative —Penguins on Edge of Ice Flow*, 1961. Oil on canvas.

PLATE 35: Margaret Eliot, *A Day at the Beach,* 1999. Oil on plywood, 21" × 24". Painted from Eliot's experiences on Ross Island, this work conflates what could be the Barne Glacier with volcanic soils and the pressure hummocks typically found in the transition zones from sea ice to fast ice held to the shoreline. These visual elements, while having a topographical basis, are juxtaposed to give the viewer a sense that the Antarctic can also appear as a dark and foreboding landscape.

PLATE 36: Nigel Brown, *Warmth is Something to be Worked At,* 1998. Acrylic on board, 1250 mm × 2460 mm. Collection Christchurch Art Gallery, Te Puna o Waiwhetu, New Zealand. Purchased 2001.

PLATE 37: Sandy Sorlien, *Peak, New Jersey,* 1996. Silver gelatin print, 18" × 18". The deliberate vignetting at the corners lends a historical atmosphere to a photo that at first appears to depict a peak in the Transantarctics, but is actually a rock on the New Jersey shore—a reverse illustration of the cognitive difficulties we experience in the Antarctic.

PLATE 38: John Jacobsen, *The White Continent* (detail), 2001. Acrylic paint and laser toner on twelve credit cards, 3⅜" × 2⅛" each.

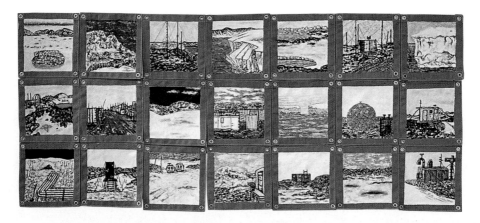

PLATE 39: Stephen Eastaugh, *Wilkes Land*, 2000. Twenty-one images, acrylic on jute, each 40 cm × 40 cm.

PLATE 40: Alan Campbell, *Shackleton's Hut, Cape Royds,* 1988. Watercolor on paper, 19" × 29½". The style of this painting, which provides a view across McMurdo Sound to the Royal Society Range in the Transantarctics, is reminiscent of field sketches made by exploration artists from Thomas Moran to Edward Wilson.

PLATE 41: David Rosenthal, *Arena Valley*, 1995. Oil on linen, 28" x 30". Sandstone mesas tower two thousand feet above the floor of a valley in the larger Beacon Valley group. The close juxtaposition of what looks like the American desert southwest with glaciers creates an otherworldly landscape.

horizon; the effect is of a bright sun pillar extending upward a few degrees. The circle is known as a 22-degree halo—so called because it is formed 22 degrees from the sun as light, on passing through millions of tiny hexagonal ice crystals, undergoes two refractions (as it enters and again as it exits the ice crystals). This halo is in turn encircled by a larger and rarer 46-degree halo—created when larger ice crystals are present—atop which is a faint circumzenith arc. On and off throughout my wanderings today I catch additional features appearing and disappearing as the ice crystals in the air align themselves differently. At one point there's an upper tangent arc on the smaller halo, and sun dogs, or perihelia, on each side alternately fade then brighten. It's the most elaborate display of daylight atmospheric phenomena I've ever seen, though not unusual here, and another reminder that landscape is a three-dimensional construct, not merely a planar one. On January 11, 1999, three Finnish observers at Pole reported observing "the great South Pole halo display," which included ten of the common halos and arcs, such as the ones I observe today, plus seventeen rare ones, the largest and most comprehensive display ever recorded.

The arcs and circles in the atmospheric ice are an appropriate backdrop as I go to the South Pole Clean Air Facility, run by the National Oceanic and Atmospheric Administration (NOAA). This time I'm dropped off some distance from the facility by the station shuttle, since vehicles are not allowed to enter the Clean Air Sector except by permit. Tony Hansen, the scientist who's been measuring black carbon aerosol pollution at Pole and elsewhere on the continent for several years, will later tell me that in the mid-1980s pollution from the single chimney at the station was detectable over an area the size of Switzerland. The pollution wasn't especially bad; it was simply noticeable in contrast to the extremely clean Antarctic air. Then too, the instruments in the NOAA facility are so sensitive they can, if the wind is blowing right, detect the exhalations of a single person walking across the ice.

NOAA traces the roots of its corps of three hundred commissioned officers, the smallest of the seven uniformed services, to the former U.S. Coast and Geodetic Survey. NOAA scientists still produce nautical and aeronautical charts, but we know them primarily as the government's oceanographers and climatologists, and as purveyors of satellite weather pictures. They maintain four baseline observatories—in Barrow, Alaska, on the slopes of the Mauna Loa volcano in Hawaii, in American Samoa, and here at Pole—from which trends in global climate and pollution are measured.

Loreen Lock, an NOAA staff member, shows me the greenhouse gas samplers that track levels of atmospheric carbon dioxide. These chromatographs both plot the chlorofluorocarbons that create the ozone hole and sample aerosol particles around which clouds condense. Having started my South Pole Station infrastructure tour yesterday looking at pipes underground, it seems fitting to end the science tour on a rooftop looking out over the plateau. A series of radiometers sit atop the building measuring the sunlight, which refracts endlessly through the ice crystals overhead and on the plateau below. Three miniature glass domes the size of plums also adorn the roof. One, mirrored and opaque, measures infrared radiation; one, made of optically clear quartz, takes in the broadband of visible light; and the third is tinted red to measure other wavelengths. Nearby is a dome protected by the shadow of a disk that moves with the sun, blocking direct rays but allowing it to measure how the sunlight is being scattered, a phenomenon with some relevance today as the halos continue to wheel around the sky with the sun, the prismatic ice crystals throwing rainbows in arcs and circles, disks and pillars, and diminishing the sunlight. In concert, the instruments—part of our effort to monitor the fluctuating ozone hole overhead—allow us to measure how sunlight changes at Pole, influenced by weather, natural aerosols, and manmade pollutants.

I end my stay at Pole by visiting three larger glass globes with Katy Jensen. It's a privilege to walk with the station manager to one of her favorite places at Pole, a pair of Campbell Stokes Sunshine Recorders, crystal spheres the size of softballs held in old-fashioned brass armatures that focus the rays of the sun onto a spool of graph paper, where they burn a track showing how much the sun shone that day. The spheres are so low-tech and human-scaled, yet elegant compared with the other instruments I've seen, that I immediately want to take one home. This is science that is comprehensible, cause-and-effect held in the hand (Plate 19).

The third ball is, of course, the South Pole itself, the mirrored ball atop the barber pole that stands surrounded by the flags of the signatory nations to the Antarctic Treaty. Katy insists that she take my picture with the ceremonial marker, knowing I'll regret it later if she doesn't. Afterward we walk over to where the U.S. Geological Survey (USGS) placed the genuine benchmark last year—as they do every January—showing where the Pole actually stood on that day. Then we pace off the thirty-three feet to where the Pole is today, and where the USGS will place a new marker in another month. The earlier markers, buried in the ice, form a gently curving invisible arc tracing how the ice cap has moved over the years as it slips toward the ocean.

At the Canterbury Museum in Christchurch, New Zealand, once you've passed the sledges used by Scott and Shackleton on the first floor and displays of early Heroic Age clothing, if you go upstairs and look to your left you'll see a sixteen-inch silvered ball in a case. Dropped by parachute in December 1956 to the first chief scientist at Pole, Paul Siple, it was used as a navigation aid by pilots bringing in supplies during the IGY, as well as by Siple to take 180-degree photos of atmospheric phenomena, including the aurora australis, the Antarctic version of the northern lights. The ball resided at Pole for eleven months before Siple took it back with him to the United States. Two decades later his widow brought it to the museum, where it remains the definitive metaphorical embodiment of one of only two spots in the world where you can circumnavigate the globe in four only steps. The curator of the Antarctic hall should open up the case, reach inside, carefully lift out the heavy sphere, and place it reverentially on a plinth at the center of the museum. There it would garner the recognition it deserves as one of the most perfect visual analogs ever designed for a place.

The mirrored spheres at Pole and in the museum represent the geosymmetry we project on the planet. They also reflect back to us our own gaze, which shows us that what we see at Pole can ultimately only be ourselves. The importance we "place" on the South Pole is the result of our attempt to project human scale onto the planet. As I stand with Katy and then turn slowly in a circle, I realize that there is nothing much else the mind can do with the South Pole. Put your back to the dome and the new station, to the buildings in the Dark and Clean sectors, to the flags whipping in the stiff breeze that is quickly taking away our body warmth—put your back to what we have built here and there is only ice and sky and sunlight, not enough for human vision to construe a sense of place. Because the ice constantly remakes itself and never stays still, and is utterly isotropic, it is the nearest thing I will ever see to pure space.

Katy was right. I'm glad I have a picture of this.

Later that evening I'm back on a Herc LC-130 flying north across the plateau. Below us the white surface seems strangely close, the sastrugi much larger than I thought they were on the way up. It's not until I perceive a line of shadow stretching hundreds of miles off to the horizon that I realize the white surface I'm looking at is a rippled cloud cover, not snow. When we can see the ice again, there's nothing beneath us but undifferentiated white until we reach the edge of the plateau. The topography, invisible under the two-mile-thick ice sheet, begins to separate the ice into individual ice streams moving at different rates toward the mountains and the ocean. Each of the streams is a lighter or darker shade of light gray, which, if you're standing on the ice at the boundary between two streams, shows as an abrupt change in surface texture. As we descend the Beardmore Glacier once more to descend toward the Ross Sea, isolated ice storms whirl in the cirques of the Transantarctics, wrapping the solitary peaks in gray blizzards. The glacier itself is polished silver in the low light behind the plane as we follow the river of ice downstream (Plate 20).

It's midnight when we approach the coast of Ross Island, and I find myself filled with a sense of homecoming. "Absurd," I think. "You've only been here for three weeks, and half that time you've been out in the field."

It's the dirt, I decide, a coastline with familiar contours set against the sea ice. And it's the shape of a social as well as a physical community that I know. The town and its residents, as opposed to being staked out in the great white of Pole, are circled up around the small harbor and nestled securely in the lee of Observation Hill, and I feel as if I live here. At Pole I was a visitor peering at maps of the large-scale structure of the universe. Here at McMurdo, I'm more likely to be walking with friends as we look at the rocks under our feet. Coming back to McMurdo gives me a newfound appreciation for the scientists who winter-over at Pole and spend months calibrating images of the universe, tethered to the earth only at mealtimes. Standing on the raft of the new station, they are sailing off the edge of the known world just as surely as if they were with James Cook traversing the Pacific.

8 THE HISTORY OF ICE

MCMURDO SEEMS POSITIVELY TROPICAL after Pole, and I work up a sweat this Saturday morning dragging my gear down to the helo hangar where I weigh and tag my rucksack and duffel for a second flight out to the Dry Valleys next week. Wherever we fly, we wear ECW (extreme cold weather) gear and carry extra clothes, a tent, and full sleep kit, and on top of that the heavy orange survival bags for everyone on board. As I walk back into the lowest level of Crary, I pass through the aquarium with its exotic denizens in water that is kept as close to freezing as possible, and pause to cool down. I watch several six-foot-long Antarctic cod slowly circle within their round metal tank, then go over to the smaller "touch tank" and put in my hands as Melissa has encouraged me to do—yet another lesson in looking for Antarctic life. I don't bother the two delicate orange sea spiders as large as salad plates, but gently caress the tentacle of a surprisingly friendly benthic octopus.

Sufficiently cooled, I go up to the next level where people are tinkering with GPS units that will be placed around the continent to measure the movement of ice. Up again and to my left are freezers full of ice cores that will be shipped back to the United States for analysis. Almost all the labs are devoted to the collection of physical specimens and related data, a somewhat archaic and surprisingly rich task on what is supposed to be the emptiest and most barren continent. Partly this is because we've only been at it here since the mid-1800s, and partly it's because the tools get better every year at probing nature at different scales, from the microscopic biota of the Dry Valleys to the entire land mass itself, which is measured in every conceivable way by satellite.

The South Pole is a place that first existed in theory, and the modern station at Pole is devoted primarily to theory-based inquiry. McMurdo, in contrast, tends, it seems to me, to embody science that approaches the world through the collection of ice, rocks, and life forms that are then subjected to tests to see if someone can figure out how they survive here. When I go out to the Dry Valleys next week, it will be to accompany a scientist who is collecting particulate carbon from the air to see if we're polluting the Antarctic atmosphere with diesel generators and helicopter engines. It's very much a nineteenth-century style of science compared with the astrophysics at Pole; while at the latter site scientists are looking for data predicted to exist by a theory, at McMurdo they are trolling the air and water to see what they find, the modus operandi during the Age of Exploration. What people bring to McMurdo from the field can still surprise the little kid in you, wonders such as petrified tree trunks and sea spiders.

As James Cook and other explorers brought back increasingly large numbers of specimens, maps, and meteorological observations, scientists were forced to organize the information through new systems of classification. Natural history, for example, which at first included only botany, biology, and mineralogy, was concerned more about exotic deviations from the known world than with devising unifying systems to explain them. Collectors placed specimens from around the world in *Wunderkammern,* or cabinets of curiosities that were sometimes arranged more by aesthetics than logic. The collections were eccentric and available only for viewing in person, but as print technology became more pervasive it became possible to compare specimens across Europe and then from around the world, compounding the information logjam. Just as the expansion of topographical knowledge provided by the explorers required new mapping technologies, so the shiploads of specimens required new ways to house them. That meant creating museums in which materials could be arranged in a systematized manner, and thus be retrieved for study. The sheer volume of information required breaking science apart into separate disciplines, then developing classification systems so that the specimens would proceed logically from one to another.

The German herbalist Otto Brunfels (1489–1543) took an early step forward when he worked with the artist Hans Weiditz to produce an herbal with illustrations drawn directly from nature, as opposed to providing only text descriptions. This allowed the reader to more accurately and efficiently duplicate the classification and selection of plants—a matter of importance to physicians and their patients, as well as to natural historians. The giant leap came with Carolus Linnaeus, who in 1753 used the external appearance of plants to distinguish them as to genus and species, extending his classification system five years later to animals. "Specimen" and "species" share a family resemblance in the Latin *specere,* which means to look at, or see. Coupling printed illustrations with the Linnaean system encouraged explorers to collect the world and bring it home to the newly established museums—institutional wonder cabinets, if you like. Experts could then place the specimens in cases where they would reside with their cousins, be they plant, animal, or rock.

The 1800s became the century of encyclopedias, with Diderot's thirty-five-volume *Encyclopédie* the best-selling publication of the times. Not far behind in sales was Comte de Buffon's *Histoire naturelle* in thirty-six volumes (1749–1785), a stupendous encyclopedia that described every facet of the natural world, and did so not in the less accessible academic Latin but in French. Slowly the public began to accept the idea that it was possible to know the world, hence the mind of God, completely and irrevocably through science and its images. Instead of knowledge being imposed on the world as a preexisting theological unity in text, knowledge was being built from the ground up by distinguishing visually between things, and only then finding patterns common among them.

It was the exhortations of Linnaeus that prompted Banks to insist that Cook bring along both a naturalist and an artist to record visual data. And it is with Cook that the historian of exploration William Goetzmann identifies the shift from the First Age of Exploration to the Second. At that moment, our worldview shifted from the stasis of Christianity, and in some ways the equally stationary clockwork universe of Newton—where every orbit in the universe was unvarying, the universe linear and predictable—to a reality in which science described how the world changed. But the theories that would allow us to realize that the sole constant *is* change could be developed only through accumulations of data massive enough to overturn the existing paradigm.

At the beginning of the nineteenth century it was believed that everything could be seen, thus known and owned by humans; in turn, humanity could then discern the hand of God in the Great Chain of Being, that natural succession of creatures from small to large, from plant to fish to mammal to man, and onward up the ladder through angels to the Creator. It was at first a fixed cast of characters, then one where new species came on stage throughout time, and finally one in which natural selection propagated only the fittest to survive from chance mutations. The accumulation of knowledge during the century was used to support religious doctrine, evolution, and material dialectics, whatever your choice.

If Linnaeus inspired the classification of the world's contents, thus moving natural history from a collection of wonders and curiosities to a table of contents, it was the Prussian Alexander von Humboldt who incited explorers to become more than adventurers traveling in search of new lands and resources to plunder, but instead to be scientists following lines of inquiry. Born in 1769, the year of the Transit of Venus expedition, he died in 1859, the year that Darwin published *The Origin of Species,* one of the greatest conceptual systems of all.

Humboldt was the son of a baron and started out studying geology and mineralogy at a mining institute, but after receiving his inheritance, liberated himself from commerce. He learned so much of everything that he was acclaimed the Aristotle of his age. Close friends with George Forster, who had taken art lessons from Hodges on Cook's

Antarctic voyage, Humboldt in 1790 realized how important landscape painting was to exploration when he visited a home in London where he saw several paintings of India done by Hodges. When he sailed in 1799 for South America, he took with him the botanist-illustrator Aimé Bonpland.

Slipping through a British naval blockade on a Spanish mail boat to Venezuela, they paddled 1,500 miles up the Orinoco to its source, traced the connection of its river basin to that of the Amazon, and climbed Ecuador's dormant volcano Chimborazo with no technical equipment (at 20,700 feet then thought to be the world's highest peak). They went on to explore parts of Mexico; headed north to Washington, D.C., where they met with President Thomas Jefferson; and returned to France in 1804 with sixty thousand specimens. The seven hundred sextant observations the two men made were the foundation for the first credible map of South America, drafted later in the 1800s. Humboldt spent the next twenty-five years of his life and his entire fortune to publish his findings in thirty volumes, which included an astonishing 1,425 plates and maps.

Humboldt's passion was to look for the underlying patterns in nature, and nowhere is this more evident than in his use of maps, which he turned from flat, two-dimensional representations of a space into vertical displays of biogeographical unity. Humboldt delighted in the seemingly chaotic profusion of the tropics, but he also knew that nature was organized by laws. While he and Bonpland were climbing up and down the volcanoes of South America, they kept track of elevations, temperatures, climatic conditions, and the distribution of flora and fauna. In 1817 Humboldt organized all of this information into a map based on isotherms, or contour lines based on temperature, to show how ecologies were organized by altitude—and how those isotherms also governed plant and animals communities within cooling climate zones as one traveled away from the equator. He discovered that gains in altitude are equivalent to gains in latitude. The 124 magnetic readings he took during his trip traced yet another contour line, how magnetism increased with latitude, a correlation that would lead

Carl Friedrich Gauss (1777–1855), the German scientist and mathematician, to deduce that magnetic fields surrounded the earth. The ancient Greeks would have found both of these maps compatible with their conception of the world's symmetry.

Humboldt intuited that similar formations were formed similarly — if you studied mountain building in the Alps, you might understand how the Andes were assembled. It was no accident that the young Charles Darwin took Humboldt's account of his travels with him on HMS *Beagle*, or that Alfred Russel Wallace (1823–1913), who was jointly inspired by Linnaeus and Humboldt, would be the codiscoverer of evolution. Humboldt's cartographic intelligence was robust enough to allow him to speculate about continental drift a century before the theory would be formulated.

During the 1800s explorers, and the scientists and artists who accompanied them, brought back so much information from around the world concerning the diversity of species, how they related to each other, and the specific visual contexts in which they lived that enough anomalies accumulated to break the existing paradigm, the Great Chain of Being, and make room for Darwin and Wallace to propose natural selection as a mechanism to account for the prolixity. Just as the word "biology" was used in 1800 to carve out a distinct niche within natural history, so geology replaced mineralogy as amateur collection became scientific discipline; this development would lead to the discovery of the Ice Age and increase both scientific and public curiosity about the polar regions. No picture of the world, no collection of its wonders, could be complete until the Arctic and Antarctic were mapped and sampled.

Charles Lyell (1797–1875), a Scottish geologist who did more than anyone else to push the age of the earth back past biblical conjecture, published the first edition of the century's most influential geology textbook, *Principles of Geology*, in 1829. Lyell was the major proponent of uniformitarianism, a theory that proposed the planet's surface had been sculpted over a long period of time by processes still active today, such as erosion and seasonal flooding. He stood in distinct opposition to the Catastrophists, who believed Earth was formed through a series of violent cataclysms, principally volcanic eruptions and huge floods. Lyell's book did much to systemize geology based on fieldwork, but it ignored the role glaciation played.

In 1815 the surveyor and self-taught geologist William Smith published a remarkable map akin to Humboldt's 1817 isotherms, but one that went down into the earth instead of up in elevation. Observing the similarity of strata across the land as they were revealed by the cutting of roads and canals, Smith noted that the same fossils appeared in the same strata from place to place, thus allowing a consistent sequence of deposition to be established even when the strata were uplifted, tilted, and otherwise made discontinuous from their surroundings. When Edward Wilson, returning from the South Pole with Scott on their fatal journey, refused to lighten his load by jettisoning the fossils he had collected in the Transantarctics, it was in part because he thought they could be important in assessing the relationship of the Antarctic to the other continents, an assumption based on the work of Smith and his contemporary Louis Agassiz.

A brilliant Swiss naturalist, Agassiz (1807–1873) had been a protégé as a young man of Baron Georges Cuvier, the inventor of paleontology, as well as of Humboldt. A major project of his, one begun with Cuvier in Paris, was an authoritative ten-volume study on fossil fish. He won international acclaim for this work, due in no small part to the five volumes of illustrations by scientific illustrator Joseph Dinkel, which made it possible for others to identify the fossils worldwide. In turn, this enabled a relative chronology for geological strata to be established, greatly extending the possibilities revealed by Smith.

Another topic of interest to Agassiz was glaciers—and on this subject, eventually, we will find firsthand experience of the Antarctic coming into play. The idea that these rivers of ice transported the huge granite boulders known as erratics had been proposed at least as early as 1815 by a mountaineer in the Swiss Alps; it was then confirmed in 1829 by Ignace Venetz, a Swiss road engineer who knew by necessity quite a bit about glaciers, and expanded upon by five years later Jean de Charpentier in a paper presented in Lucerne. Agassiz attended that lecture, yet he remained unconvinced, subscribing instead to Lyell's theory (one that confirmed the biblical story of a great flood) that flood waters and icebergs were responsible for depositing the erratics.

During a summer vacation in 1836, however, Agassiz found himself in the company of and arguing with Venetz and Charpentier about the matter. To resolve the dispute, the men went into the Alps, where they prowled around Zermatt at the base of the Matterhorn, then climbed the flanks of Mont Blanc, Europe's highest mountain, to inspect its largest glacier, the Mer de Glace. Observing over five months the parallel walls of moraines pushed up by the glaciers, and the scoriation of granite by the ice—ample evidence that all of Switzerland had apparently been glaciated—Agassiz became a convert. Realizing that the same evidence was found across Europe, he began to theorize that ice had stretched from the North Pole to the Mediterranean. By early 1837 his colleague Karl Schimper had coined the term *Eiszeit*, or Ice Age, and thus the history of ice was born, a story still being written as the ice cores in Crary are deciphered.

Agassiz and his friends, though, faced an uphill battle of immense magnitude, much like the one faced by Darwin and Wallace. Even mainstream scientists who were willing to accept that Earth was older than the biblical six thousand years believed the planet had progressed steadily from a hot volcanic sterility to a slowly cooling body. This progression, they maintained, was paralleled by the successive appearance of creatures in the Great Chain of Being, from the lowly insect to the exalted human, which led inevitably upward to a supreme creator with an intelligent design in mind. Why would such a tidy and self-evident progression be interrupted by a period in the earth's history cold enough to produce glaciers a mile thick over Europe?

In 1837 Lyell, still dismissing glaciation, wrote to the young and admiring Charles Darwin (who a few years before had returned from charting the coastline of South America and visiting the Galápagos) that his travels in Norway convinced him that erratics there had not been transported by floods, but dropped by melting icebergs. Three years later, as Agassiz was writing his first book on glaciers, Lyell was preparing the sixth edition of his textbook, which he periodically revised. By then he was ready to mention the existence of glaciers, but only as static blocks of ice, not as rivers of ice capable of strewing granite boulders about, much less carving entire valleys.

In the summer of 1841, while Agassiz was fielding an entire team of specialists on a Swiss glacier to study it—a practice still followed in the Antarctic today—Lyell was touring Niagara Falls. Despite a profusion of erratics and other evidence of glaciation in North America, he clung to his notion that the rocks were waterborne, notwithstanding the absence of marine fossils nearby or other corroborating evidence. An Ice Age was entirely too much of a catastrophe for him to contemplate, and ice aggregated into continental sheets was a thought that even Humboldt declared to be fearsome.

In order for Lyell, much less the public, to accept glaciation, a massive dose of visual evidence would have to be accumulated to contradict biblical certainty and uniformitarianism. And here we meet up again with our intrepid explorers and their artists—but this time it is men venturing to the polar regions that tipped the scales of belief.

Following the success of Cook's first voyage in the Pacific, the Royal Society convinced the British Admiralty to attempt a journey to the North Pole in 1773, the same year that Cook first crossed the Antarctic Circle. During the northern summer, HMS *Racehorse* and HMS *Carcass* crossed the Arctic Circle, making it to 80°48' N before being turned back. Roughly six months later, during the Austral summer of 1773–1774, Cook reached his southernmost point at 71°10' S.

Hodges, of course, brought back from the south his sketches of icebergs, although the exact source of those ice islands was still unverified. Cook thought they had fallen off a continent of ice somewhere farther to the south than he was able to sail, prevented from doing so by the pack ice guarding the region. When the educated and articulate British whaler William Scoresby sailed north in 1806, he mapped almost a thousand miles of the east coast of Greenland, reached past 81° N, and returned home with sketches ranging from the structure of snowflakes to icebergs. Ten years later the ambitious John Barrow was named Second Secretary to the Admiralty, and over the next three decades more than twenty major expeditions were sent out under his direction. In Africa they traversed the Congo, reached the legendary Timbuktu, and traced the course of the Niger. But it was in polar exploration that "Barrow's boys" are most remembered (and whose exploits are recounted in a book of that title by Fergus Fleming). Barrow, ever alert to commercial pressures as well as scientific ones, started with the Arctic. Although the handful of Antarctic watercolors by Hodges had initiated the representation of the polar regions in artistic and scientific images, it would be the flood of images produced during the search for the Northwest Passage that would convince the public that ice once covered vast portions of the earth.

In 1818 Barrow sent out John Franklin in the first serious foray since 1741 to find a passage from the Atlantic to the Pacific. Together with David Buchan, he explored the Greenland Sea to the east of the world's largest island while, simultaneously, John Ross and Edward Parry sailed up the Davis Strait to Baffin Bay on its west coast. Ross accomplished much on his voyage, including the development of a classification of icebergs still in use today, but he turned back when confronted by what he took to be a chain of impenetrable peaks at the end of Lancaster Sound, which he named the Croker Mountains. Parry returned two years later and sailed directly over the position of the supposed mountains. Ross had been repelled by no more than a looming mirage.

Franklin returned to the Arctic in 1825–1827, taking with him, as before, the officer and artist George Back (1796–1878), who remains the definitive exploration artist of the northern polar region. The practice of the British Admiralty to train its officers and sailors in art was by then so deeply entrenched in naval culture that it seems as if every captain produced his own sketches and even oil paintings, Ross and Franklin being no exceptions. The results varied from spectacular collisions of ships with gothic ice-flows, which Ross favored, to more sober views delineating the methods of exploration and the liniments of the landscape. Back's work epitomized this later category at its best.

Attempting to salvage his now tarnished reputation, the argumentative and ill-tempered Ross convinced a private patron to send him north again in 1829 and, in the summer of 1831, during the middle of the four-year expedition, found himself on the Boothia Peninsula of Baffin Island. Accompanying him was his eighteen-year-old nephew, James Clark Ross, the man for whom the Antarctic's Ross Sea is named. Together they measured the north magnetic pole—1,250 miles from the geographical pole—to be within sledging distance of their ice-locked ship, the Victory. The historical pull to be the first to stand at one of the two centers of terrestrial magnetism was too alluring for the younger Ross, who was fascinated with geomagnetism, to resist, and he set off with a dip compass and a small party. (The dip compass, invented in 1576, has a vertical circle instead of a horizontal one, and points downward more or less to the center of the earth—which led its inventor, Robert Norman, to hypothesize correctly that the earth is in essence a spherical magnet.)

At 8 A.M. on June 1 Ross found his needle pointing directly downward, and he spent the next day and a half painstakingly measuring his position to be 89°59'. Given that the magnetic pole can wander as much as thirty minutes in an hour, it was fair to say that he was on the spot, an achievement that stood unmatched until the 1990s and the deployment of GPS units. His achievement earned both John and James an audience with the king upon their return in 1833, and the owner of the great Panorama at Leicester Square—a viewing space completely in the round—painted the ninety-foot-long View of the Continent of Boothia, discovered by Captain Ross based on sketches made by the former.

The panorama (meaning to "see all"), invented in 1787, at first showed elevated views of cities, the tourist destinations of Florence, Rome, and Athens being popular subjects. Spectacular in scope and in its sense of realism, it was a way for citizens to regain a sense of ownership; providing an illusion of control, it turned an increasingly impenetrable urban space into personal place. It was also a medium well suited to presenting heroic themes such as military battles and expeditions of discovery—including vistas of the polar environment. The Royal Gardens at Vauxhall devoted 65,000 square feet to the exhibition of huge paintings depicting both the open waters into which the Rosses had sailed in the *Victory* and the sea of ice that eventually beset her. The showings were wildly successful, and helped stoke the fires of John Barrow's ambitions.

Ross's achievement also fueled Humboldt's desire to establish an international network of geomagnetic observatories, which would go a long way toward establishing the true shape of the planet as well as providing the data necessary for navigators to make compass corrections while mapping the oceans and continental interiors. Geomagnetism was for Humboldt yet another way of demonstrating the unity of nature, and in his quest he enlisted the help of Gauss, who in 1833, two years after Ross had stood at the north magnetic pole, published his theory that allowed the prediction of magnetism anywhere on earth. To verify the theory and complete the geomagnetic map, it would be necessary to find the south magnetic pole. James Ross was sent south to the Antarctic in 1839. The public, primed by the Arctic panoramas six years earlier, eagerly awaited his results.

The exploration of Antarctic waters since James Cook had proceeded slowly during the early part of the nineteenth century, dominated more by American sealers than by Europeans, who were otherwise engaged in warfare. By the early 1820s, however, with more than two hundred American ships plying the sub-Antarctic waters, the fur seals were virtually extinct, and the Napoleonic Wars were over. It was a Russian explorer, Thaddeus von Bellingshausen, who first saw the Antarctic mainland—or, more accurately, one of its ice shelves—in 1820. Sighting the continent at almost the same time were the American whaler Nathaniel Palmer and the English naval captain Edward Bransfield.

A decade later the first scientist to visit the Antarctic, the American geologist James Eights (1798–1882), found the first fossil on the continent, a piece of carbonized wood. From 1837 to 1840, Jules Sébastien César Dumont d'Urville, the urbane Frenchman, would-be scientist, and discoverer of the Venus de Milo, sailed Antarctic waters in search of the magnetic pole, but failed to locate it. His expedition produced an extensive visual record, including several sketches by Louis Le Breton (1818–1866) of a landing on Adélie Land, one of which Edward Wilson later called a prototypical image of Antarctic exploration. In it, officers stand on exposed rock with architectonic cliffs of ice rising behind them, and penguins observe a toast being raised as if they were an admiring audience.

The Americans also launched a national exploring expedition in search of the magnetic pole, in parallel with the French, who based their search on Gauss's early calculations of its location. This was the young country's first official scientific voyage, and it was conducted under the unfortunately contentious leadership of Charles Wilkes. Sailing on a five-year voyage that lasted from 1838 to 1842, Wilkes took with him numerous artists and naturalists (the latter a post to which the writer Nathaniel Hawthorne unsuccessfully applied). Among the artists was Titian Ramsey Peale (1799–1885)—who had been on the government's overland expedition in 1819–1820 that first produced images of the Rocky Mountains—as well as the topographical draftsmen Joseph Drayton and Alfred T. Agate. Wilkes was not exactly enamored of the "scientific corps," however, and left most of them behind in Australia and New Zealand before sailing south beneath the Antarctic Circle.

Despite his disdain for the "scientifics," among Wilkes's notable achievements were the mapping of nearly 1,500 miles of Antarctic coastline, publication of the first charts to declare the landmass a continent, and the collecting of so many specimens that the United States would build what would become the Smithsonian Institution to house and study them. Wilkes was a meticulous surveyor, using a camera lucida to aid in the sketching of coastal profiles, and he amassed thousands of triangulation points in his running surveys. His charts became the core around which the U. S. Hydrographic Office would build its collections. The natural history illustrations and landscapes produced in various locations across the Pacific by Peale, Agate, and Drayton— when they were allowed to accompany shore parties—were extraordinary, and it's a shame that Wilkes left them behind when mapping the Antarctic coastline. Wilkes was himself a trained artist and produced both sketches on the spot and, in later years, a series of oil paintings depicting the Antarctic; but the more cosmopolitan d'Urville had kept his artists on board, and as a result his visual record of the continent was much more extensive.

When James Ross set sail for the south, it was aboard the HMS *Erebus;* accompanying him, under the command of Lt. Francis R. M. Crozier, was HMS *Terror.* The two ships, which would play remarkable roles in the exploration of both poles, were bomb vessels massively reinforced to absorb the recoils produced when launching mortar bombs at the shoreline. Because they were smaller, more nimble, and stronger than Wilkes's vessels, and Ross a far more experienced sailor with eight winters and fifteen summers under his belt in the Arctic, he would be able to establish the southernmost port in the world. It also helped that, when Ross called in at Hobart, Tasmania, on his way south and visited with governor John Franklin, waiting for him was a letter from Wilkes with a copy of his new Antarctic chart, a gracious gesture all too uncommon in the early history of national expeditions. (Franklin would himself soon be agitating with John Barrow to be sent again into polar waters—not south, but north, in pursuit of the ever elusive Northwest Passage.)

Ross sailed out of Hobart in November 1840 and in early January spent four days ramming his way through the ice pack, a fight that other ships simply could not have handled. What Ross found was at first supremely disappointing: the south magnetic pole was currently located hundreds of miles away on the other side of the Transantarctic's Admiralty Range. Nonetheless, he continued to sail south along the mountainous coastline. Joseph Dalton Hooker, serving as botanist on the journey, thought the range, with its glaciers flowing from the peaks right down to the sea ice, one of the most wonderful sights he had ever beheld. (Hooker would later become the foremost botanist of the century, succeed his father as director of the internationally renowned Royal Botanic Gardens at Kew, and be an adviser to Scott's expeditions.)

What Ross discovered at least partly made up for the unattainable magnetic pole. First was what looked to be wind-driven spindrift from the top of an island peak. It turned out to be the plume of a volcano, its underside reflecting the red glow of an eruption. The discovery of a live volcano at 79° S astounded the crewmembers and for Hooker was awesome evidence of the Creator. They sailed to the coast of Ross Island, named the smoking mountain Erebus and the smaller, extinct volcano next to it Terror, then continued east to what Ross called on his chart a "Perpendicular Barrier of Ice" three times higher than their masts (Plate 21). More than a week later, still following the Ross Ice Shelf, crewmen were able to climb the masts and peer over a low point, finding nothing but a white plain as far as the eye could see.

Ross hoped to winter near the future location of McMurdo, travel overland to reach the magnetic pole, and climb Erebus. Weather and ice prevented him, and just as his uncle had been fooled by a mirage in Lancaster Sound, so the younger man descried a range of mountains beyond Mt. Erebus and stretching across the ice sheet. Scott later sledged across where they were supposed to have risen, finding only sastrugi. Although traveling to the magnetic pole and ascending Erebus would have to wait until Shackleton came in 1907–1909, Ross had found the gateway to geophysical symmetry, an island reachable by ship from which to launch an expedition to the geographical South Pole.

On his return to London in 1843, after having been gone for four years and five months, James Ross and his expedition were memorialized in another panorama at Leicester Square. Lyell, when discussing the presence of an ice sheet covering Scotland, compared what it must have looked like with Ross's account of the ice barrier. But it would be images of the frozen north, not the south, that would lead both scientists and the public finally to accept the Ice Age, despite the fact that Ross had discovered a place on earth where it had never ended. Franklin would get his wish—Barrow would send him north in search once more for the Northwest Passage—thereby setting off events that would ultimately create the Heroic Age of Antarctic exploration.

Two years after Ross's return, the *Erebus* and *Terror* were pointed north, Franklin in command of the former, Crozier once again captaining the latter. The two ships had been additionally reinforced and given auxiliary steam power. It was the best-equipped polar expedition the world had assembled to date: the stores included 7,088 pounds of tobacco, 3,600 pounds of soap, and libraries of 1,200 volumes for each vessel. They were provisioned to sail from England to Baffin Bay, across the top of Canada, down through the Bering Strait, and south to the Sandwich Islands, and took enough food for three years, including hundreds of thousands of pounds of meat in 8,000 tins. On July 26, 1845, two whalers noted that Franklin's ships were parked at the entrance to Lancaster Sound waiting for the ice to break out. The two sturdy little ships were never seen again.

Two years later, with no word from Franklin, Barrow, James Ross, and Lady Jane Franklin were beginning to worry, and over the next decade forty ships would be dispatched from both England and America to find the expedition. A total of 40,000 miles were covered on sledges and 8,000 miles of coastline traced and retraced until finally notes left under a cairn revealed that the two ships had been trapped by ice in 1846. Their crews had lived on board for eighteen months, then abandoned ship, all of them eventually perishing. Autopsies conducted during the 1990s on three of the mummified remains revealed that the crewmembers had suffered extreme lead poisoning from the faulty soldering of the tinned food. Ironically, what was then a new technology that was designed to enable them to extend their exploratory range instead killed them.

One of the searchers was an American adventurer, Elisha Kent Kane, who declared two reasons to sail north. One was to look for Franklin, the other to seek the mythical "open polar sea." Kane had first shipped into Arctic waters as a member of a U.S. Navy party searching for Franklin in 1850. Three years later he set off again, this time also, and perhaps more importantly in his own mind, to find once and for all an ice-free route across the North Pole. He sailed blithely into disaster and emerged a celebrity hero.

During the first half of the summer of 1853 Kane made his way up Baffin Bay to the southern end of Melville Bay, a place so packed with ice floes and bergs that even the whalers avoided it when possible. Instead of attempting to pick his way through under sail, Kane anchored the *Advance* to a succession of bergs. Whereas the floes were spinning south with the surface current, the icebergs, with their deep keels, were caught in the northerly West Greenland Current, and he was pulled safely through the 150-mile bay and into the relatively clear water of Smith Sound. Proceeding north past the site where Thule Air Base sits today, he ventured into what the map now calls Kane Basin, which that season was choked with ice of every kind, including massive icebergs. He parked his ship in a harbor with a river of freshwater, an anchorage from which it would never stir again.

Scouts from his party explored the nearby coast and trooped inland until they could go no farther, stopped by the Greenland ice sheet. As Edmund Blair Bolles notes in *The Ice Finders,* a book that does much to rescue the importance of Kane's journey, they were gazing on more ice than all but a handful of Antarctic explorers had ever seen. Like Antarctica's polar plateau, Greenland's ice moves out and down to the coast in all directions, and was the source of all the icebergs Kane's party had faced. If it melted, it would raise the sea levels worldwide by twenty feet. That winter temperatures fell to −75°F, killing both the sled dogs and Kane's illusions about an open sea to the north. The next spring, Kane climbed to the ridge from which his scouts had peered the previous year, and looked down on what he named the Humboldt Glacier, with its sixty-mile-wide terminus one of the largest glacial edges in the world. Before leaving New York, Kane had written Agassiz to query him about the nature of icebergs, thinking that they were composed not merely of compacted snow, but of glacial ice. Here was proof, continental ice pouring off a landmass and creating entire fleets of bergs every summer.

The next winter Kane ate rats, the crew cannibalized the ship's timbers for fuel, and his journal compared Greenland to a Dantean landscape: "inorganic, desolate, mysterious . . . a world unfinished by the hand of its Creator." In the spring of 1855 Kane led his men through a desperate eighty-five-day retreat back down through Smith Sound and across Melville Bay, where later in the year the surviving members were rescued by an American steamship. Franklin's death, they now learned, had been confirmed by Eskimos the previous year in a location a thousand miles to the west.

Although his exploits on the west coast of Greenland aren't listed in most exploration atlases—he discovered no new lands—Kane contributed uniquely to the history of ice by grasping the extent of Greenland's ice sheet, second in size only to the Antarctic's. And the images of Greenland's glaciers and ice cap that he brought back convinced the public that an Ice Age was possible. Kane died in Havana in 1857, his health broken by the ordeal, but not before he had seen into publication his two-volume *Arctic Explorations*. Even today the account—which, Bolles points out, was displayed in many American homes as a "centre-table" book next to the Bible—reads like an adventure yarn, and it was illustrated with more than three hundred engravings of glaciers, icebergs, and all the paraphernalia of polar exploration. The images of his ship nipped in ice and threatened by towering icebergs were as exciting as an action movie would be today, and his account became one of the most popular books of the nineteenth century.

Kane included pictures of an ice river that was more than twice the width of the Dover Channel. The images of the Humboldt Glacier were proof again that masses of ice much larger than the glaciers of Switzerland could exist and move, transporting boulders, dismantling mountains, and carving valleys. The year that Kane died, Lyell went to Switzerland and walked up to the foot of a receding glacier to examine the rocks it was leaving behind. He returned a convert, and the future of the Ice Age, so to speak, was assured. Kane had provided Americans with a genuine, if flawed, polar hero, whereas the British were left with the most famous failure in all of polar exploration. They would be looking for ways to rectify that situation early in the next century.

Antarctic exploration would continue only fitfully after d'Urville, Wilkes, and Ross until the meeting of the International Geographical Congress in London during 1895. In the meantime, exploration and science made progress elsewhere. Under Francis Beaufort, a maritime surveyor who was appointed in 1829 as the Admiralty's hydrographer, the collection of official British charts available more than doubled by his retirement in 1855, from approximately a thousand to some 2,500. Now the broad outlines of the globe were completed for all the continents, save Antarctica.

The continental interiors were being inventoried as well. And in this effort, very slowly, the balance among painting, photography, and cartography began to shift irrevocably, most notably during the exploration of America's Transmississippi West. By the time Scott occupied his hut at Cape Evans, the transition from eye-based to optical-based representation of terrain was almost complete.

After completion of the Pacific Railroad surveys in the 1850s and 1860s, four great government surveys were sent out to finish the reconnaissance of the West. Their mission, undertaken between 1867 and 1879, was not only to assess the terrain in the interest of science, but also to convert it into territory for colonization and resource extraction. Between 1820 and 1860 the government published more than sixty reports on the expeditions, in some cases spending more money on the books and their illustrations than on the expeditions themselves. At one point as much as a third of the federal budget was devoted to the printing and distribution of these reports. Their purpose: to promote the fulfillment of America's "manifest destiny," the settling of the West.

The reports from the railroad surveys led to seventeen volumes of cartographic and natural history information containing more than seven hundred pictures, but no photographs. The enormous swaths of land being surveyed simply weren't capturable within the narrow view of mid-nineteenth-century cameras, and only a draftsman could see through the atmospheric distortions of this vast, arid land. (This was the same problem Ponting would face when attempting to photograph the Transantarctics.) In any case, the public had not yet adapted to viewing photographic representations of landscape. Human vision and painting both excerpt heavily when viewing empty terrain, part of the cognitive mediation that turns land into landscape. The photograph captures every last detail, however; it also presents objects in the background as much smaller than either vision or painting does. This "photographic distortion" was an issue that would be overcome only through acculturation.

Although Joseph Niépce took the first permanent photograph in 1825, and photographers with their daguerreotype equipment were passing each other up and down the Nile as early as 1839, painters and draftsmen were still critical to picturing new lands and the knowledge they represented. Ross took a daguerreotype camera with him in 1839, but it never left the case. It would take the Crimean and American Civil wars to spur the development of methods of field photography suited to the combative environment of the American West, which would later be applied to the Antarctic.

The first major deployment of a photographer on an exploration came in 1867, when the geologist Clarence King invited Timothy O'Sullivan (1840–1882) along on his survey of the fortieth parallel. King was a friend of Agassiz, then teaching at Harvard, who suspected that photography could provide incontrovertible evidence for geologic processes. O'Sullivan, a large-format, wet-plate photographer who had worked with Matthew Brady during the Civil War, was no stranger to working under adverse conditions.

When Ferdinand Hayden led the first official expedition into Yellowstone in the summer of 1871, he took with him both the photographer William Henry Jackson (1843–1942) and the painter Thomas Moran (1837–1926). Like his contemporary Albert Bierstadt (1830–1902), Moran aspired to be a painter of the American West. Both Bierstadt and Moran were following close on the heels of Frederick Church (1826–1900), who had been inspired by Humboldt to travel to South America and paint scientifically accurate panoramic scenes of what he saw, huge encyclopedic canvases that became immensely popular. Humboldt had urged landscape painters to depict accurately the color of the sky, the angle of the sun and shadows, the density of haze in the atmosphere, the relative brightness of foliage, and the profiles of mountain ranges. In short, he promoted landscape paintings as scientific documents, seeking unity between art and science.

Like Church, Moran was a great admirer of the work of the English painter J. M. W. Turner (1775–1850), whose style combined topographical accuracy with certain overt exaggerations. Both Church and Moran felt free to move topographical features to suit a composition, if they felt the changes better conveyed the spirit of the place. Although Jackson's photographs of Yellowstone were of great interest to members of Congress (Hayden gave them prints as gifts to increase his chances for future funding), Moran's watercolor sketches of the polychrome geothermal wonders were ultimately more influential in the decision to declare Yellowstone the first national park.

Thanks to the Wilkes, King, and Hayden expeditions, the tradition of employing artists on American exploratory missions was now firmly rooted. Although their use as scientific illustrators diminished as the public became accustomed to reading photographs, their political value remained high, for in order to finance large-scale explorations, whether for military, commercial, or scientific purposes, the permission and support of Congress was essential. That required public support—which in turn meant selling the public, a task accomplished most effectively with beautiful and evocative pictures. The practice continues today with the National Science Foundation's Antarctic Visiting Artists and Writers Program.

Turner's name appears everywhere in the journals of nineteenth-century exploration artists, and he remains the artist most cited today by painters working in the Antarctic. Turner was a close boyhood friend of James Alexander, who followed in the footsteps of Hodges to become one of the foremost topographical artists in the British empire. Both Turner, who trained first as an architectural artist, and Alexander taught drawing to military men, and despite Turner's increasing experiments with the fluidity of paint, he continued to produce topographical work his entire life.

When Turner took his first tour of the Alps in 1802, landscape art was still dominated by the picturesque. Bound volumes of carefully framed views directed tourists to "beauty spots," both picture and reality organized more by the aesthetic sensibility of Claude than by nature itself. Beginning in 1812, however, Turner radically subverted the traditional compositional techniques of both Claude and the topographical artists with *Snowstorm: Hannibal and His Army Crossing the Alps*. The large canvas, though following the traditional geometry of landscape compositions, is dominated by a great vortex in the sky that seizes the viewer's eye, making the painting less a literal image of a storm than an emotional equivalent for it. Turner hiked the pass himself, and the storm derived from an actual experience he'd sketched on the back of an envelope a year or two earlier. Overtly, then, this is a history painting set within real topography—but more than that, it is a painting about what paint and the artist can do to move beyond representing nature. Turner didn't attempt just to capture literal reality; rather, he sought to create within the viewer an emotional reaction to unbridled nature. Until his death in 1851, Turner defined the world in terms of light and cloud, storm and fury. One of his most important techniques—facing directly toward the sun and letting halation dissolve the scene—was adopted from Hodges.

From the time of the snowstorm painting onward, Turner's influence on the romantic painters of the century was immense. Increasing industrialization made it appear as if science and commerce were conspiring to ruin the natural landscape even as they depersonalized the individual. In response, the artists and writers of the romantic movement sought to present a view of the world where feeling was as important as thought, where wild nature was a refuge from the coal mines and mill machines. Turner's sublime storms of paint made him a hero to the movement.

The German Caspar David Friedrich and the Americans Church,

Bierstadt, and Moran, romanticists all, painted epic polar pictures with shipwrecks set among the looming architectonics of ice. These allegories, based on romanticism's deep pessimism about the failure of rationality to serve mankind, often used Turner's vivid palette, wild atmospherics, and scumbled brushwork to accentuate the untamed and chaotic in nature. Yet ironically, Turner's escape from the classical conventions of his craft was enabled in large part by his own extraordinarily restless and wide-ranging curiosity about science. From 1814 onward his circle of friends included notable scientists of the day, such as Michael Faraday, Charles Babbage, and the remarkable mathematician Mary Somerville (1780–1872). Somerville was the best-selling popular science writer of mid-nineteenth-century England as well as the translator of the French astronomer Pierre Laplace's encyclopedic summation of mathematical astronomy, *Mechanisms of the Heavens* (1831). She herself conducted experiments in the perception of light and magnetism, and she provided Turner with a scientific justification for transcending literal reality in the interpretation of landscape, asserting that vision is more a matter of neural processing than a transcription of absolute reality. In his snowstorm painting, concordantly, Turner, rather than presenting an illusion of observed, objective reality such as a static composition based on rectangles would provide, instead thrusts the viewer into a much more subjective realm with his dynamic vortex of color. For Turner, nature was always changing, never still, and light was in perpetual flux. In his innovative approach to the observable Turner didn't just inspire the romantics; he also prefigured modernism, a period in which the observer, whether painter or physicist, would construct reality in collusion with it.

Turner's influence on American landscape and exploration art was likewise profound. Thomas Cole (1801–1848), the founder of America's first major landscape school of painting, the Hudson River School, had gone to England to study his work, followed by Thomas Moran. One of Moran's early acquaintance's was James Hamilton (1819–1878), a prominent marine painter who was a close friend of Turner's and who in the 1850s created from Elisha Kane's drawings the plates for his Arctic books. Hamilton taught one of Thomas's older brothers, and Moran soon found himself in possession of Turner's *Liber Studorium*, the artist's guidebook to landscape painting styles. Moran went to England in 1862 on the first of seven trips to Europe that spanned the years until 1890. He copied Turner's paintings in the London's Tate Gallery and followed his footsteps to Wales, through Italy, and across the Alps. He also met with the critic John Ruskin, a champion of Turner's work. Ruskin defined two kinds of landscape painters: those who were topographically adept and those who were able to go beyond faithful representation to achieve a psychological connection to the sublime. The latter was an aesthetic ideal derived from his analysis of Turner's work, and it was this goal that Moran promoted to his friend William Henry Jackson.

Moran never pushed his craft as far as Turner did, much less as far as the European avant-garde, which increasingly would overwhelm the topographical aspect of art. The Barbizon school in Paris had begun painting outdoors in 1840, a working method that the Impressionists, who were also studying the physics of light, soon used in the forest of Fontainebleau. Monet and Pissarro visited London together in 1870 to view Turner's works, and in 1872 Monet painted *Impression: Sunrise,* the painting that lent its name to the movement. The movement, which was based on observing directly the effects of light and color during specific times of the day, owed much to Hodges and Turner. At the same time, Cézanne was organizing the view of La Montagne Ste. Victoire outside his window in Aix-en-Provence into increasingly geometric schemes, which helped give rise to Cubism early in the twentieth century, a movement that had its own effect on landscape painting.

The same year that the French painters were first taking their easels outside, Turner studied the daguerreotype and found it to be no threat to the livelihood of artists. Painters, in addition to being able to encompass wider views than the early cameras, and to address cognitive difficulties of size and scale in large landscapes, worked in color, which was still beyond the chemistry of the darkroom. The history of ice would continue to be imagined and imaged in paintings, and Turner's hand would be evident throughout.

Nevertheless, photography was making inroads. A friend of Albert Bierstadt's, the American maritime painter William Bradford (1823–1892), sailed into Arctic waters in 1861, the same year that Church finished *The Icebergs,* a famous allegorical painting of Franklin's tragic expedition to the North Pole. He returned six more times, finishing in 1869 with a three-month-long voyage into Melville Bay with two professional photographers, John Dunmore and George Critcherson. The resulting book, *The Arctic Regions,* had 141 albumen photographic prints individually pasted into each of the 350 copies produced. By the end of the century, Bradford had become the definitive imagemaker of icebergs, on occasion even achieving the sublime exuberance that Turner seemed to capture so effortlessly. Although not an innovator like Turner, in his art Bradford recapitulates the movement from topography to romanticism, for even as his renderings were acclaimed by geologists to be faithful to the topology of ice, his images of ships beset among icebergs evoked heroic memories of Franklin and Kane.

Bradford's life and work demonstrates the assimilation of the northern polar region into European culture as it progressed from an environment to be cataloged to an exotic stage for historical drama. The coastal profiles, topographical art, and exploration narratives produced during the search for the Northwest Passage were converted by Friedrich, Church, Bradford, and other artists into a theater on which to set the metaphorical drama where exploration—symbolizing the greed of the Industrial Age—would founder in the face of Nature.

After the mid–nineteenth century romanticism began to decline. Art, science, and cartography were now diverging on their paths, and the dialogue among them became much less visible to the general public. Science moved, in large measure, from the collection of physical specimens to the collection of images on paper and film. Increasingly scientists turned to photography—x-ray imagery, spectrographs of stars, microphotography—to provide an exactitude of record keeping that could match the precision of their measurements. Within short order the public would follow their lead and embrace photography as reality.

The emphasis in most scientific disciplines now swung from categorization of the world to theories about how it worked. In geology the shift came about through the theories of continental drift and plate tectonics, as the job of mapping strata devolved from the scientific community to mining companies. Astronomers continued to find new objects to catalog, but increasingly found themselves concerned with the physics of first principles. Biologists and botanists were still finding new species to add to their classifications systems, but they began now to investigate what caused the differences among all those millions of specimens. Their quest would culminate in the parsing of the human genome.

Only the Antarctic remained as a redoubt of traditional natural science, a space so difficult to traverse, map, and catalog that it would take several international efforts most of a century to accomplish those tasks. And it would not be done on foot, but mainly from the air, the only vantage point from which it is possible to gauge the scale and flow of the ice rivers. Its purity, isotropy, and sheer strangeness resisted the efforts of artists to use it as a symbolic theater for history. Such images would be possible to make, but more often it was the photographers who succeeded, not the painters.

9 TRANSANTARCTICA II

I HAVE THIS THING about helicopters: they fall down more often than fixed-wing aircraft, and their accidents are more often fatal. Flying this morning with Barry James at the controls of the compact helicopter is therefore a mixed blessing. Although the bubble cockpit of the A-Star affords fine panoramic views of the mountains as we fly across the sound, it's a much smaller aircraft than the twin-engine Bell 212s on station, and has only a single engine. Barry, a genial bearded man with a slight Texas drawl, has flown in deserts worldwide as well as among the mountains and glaciers of Alaska, and he's been working out of McMurdo since 1998. But it doesn't reassure me that, as we pass from open sky to a solid overcast, surface definition on the sea ice below us is suddenly and severely reduced, the ice and the sky becoming the same shade of gray.

Out on the sea ice on a overcast day you can lose all horizon referents, and the lack of shadows means you can't see the sastrugi should you have to land. "Two Navy guys were flying out over the sea ice on the Ross Ice Shelf," Barry tells me, "and the coastline disappeared. They turned toward land, hoping to pick it up again, but hit ice, busting out their chin bubbles before they knew they weren't flying. They had crossed the coastline and were flying over rising ground and didn't know it.

"Sometimes you'll see a layer of blue sky in between two layers of cloud. It isn't much, but it's something to see and to fly toward. I was the number two aircraft this one time, flying across on the other side of Mt. Discovery trying to get about two hundred miles south. There was an overcast sky with layers in between. We could see part of Minna Bluff to our left, and part of Mt. Morning with rising terrain to our right. So those were both brown terrain. To the left there was a low saddle and we could see sky there—and in front there was a layer of sky for us to fly toward. We had both horizon and sky, so it looked okay.

"We were really close to that blue streak, within two or three miles, when the guy in front said: 'I don't think that's sky; I think it's ice, and I'm turning. Now!'

"We had terrain out to either side at forty-five degrees; the ground was rising in front of us but we couldn't see it. The guy in front had read the book about the Air New Zealand crash on Mt. Erebus, and in there they mentioned something like this, which they called 'sector whiteout.' When I did an Internet search, that was the only relevant mention I found, where it said that the pilots hadn't been aware of it. But it didn't define it."

Cognitive dissonance is a serious problem for pilots flying over the ice, as it is in any isotropic environment. When Barry said that they were within two or three miles of hitting the ice, given that these helicopters fly forward at around 100 mph, that's a potential crash within ninety seconds. So here's a pilot who has been selected for, among other things, the extent and quality of his peripheral vision—which means his mind excels at taking information from the outside edges of his vision and extrapolating to fill in the middle, smoothing out the possibilities. Because of this skill, however, he is inadvertently liable to fall prey to this kind of illusion, and only the collective memory of colleagues is there to preserve him.

When Barry calls out to his passengers the features of the land he's flying over, or the fact that the sea ice below us is reconsolidated pack ice from last year, he's not just being an affable tour guide, he's also reciting the topography as a mnemonic. If the Dailey Islands are to our left, then we're within x number of minutes from a landing site at New

Harbor. If it's refrozen pack ice, that may mean it's still safe to land on this late in the year. Pilots, but especially helicopter jockeys, must know the terrain to increase their odds of weeding out illusion from reality.

Minutes after we bank sharply up into Taylor Valley, the immense Canada Glacier comes into view. It is snowing up on the peaks, and the alpine ice flows out of the clouds and clear across the valley, the glacier separating the Fryxell and Hoare Lakes, both of which are permanently frozen, save small moats around their edges that occur during summer. We pass over Fryxell and then the deep corrugations atop the massive ice flow, setting down briefly at Hoare to let out Antonia Fairbanks, an NSF geographer who's working on new environmental protocols for visitors to the Dry Valleys, and to pick up Tony Hansen and his assistant, Joe Mastroianni. We then lift off again for the five-minute ride to Lake Bonney. Taylor Valley sits just south and over the Asgard Range from Wright Valley, where I was a month earlier, but the two valleys are quite distinct from each other. Lake Vanda sits in a broad, U-shaped gravel trough. Taylor is narrower, the Asgards on this side steeper. Frozen lakes and streams are interspersed all the way down from the Taylor Glacier at the upper western end of the valley to the piedmont glacier bordering the sea.

Barry sets us down almost imperceptibly at the wooden landing pad at Bonney and kills the engine so we have some peace and quiet in which to unload. Tony is a voluble man in his early fifties, with a shock of white hair and a short beard. His English accent has survived thirty years of working in the States, most of it in labs at the University of California, Berkeley. Joe, a strapping guy ten years younger, is a published science fiction writer and a minor scion of Silicon Valley. Both men own their own companies. They met when Joe, who's wanted to come to the Antarctic since he was a kid, contacted Tony, who was looking for someone this last year to write computer code for his "Aethalometer," a machine that measures the combustion of effluent carbonaceous aerosols—particulate carbon from the camps, in other words.

We're in the heart of one of eighteen places worldwide that are supported by NSF as Long-Term Ecological Research sites. Most of the LTER sites are in places such as the rainforests of Puerto Rico, where the ecosystems are incredibly complex and require decades of patience to understand. Here, at the extreme edge of where viable life is found, the relationships are fewer, simpler, and more easily monitored. Every effort is made to minimize human impact—not just footprints in streambeds, as during my walks in Wright Valley, but also the use of generators and the number of helo flights.

The Bonney Lake camp is part of a limnology project designed by John Priscu from Montana State University at Bozeman, and the fieldwork is run by Craig Wolf, a burly and balding scientist who greets us somewhat somberly. His team members, three women in their twenties and thirties, are somewhat more enthusiastic, but it's obvious that everyone is intent on getting back to work. The Dry Valleys, the coldest and driest site in the worldwide LTER network, are a highly desirable place for limnologists to work. Although its biological systems are limited to microbes, microinvertebrates, mosses, and lichens, that's enough to create complex life cycles based on six months of sunlight, fresh meltwater flows from the glaciers, and windblown matter. Because the work season lasts less than twelve weeks, everyone is very focused.

Priscu's first six years of study established that, while variations in year-to-year local weather affect the biology of these organisms, long-term climatic history is also a strong factor. The glaciers, for instance, which here move only inches a year as opposed to yards, are still reacting to events two thousand years in the past. Current studies are assessing those climatic legacies, looking at the hydrology of the lakes and their interrelated biogeochemical processes.

The Priscu group is drilling holes through the frozen surface of the lake, taking 150 samples during the season from sixteen different depths within the 100-foot-plus-deep lake, then filtering and analyzing the samples to determine the microbial food webs. While one of the scientists analyzes evidence of what nutrients are being processed, another looks at what nutrients are concentrated where within the water column, and thus seeks to predict what kind of organisms should be present. The LTER work is interdisciplinary, complicated, and should probably be extended throughout a full twelve-month year to allow a more thorough understanding of how this extreme end-use environment works. Tony and Joe will be complicating the picture even further by looking at how diesel generators and helicopter flights change the chemical composition of the region's air by injecting black carbon into it.

We complete the unloading in less than ten minutes, and Barry takes off. The limno team disperses back to their drilling sites and small lab shacks where they filter the samples, while we three pick up the hundred-pound black plastic box containing Tony's instrument—which he built in his home shop for peanuts—and the five hundred feet of armored cable necessary to connect it to the station's power supply. Staggering up to a small gravel bench well above the lake, we set down the contraption and plug it in. And that's that. The contrast with the complicated military seismology work done in Wright Valley last month couldn't be more profound.

Tony has a formal background in physics and engineering, but he's really another one of these basement tinkerer types so common to Antarctic science. He invented a way to suck air in through a plastic tube and run it through a ribbon of quartz fiber tape that advances every five minutes. The ribbon carries forward a little circle of collected material that's then scanned with light in the visible and infrared spectrum, the results graphed and then telemetered out. You see spikes when helos fly in or the generators fire up. Because the LTER project with its multiple sites depends on environmental purity for its work, it needs to measure its own presence in the valleys. The team also needs to see if combustion products are drifting across the sound from McMurdo. By fingerprinting pollutants for three years, Tony seeks to help NSF convert field camps from diesel power to solar and wind energy.

The direct imaging of the air is refreshingly tangible compared with the computerized colorization of data sets done by the astrophysicists at Pole. The Aethalometer, conceptually closely related to the sunshine recorders there, is simple and self-contained, a model for remote-sensing "telescience" packages that will follow in years to come. Tony's instrument is named after the Greek word *aethalo,* which means to blacken with soot, a term used in classical theater to refer to the make-up applied to the faces of characters portraying evil (as opposed to those portraying good in the world, who wore whiteface). His Aethalometers sit in remote research stations around the world, as well as in urban areas measuring the components of smog. Whereas the sunshine recorder burns a line in black paper to measure light, the Aethalometer puts black spots on white paper to measure the blockage of light. The ancient Greeks would have appreciated this cause-and-effect symmetry.

Everywhere I look here things seem to come in contrasting pairs, whether it's the valleys or the instruments, the resonance between being on top of a lake or under a dome, and it makes me wonder about that tendency we have in deserts, given the lack of visual distractions, to see the world in dualistic terms. I suspect that what I'm experiencing is not so much a tendency of things to pair off in the Antarctic, as simply how a human mind seeks to process sensory input here. The basis for vision, that sensory perception through which we obtain most of what we know about the world, is boundary recognition, and that means parsing everything we see into darker and lighter, still or in motion. Seeing is a mental construction; to an enormous degree, what we see is what we think, and what we think what we see. The harsher the conditions for life, the more the gray scale of indeterminacy seems to diminish, and we parse what we see in the Antarctic more quickly and firmly than in temperate climes.

We're free to wander up the valley for the rest of the afternoon, so head first uphill toward the nearest glacier, the Hughes, which laps down from the Kukri Hills like a spatula-flattened tongue. Unlike Wright Valley, where the glaciers were just out of convenient walking range, in the Taylor they come down far enough into the valley that you have to walk around them to get anywhere. At the foot of the Hughes, freshly fallen white rubble litters the ground, debris from the sixty-foot-high face that we stay away from, conscious that the calving is a constant process. We turn right to hike upvalley toward the Taylor Glacier proper, which is not an alpine body spilling out of the mountains but a much larger body, a finger of the polar plateau seeking the ocean.

Halfway there we find the body of an Adélie penguin lying on its side. Although sand has collected in its feathers, the carcass doesn't look that old. Mummified seals are common, but this is the first freeze-dried penguin I've seen in the Dry Valleys. Joe and Tony spotted a live one a couple of days ago down by Lake Hoare, headed inexplicably upvalley, and Joe had a difficult time restraining himself from picking it up and turning it around. We're forbidden by the Antarctic Treaty from committing such interference, and the only way any of us can distance ourselves is to put it in terms of evolution. Personally, I frame the carcasses not exactly as the oft-quoted culling of the gene pool that's going on, but as the process of nature learning through mistakes.

Anthropomorphizing a penguin or anything else not human is fallacious to a high degree, and ascribing to the Adélie a drive to explore is dangerous—yet *something* compels both the seals and penguins to wander up the valleys fifty miles from their habitat. One theory is that some penguins waddle long distances to their rookeries and perhaps those in the Dry Valleys have lost their sense of direction. Birds have evolved very sophisticated mechanisms for navigation, which include orienting themselves to the sun and the stars at night as well as the polarized light at sunrise and sunset. Some of them sense the earth's magnetic field, or calibrate the low-frequency sound waves generated by trade winds and ocean surf to their inherited memories of location. Such sophisticated mechanisms may fall prey to disease or other environmental factors such as stress.

Penguins, however, are very primitive birds, and it may be that they lack such organic analogs to the instruments in airplanes and ships. A hypothesis that interests me is related to nature's propensity to use mistakes created by miscopies in genetic code to improve the lot of a species over time. The avian DNA of Adélies mutates two to seven times faster than that of related species. Perhaps the Dry Valley penguins and seals are members of their species with minor genetic miswirings—

mistakes in the sense that they do not stay within their habitats to perform optimally, but wander. They are random probes continually sent
out from within the species to see what's new and what's available to
inhabit. They may not be exploring consciously, but if they were to discover suitable habitat, new colonies would establish themselves and
thus broaden the range of the species. Extending range is an important
strategy exercised by most species to survive climatic changes. Nature,
in a sense, loves a mistake because it creates information—you find out
something you weren't expecting. And nature doesn't care much about
the fate of individuals, only species.

Whatever the cause, it's startling to see penguin tracks in the sandy
slope hundreds of feet above the valley floor and headed toward the
polar plateau. I mention the article that hangs in F-Stop, clipped from a
tabloid, that brings us the shocking news of a herd of crazed king penguins living near Pole, apparently enraged by the presence of scientists,
that devoured seven people, leaving behind only the tattered remains of
their red parkas. This sets Joe off on a series of equally fictional speculations, first about the errant penguins, and then about the even more
improbably wandering seals whose remains we constantly stumble
upon while hiking.

"I mean, seals don't have arms or legs. How could they possibly
come this far? I think there's volcanic activity underneath the permafrost, and there are underground rivers here that they swim up."

"I think that penguins actually can fly," I respond, "and carry seals
with them for food."

"Caches!" he exclaims.

"Exactly."

Thus starts a running joke that will last for the four days we're in
Taylor Valley and constantly finding dead animals—another mechanism that allows us to swallow the pathos.

We finish our hike on the Bonney Riegel, one of the transverse
ridges common in glaciated valleys, by tucking into the side of a cavernously weathered boulder. Before us the Taylor Glacier rises up and
turns south toward the plateau. Tony busies himself with his video

camera, getting footage to share with school kids back home. Joe leans back and just soaks it all in.

If Tony is taking the measure of Antarctica as a pristine baseline environment for the rest of the planet, then Joe is taking its measure as a metaphorical locus for the imagination. Part of the novel he's currently working on is set here, so there's a personal reason for his trip, in addition to the work for Tony. But he's also conceptualized the Antarctic as an analog to the Hopi *sipapu*, the hole in the floor of the kiva out of which life emerged. For him the white continent is the imaginary locus of all mystery on the planet. Joe is on his own kind of quest for new territory, an interior one, and he's finding that the easiest way to integrate the Antarctic into his experience of the world is by constantly making up stories about it.

What intrigues me most at the moment, however, is the terrain that lies above and beyond the glacier. Once again I've been looking wistfully at the sandstone-and-dolerite-banded peaks on the horizon of the Dry Valleys, huge cliffs topped with rugged summits, the wall at the end of the world beyond which there is only the plateau stretching to Pole and across the entire continent. Beacon Valley is up there, the highest, coldest, most arid and remote of the Dry Valleys. The ice-locked oasis of dry land represents for me the ultimate conjunction of ice and rock in the Antarctic, a landscape that Porter photographed, and one I would very much like to visit. It's within helicopter range of McMurdo, and I have hopes for a trip later in the season.

By the time we return to camp, it is seven o'clock and dinner time. Tony has managed to smuggle in a shipment from the States: some bags of highly pressurized frozen guacamole, salsa, and chips, plus the ingredients for margaritas. The limno team is cooking chicken and beef fajitas. Together we have a leisurely Mexican dinner as the temperature falls to twenty below.

Tony and Joe spend the next morning testing the Aethalometer and doing an energy audit of the camp. The generator here puts out electricity on two circuits. In order not to stress it, you have to load each circuit more or less equally; this means plugging in appliances on one circuit to balance the number of vacuum pumps filtering water on the other. The crew is therefore forced to turn on electric heaters, which are placed outside the small lab units so the scientists don't overheat while working. Running a diesel engine and using half its power to heat the Antarctic is perhaps not the most efficient energy equation that could be devised, especially since a few solar panels would provide all the necessary power without the balancing problems. Tony and Joe are also aware of the irony that it takes diesel power to measure the pollution, which in itself creates pollution to be measured—quite a noticeable feedback loop in an environment as clean as the Dry Valleys.

While Tony's poking around, Joe works on the computer, and I take stock of the visual culture in the Jamesway, which was originally deployed by the New York U.S. Army quartermaster in 1951, according to stenciled lettering on the struts. Jamesways are constructed on arches of wood spaced four feet apart for as long as you like; this one is sixteen by forty-four feet. The canvas in between has been stitched into pillowed segments with wool felt for insulation. Sporting pink flamingos, plastic ferns, Christmas lights, family pictures, cartoons, maps, instructions for lighting stoves, and goodness knows what all else, the place has layers and layers of visual embellishment pinned to the walls and strung across the ceiling, as in field billeting, military or otherwise, all around the world.

We are, as Tony puts it, "at the end of the world's wires": the Internet is here and very much in evidence. Once people troop in and take care of the immediate need for high caloric consumption, e-mail is the next priority. Everyone has a digital camera and posts pictures on both the walls and the Web to family and friends, augmenting the physical space of the Jamesway with cyberspace, almost as if there's another room in camp where people go to talk. Last year, Tony was storing digital information on disks and having to retrieve them annually in person; now he's building machines that can send out the information over a wireless phone. Soon he'll be operating his instruments just as the

AFTAC guys do, running things on the Internet from a laptop in Berkeley via satellite dishes. Next year Tony hopes to install webcams next to the Aethalometers so they can correlate camp events visually with the graphs. Eventually they, too, will be live on the Internet, joining the stream of images from McMurdo, Pole, and the crater on Erebus. These are places where what we imagine about them from afar is now being imaged in real time.

In the afternoon we take an all-terrain vehicle across the frozen lake, steering through the narrows framed by the riegel to our left and the Asgard Range to our south. This brings us to the west lobe of the lake and the foot of Blood Falls, a giant orange stain on the front of the Taylor Glacier. The Taylor is as white and blue as every other glacier in the Antarctic, but it's also gotten tangled up with something as yet unidentified containing a lot of iron, and created an Antarctic landmark.

Before investigating the discolored icefalls, we're diverted by an even more astounding phenomenon—the sound of running water. It's like hearing music for the first time in weeks. Prodigious streams pour out from both the southern side of the Taylor and the nearby eastern edge of the Rhone Glacier, only a few hundred yards away. Where once the two ice streams met and carved the valley, the glaciers receded in the past and now just their meltwaters braid together and flow into Lake Bonney. We follow the Taylor upstream for a mile, eat lunch, and watch dinnerplate-sized pieces of the glacier peel off, falling into pools of green slush.

The glaciers here are actually growing slightly again, responding to events in millennia past—unlike the alpine glaciers of Europe and America, which at their snouts may reflect the snowfalls or droughts of only twenty years ago. The growth isn't dramatic, but it is clearly measurable by comparing photographs taken by New Zealand scientists in the 1970s with those taken today. The Canada Glacier down the valley is also growing, but held in balance by almost four feet of ablation per year, 70 percent of which is through sublimation, the ice phased straight to vapor by the intensity of the solar radiation, which pours this month down the valley from a low summer azimuth that virtually targets the face.

We walk back down to investigate the iron-stained falls, finding that they're getting soft, a mess of gravel, meltwater, and slush. Tony jokes that it's an alien spacecraft, oxidizing in there somewhere. Scrambling up the bottom third of the fall, we find meltwater pools on the ice, springs from hidden channels, and huge icicles. The face is decaying so rapidly, the absorption of the sunlight magnified by the dark material, that we stay just long enough for some photographs, then scoot back down.

After a more modest dinner than the extravaganza of the night before, Craig reminisces about the Christmases with his family that he has missed, and states that this will be his last trip. What has kept his attention here for so long is the tenacity of life.

"Life is anywhere on the planet you look for it—at the bottom of the oceans, under extreme pressure in rocks. There's microbial life everywhere, you just have to pick the right scale. And it doesn't have to be photosynthetic. Chemosynthetic microbes were the first to evolve. It's amazing to be involved at looking at life at that level." He pauses, takes off his glasses, rubs a hand through his short brown beard. "The amount of science here at Lake Bonney, though, is diminishing. There are still unanswered questions that will be worked on—why the partic- ular chemistry here, how it affects the organisms. But the focus is shift- ing to Lake Vostok and the other lakes under deep ice. Vostok is the largest, but there are probably hundreds of them. And we know there's life there."

He's referring to a body of freshwater the size of Lake Ontario buried under 2.4 miles of ice in the East Antarctic. Lake Vostok is 150 miles long by 31 miles wide and, at 1,640 feet, deeper than Lake Tahoe in the Sierra Nevada. It's one of the fifteen largest lakes on the planet, almost more of an under-ice sea. A body of water under the ice cap there had been suspected since an airborne radar survey of the area in 1974–1975 indicated that the surface ice was ten times flatter than the surroundings. By 1995 the Russians, who had a station fortuitously located at one end of the lake, had drilled down to within 495 feet of it; at that depth, they determined, the ice had last been at the surface 400,000 years ago. They stopped, fearing to contaminate a body of water that may have been isolated from the earth's atmosphere for as long as 15 million years.

In December 1999, John Priscu announced that viable microorganisms related to common soil bacteria had been found in an eighteen-by-four-inch segment of core brought up from within 400 feet of the lake—organisms up to 200,000 years old in ice that had once been lake water. When Craig talks about life existing everywhere we look, he means in time as well as space. Microbes have been on Earth for at least 3.7 billion years, and viable microorganisms have been dug up out of the Antarctic ice cap from as deep as 7,300 feet.

Not only is the subglacial Vostok environment perhaps similar to the earth's environment 750 to 543 million years ago, a period that saw ten major planetary glaciations, but it may be an analog for the water under the ice on Europa, one of Jupiter's moons. At 483 million miles from the sun, and with exterior temperatures of −250°F, the fact that enough heat is present under the Jovian moon's ice to keep water liquid makes it the most likely candidate in our solar system for extraterrestrial life—more likely, in fact, than Mars, according to Ralph Harvey, whose team works out of McMurdo collecting meteorites on the ice. Robbie Score, the woman who now supervises Crary Lab, was on Ralph's team in 1984 when she discovered the iron meteorite from Mars that people have been arguing over for years. Does it or doesn't it contain fossilized traces of microbial activity? Harvey says no. When giving his annual science lectures at McMurdo, Harvey urges audiences to think harder about looking for life on Europa than on Mars.

It's clear from their comments that the graduate students working here for Craig this summer have exobiology in mind. The work they're doing at Bonney will help others understand what they find when they punch into the deep lake. The experimental protocols for sterilization and such developed at Vostok will be applicable to how we sample water on Mars or Europa. The researchers sense the thread of exploration running through their hands as they sample the water column, and it keeps them getting up at 4:30 A.M. in the endless daylight to pull up the collecting bottles.

The next morning a helo comes to pick up Tony and transfer him to the Lake Hoare camp; Joe and I opt to hike the ten miles along what is slowly becoming the first classic Antarctic trail. We leave at 10:45 A.M. to contour around Bonney, careful to stay high enough so that we're not disturbing the lakeshore. We find ourselves walking past penguin tracks headed upvalley, braided with human ones among rock-paved sandy dunes and along multiple pathways, evidence of how both scientists and penguins have attempted to find the easiest course. Overall we follow the meltwater streams flowing out of the glaciers and feeding into the ponds along the way. Often the paths utilize the natural troughs created by the ancient and strongly sorted polygons, a maze of intersecting geometry that does not lead anywhere. Antonia Fairbanks will parallel our walk later in the day and high up along the ridgeline so she can survey the route, which she notes has not consolidated yet into a trail.

The wind, a relatively warm katabatic flow from the polar plateau, is at our backs for about an hour. It is warm because, as the falling air loses altitude, the molecules rub against each other and heat up through friction. When the wind turns, as it does most days, and flows up the valley—a slot that acts as a giant barometric pressure relief valve between the interior of the continent and the coast—the air is much cooler. By noon we're forced to button up and raise our hoods as we walk toward the Seuss Glacier, which launches off the Asgard Range, falls three thousand feet almost straight down, flows across the valley—which at that point is only a few hundred yards wide—climbs a few feet up the foot of the Kukri Hills, and then just stops (Plate 22). The gap between the glacier front and the rocks is the only way up or down the valley floor.

Our route is also followed by the seals, and at one point we find ourselves in what is almost a boneyard. We've passed some crabeater carcasses, and even one of a much larger Weddell seal, but deep into the dunes we notice that we're walking on bone fragments, mostly digits from flippers that at first glance are disconcertingly human in appearance. The evidence of how deep time is in the Antarctic isn't brought home very easily by staring at an ice core, which takes careful and patient interpretation. But carcasses that have been on the ground so long that even the mummified digits have been scattered by the wind— that's a story anyone can read. We pause in the boneyard, walk in small circles, lift our heads up and smell the air, which has no odor except cold brilliance itself, more a tactility than a smell (Plate 23).

By two o'clock we're headed into the Defile, the narrow gap between the Seuss Glacier and the Kukri Hills. We walk slowly up into the deeply shadowed slot. I put one hand on the dense ice and the other almost to the hillside, millions of tons of ice pressing into my palm. If the ground were to warm just one or two degrees, if the bottom of the glacier were to be just a little wet, thus lubricated and freed from the friction holding it in place, there would be no gap here through which to walk. The pressure is palpable, like being a hundred feet underwater.

To my left, then, the white ice with its tincture of blue; to my right, a shattered marble bluff, the stones broken into pieces the size of my fist. I chant, "White rock, white ice," which sounds both very much like early poems of mine about the Nevada desert, and like the poems of a Chinese poet invented by the novelist Kim Stanley Robinson for his book *Antarctica*. That character had visited the ice much as I am doing, as a visiting writer; on leaving, he was reduced to uttering poems so minimalist that they made haiku seem like effusive epics. When I first read the novel, I contacted Robinson to see if he knew of either my work or the work of Robert Lax, from whom I'd borrowed my own minimalist technique. He said no, but that he had spent time contemplating the Great Basin and Mojave deserts. Stan was one of the people who recommended that I take this hike.

I grew up in the highest, driest, and coldest desert in North America, the Great Basin of northern Nevada. Lax lived as a hermit on a bleak Greek desert island hillside where there was nothing but "blue sky, blue water, white stone." The evolution of a desert aesthetic to match such severe landscapes makes perfect sense in the Defile, and I continue to chant "White rock, white ice" to myself as we walk. Joe thinks I've gone around the bend.

We crest the small pass in between the glacier and the mountainside, and there below us is Lake Hoare, yet another expanse of frozen water. The camp at the far end is invisible from this far away, with still a third of our hike to go. As we exit the Defile, the Seuss curves away to our left in elaborate hanging terraces of icicles, its eastern face sunlit and running everywhere with water. Flying buttresses of rotting ice project out and downward for twenty and thirty feet, great masses of clarified glacier melting in the sun or evaporating in the wind, phase shifting from mineral to gas or liquid, depending on the time of day and the weather.

We pursue the running waters down to the lake and follow the shoreline around to camp, which is a hive of activity. The nine buildings and ten tents, spread out over a square acre, are managed by the efficient and unflappable Rae Spain, who, as we walk into the main building, has paused—in the middle of making bread, baking brownies, marinating t-bone steaks, and thawing out lobster tails for dinner—to talk with a radio in each hand to two incoming helos. She puts everyone on hold just long enough to tell us which dome tents we're in, adding that gin and tonics will be served in an hour.

Dinner that evening with thirteen people spread around the table is leisurely, held during the only time the sun, shaded behind the mountains, is not shining directly into camp, a break from 4:30 in the afternoon until seven. Thomas Nylen from Portland, Oregon, the resident glaciologist, has just come down from the Canada Glacier, the hundred-foot face of which stands majestically a stone's throw—literally—out the kitchen window. He barbecues the steaks, the carbon signature from which will show up on Tony's Hoare recorder the next day. A crew of three painters and two carpenters have flown in to refurbish the outside of the camp's blue buildings and to replace kitchen countertops.

Antonia has returned from her hike and we compare notes. NSF is concerned about the increasing tourism in the Antarctic, nowhere more so than in the Taylor Valley. When the passenger ships can get into McMurdo Sound, they launch helicopters with shore parties to visit the valley on the other side of the Canada Glacier. The passengers are not allowed into the most sensitive of the LTER areas, but scientists are nervous about the potential pressures. The Antarctic has been visited by an estimated seventy thousand scientists and support personnel in the last fifty years, and about fifty thousand tourists. Most of the latter step ashore only on the Antarctic Peninsula, but the numbers are growing steadily, and the fervor to visit the Ross Sea area, the most historic region, has been fed by a recent spate of movies about Shackleton.

In 1999, 14,623 ship-based tourists visited the Antarctic, about the same as visited during all of the 1980s. The next season, 131 passenger ships cruised below the Antarctic Circle, though only five of them made it as far as the Ross Sea area. Out of the 12,248 tourists on private expeditions that year, only 385 landed in the region. Taylor is the Dry Valley most accessible from the coast, and the only one visited regularly so far—a total of 715 people have landed on the other side of the glacier.

Antarctic tourism is projected to exceed 22,000 people in 2005–2006. What Antonia was conducting above our route today was part of a GPS survey of human activity in the Dry Valleys, research that NSF will use to decide where the boundaries of the science camps should be set, as well as how to channel foot traffic to limit human impact. Both the Antarctic Treaty and the expense of mining on the continent may prevent the extraction of natural resources for a very long time, but hotels cropping up on the continent aren't prohibited, nor are they out of the realm of possibility. And I am very aware, even as I take notes of our conversation, that both the hike today and my writing about it are part of the process she has to measure.

The dishes are done promptly after dinner, and e-mails answered by nine, but it being the Antarctic and with sunshine now pouring down the from west end of the valley and bouncing off a half dozen glaciers before hitting our camp, we're ready for some exercise. Rae picks up a frisbee, Thomas grabs an inflatable ball, and we're off to "The Beach," a strand of sloping sand twenty yards wide that separates the Canada Glacier from Lake Hoare (Plate 24). We take care crossing the alternately frozen and thawed streambed from glacier to lake, but once on the sand roll up the pantlegs of our insulated bibs, strip off our boots and socks, and begin throwing things around. Retrieving missed catches from the surface of the frozen lake in bare feet is a bracing reminder that the summer sun lasts only a few weeks. The activity is a sweet release from the tension that Rae labors under while balancing the logistics of the entire Dry Valleys region from her hub, a job from which she has no real break once she arrives in mid-October until she leaves at the end of January. And it keeps Thomas anchored to reality after a full day tromping alone over snow bridges atop crevasses.

Barry Lopez has spent time in both the Wright and Taylor dry valleys as a visiting writer, and he published a striking piece about his experiences titled "Informed by Indifference." He notes that he "found the dry valleys unfetchable," that his attempts to establish a connection to the place "met almost always with monumental indifference." He posits the sense of age that we feel here by equating it to human terms: "I have never felt so strongly that unsettling aloofness of the adult that a small child knows, and fears." Although not a hostile place, the valleys struck him as utterly impersonal.

I interpret the frisbee and beach ball to be deliberate attempts to counter that indifference. Lopez ends the essay with a sentence that is slowly passing by word-of-mouth into Antarctic lore: "If you returned it would be to pay your respects, for not being welcomed." That Rae has made us all feel as if we'd like to return to Lake Hoare says much about the ability of humans to convert Archeozoic land into a landscape contemporaneous with us and our needs. It makes me think of the Antarctic diatoms surviving in liquid nitrogen, and what Craig Wolf said about looking for life—but only at the right scale.

The indifference we feel may be another facet of dissonance brought about by our limited perceptual abilities. Our eyes and ears, our tactile and olfactory and taste senses, all evolved to derive the maximum amount of information with the least caloric expenditure, following Buckminster Fuller's description of nature as the most efficient designer. Our eyes deal only with that densest part of the electromagnetic spectrum, where the universe emits immense amounts of data. The only way for us to physically transcend those biological limitations in places where life exists at scales far from human, or the information is less dense and spread out in other parts of the electromagnetic spectrum, is to extend our senses through instrumentation and imagination. We are required to peer through electron scanning microscopes to examine diatoms from the Ross Sea and deploy photomultiplier arrays at Pole to detect neutrinos. When doing the latter, our instrumentation is so extended that we're not seeing anything directly at all, but are reduced to observing secondary effects. At some point our observation of nature becomes so distant from our own sense of scale that we have to reinforce our faith in the observations with cultural means, with imagination. An example is the work of the New Zealand artist Virginia King with her enlarged sculptures of the diatoms from Lake Vanda.

The landscape of the Dry Valleys, far from being the lifeless wasteland described by Scott, is increasingly seen by both scientists and artists to be one permeated by life. But to perceive it, you have to step beyond our genetically evolved senses and perception of scale, then return to make visual/visible representations of what you have found. These efforts produce another kind of mapping, one that we will require if we are to find and understand how life manifests itself on places other than Earth. That progression is a reason why scientists are increasingly replacing the word "mapping" with "imaging," acknowledging that we have to move beyond the nineteenth-century paradigm of maps as the ultimate visualization for understanding the world.

10 ORBITING ANTARCTICA

THE WEATHER IN MCMURDO is calm this afternoon as I write up my notes from Taylor Valley. Every now and then one of the dozen people tapping away on the computers in the library gets up to stretch and look out the windows across the sound to the mountains. The most popular excuse for a break is peering through the telescope to check out the seal that has taken advantage of a hole in the transition zone between shore and sea ice to haul itself out and bask in the sun.

A steady stream of scientists, teachers, and journalists occupy the workstations in the library. Joe sits on my left working on his novel, while behind us a Canadian pilot in his twenties is editing on his laptop the minivideo of a recent flight through the Royal Society Range, preparing to e-mail it to friends. The most active users recently are the astrophysicists and engineers who are tracking a high-altitude balloon as it circumnavigates the continent. The helium-filled sack, which was launched from one of the ice runways a few days ago, is flying up to 120,000 feet high in the stratosphere, its gondola carrying a small instrument measuring Cosmic Microwave Background Radiation. The circumpolar winds should bring the huge translucent balloon back to this side of the continent within several days, when the scientists hope to retrieve it—a race against the inevitable cyclonic storms also circling the Antarctic. Every hour someone pops in to monitor its progress and altitude along the flight path via remote telemetry on a laptop.

Next to me Jason Anthony is frantically typing e-mails before he catches one of the Twin Otters back out into the field. He is one of two people who maintains a blue-ice runway on the Odell Glacier, an emergency airstrip on the far side of the Transantarctics by the Allan Hills, where the search goes on for meteors. Jason, who has a master's degree in creative writing, is also working on a book about the Antarctic, a meditation on his experiences here over the last several years. He's juxtaposing his story with extensive quotations from other authors about the nature of whiteness, emptiness, silence, and absence—in short, the primary attributes of the continent. His sources range from the existentialist Albert Camus to the contemporary American poet Charles Simic, but much of his material is drawn from the literature of the Heroic Age, and he invokes passages from Scott, Shackleton, Apsley Cherry-Garrard, Douglas Mawson, Robert Byrd, and others in order to explain both the toll extracted and the revelations experienced by being on the ice. Like many people who work here, he admires their accomplishments, yet at the same time remains conscious that their egos were harnessed to the strategic needs of their countries.

Jason writes: "To work down here is to take advantage of the reputation that precedes us. Either we allow vanity to take pride in our sharing the hallowed ground, or we allow vanity to pass judgment on men of a different era whose dreams were couched in the language of empire that now evades us." I look around the library and realize how much of our work in and view of the Antarctic is now constructed from aerial vantage points. The Heroic Age marked the transition from ground-level to airborne exploration, and the connection between flight and vanity is longstanding in our culture. But it was also an inevitable evolution, for science needed literally to get higher in order to obtain a unifying view of the world.

James Clark Ross sailed toward the South Pole as far as 78° S when he was stopped by the Great Ice Barrier—the Ross Ice Shelf—part of which is visible from the windows over my left shoulder. No one would break that record until 1900. Although the sealing industry had collapsed in Antarctic waters, whalers continued plying the waters until their prey, too, was exhausted in the 1890s. In January 1895, the whaling captain Henryk Bull landed at Cape Adare, up the coast at the end of the Transantarctic Mountains. It was the first landing on the actual continent outside the Antarctic Peninsula. One of his crewmen, Carsten Borchgrevink, had already found lichen on an island just offshore, the first plant life discovered inside the Antarctic Circle, and Bull now found the same species again.

In July of that same year the Sixth International Geographical Congress met in London and passed a resolution urging exploration of the Antarctic before the nineteenth century was over. Just ten years previously it had been estimated that less than one-ninth of the world's landmass had been mapped. The contours of the coasts and the major geophysical provinces of most continents were known; the Antarctic, protected by the roughest seas in the world and the constant circumpolar storms, remained the major exception. It was as if both history and the lines of longitude were converging on the continent.

The resolution would set off a spate of national expeditions, including those of Scott and Shackleton, but as the delegates were affixing their signatures, Adrien Victor Joseph de Gerlache was already planning the Belgian Antarctic Expedition. His ship, the *Belgica,* left Antwerp in 1897. Aboard were a twenty-five-year-old volunteer from Norway, Roald Amundsen, and the ship's doctor, Frederick A. Cook. In January 1898 they cruised down the western shores of the eight-hundred-mile-long Antarctic Peninsula, which had not been visited in sixty years, and in mid-February crossed the Antarctic Circle, which bisects the icebound mountain chain and islands that make up the peninsula. In early March at 71° S they were beset in the ice and became the first party to overwinter inside the circle. Men went mad that winter, but Amundsen was a solid mate and Cook an excellent doctor. Between them they kept the ship functioning and managed to keep a scientific program running. In March 1899, more than a year later, the ship was able to break free of the ice and sail home.

Cook was not only the expedition physician, but also its photographer. Much had changed since Bradford published *The Arctic Regions* in 1869. Not only had photographers probed into the most daunting landscapes almost everywhere else on the planet, but in 1888 Kodak had brought out its first portable camera. The public was by now used to the ubiquity of photographic images and expected them from expeditions. Cook did not disappoint them. His book about the journey, *Through the First Antarctic Night* (1900), contained reproductions of both his black-and-white and color photographs, demonstrating the first extensive use of photography during an Antarctic expedition. The ship frozen in place, the red hues of a low sun, the mind-numbing expanse of sea ice, all were views that the readers of Bradford's Arctic work would have recognized.

Amundsen went home, raised enough money to buy a herring boat, the *Gjoa,* and sailed for the Arctic with six companions in 1903. He had read as a boy about Franklin's search for the Northwest Passage, which had inspired him not only to become a polar explorer but also to attempt for himself the first sailing of the passage. The first party to complete the traverse had been Robert McClure in 1850–1854, who started from the Bering Strait and worked eastward. His crew was forced to abandon their ship to the ice in 1853, however, and to finish the trip sledging and then on board a rescue ship. Amundsen likewise spent four years on his trip, starting from the opposite direction in Lancaster Sound, and became the first person to complete a navigable route to San Francisco, which he reached in October 1906. The North Pole itself would be attained in 1909 by Robert Peary, with whom Cook had explored in north Greenland before joining the *Belgica.* Amundsen was on the verge of attempting the North Pole himself in 1910 when he learned of Peary's achievement. He secretly changed his mind and sailed south, thereby entering into a race with Scott to capture its southern counterpart.

What compelled these expeditions? National pride, ego gratification, the cultural pressure to have heroes, the deeply embedded genetic need that humans carry to explore new territory? All of those in varying mixes, perhaps. Shackleton, quite typically for the age, claimed that adventure, science, and the lure of the unknown were the primary factors motivating him. From the distance of a century later other reasons commend themselves, among them the search to find a primeval version of the world, something closer to what it was in the beginning, a romantic antidote to the spread of industrialism. If the Grand Canyon could give us a deep past in its neatly organized strata, what could we find in a place where everything was frozen in time? Was there a lost world at the South Pole, an open land corresponding to the earlier myth of an open polar sea at its antipode? If we find that a wild idea today, what would we have thought if we had been reading about a live volcano discovered on the edge of a frozen continent?

The nineteenth century had completed the initial cataloging of nature's surface but was struggling to develop theories to encompass all the collected data. Humboldt offered a way to begin assimilating geography visually into ecologies, and Gauss and Faraday shaped a picture of a geomagnetic field that was generated by and surrounded the planet. They were, in short, unifying observations into models that could then be used to predict what you would find anywhere in a particular field—both in a field of knowledge and on a physical field trip. Humboldt climbed physically upward to obtain his synthesis of data, while the two physicists imagined a reality at an even higher altitude.

Field theory depends on knowing distinct points within it. In terms of the sphere of the earth, this most definitely meant pinning down the geomagnetic and geographical poles. They were the prime coordinates from which to measure the field of the earth, the first and last places on the planet. Attaining the poles would fulfill finally the geometric imagination of the Greeks, complete the surveying graticule that had been pulled over the planet, and close the last drawer in the cabinet of collections. Reaching the poles would signify that the planet had been unified on foot. (And not coincidentally, reaching the South Pole would allow the British Empire to girdle the globe vertically, from South Africa on one end of the Southern Ocean to New Zealand on the other.) The only new vantage point that we could reach afterward to assemble a larger visual framework would be above the planet's surface.

In 1898–1900 Borchgrevink returned to Cape Adare as the leader of the British Antarctic Expedition; he and his party overwintered in two prefabricated huts, the first permanent human structures to be erected in the Antarctic and the oldest "first wooden buildings" of any continent still standing. Scott followed him the next year, erecting the *Discovery* hut at McMurdo. On February 4, 1902, he ascended eight hundred feet in a tethered balloon to observe the ice shelf; later that day Shackleton took a turn and snapped the first aerial photographs of the continent. The most significant revelation was the seemingly infinite extent of the Ross Ice Shelf to the south. Edward Wilson, as befit his role as a more traditional imagemaker, a painter, refused to go up in the balloon, thinking it too dangerous. It would be the last time an artist in the Antarctic refused an aerial view of the surroundings.

Wilson was a self-taught and accomplished watercolorist who began drawing when he was three. At nine years old he was already collecting butterflies, flowers, shells, and fossils, intent on becoming a naturalist. Darwin's *The Voyage of the Beagle* inspired him to start keeping a journal, and he spent years studying and copying Turner's works at the National Gallery. All three activities prepared him to sail with Scott to the Antarctic as the physician and science officer on both his expeditions, and it is in the latter capacity that he produced more than four hundred finished landscapes and natural history paintings, and perhaps as many as a thousand additional sketches, one of the most comprehensive visual records of the continent made by a painter.

As Scott's first expedition sailed through the Ross Sea, Scott ordered Wilson to make a running coastal profile of the South Victoria Land coastline, and the artist left a standing order with the watch to be called when any land was clearly visible. His panorama of the Transantarctics from Cape Adare to Ross Island ran longer than a hundred feet when pieced together. When Scott took angular measurements to check the paintings against the survey work, he was astounded at how accurate the drawings were. Once on land, while the others were away on depot-laying trips, Wilson spent hours atop Ob Hill sketching the Trans-antarctics during the long autumnal season; when winter descended he retreated indoors to paint watercolors from his carefully annotated sketches (Plate 2). His aesthetic was derived from a close adherence to Ruskin's dictum that the artist must follow truth in nature, and as his biographer George Seaver notes, his images represented accurately rocks, icebergs, and the sea ice. He was able to capture with great precision in his watercolors both the geometry and color of sundogs, halos, perihelia, and other atmospheric phenomena, an accomplish-ment that cameras could not match for almost another hundred years.

Wilson was a religious man, though private about his practice, and a great admirer of Seton Thompson, the co-founder of the Boy Scouts. Thompson published a series of illustrated books throughout this life, natural history and adventure narratives meant to inspire both wood-craft and wonder, and it was Wilson's goal to someday publish a book modeled after them. Although he was not to see such a book during his lifetime, his published journals from both the Discovery and Terra Nova expeditions were designed with Seton in mind, and are illustrated in a like manner. Wilson was the last expedition painter to succeed where the camera had not, where the painter's table was accorded precious space on shipboard equivalent to that for the chemist's bench. On his return to England, his works were exhibited and published alongside the photo-graphs of the journey made by the chief engineer, Reginald Skelton.

When Shackleton returned to the Antarctic in 1907 he tried to anchor along the Ross Ice Shelf as close as possible to the South Pole, but found that the landing selected previously had collapsed into the sea. He continued to cast about, but found twenty miles of sea ice be-tween the Nimrod and Hut Point. He settled on Cape Royds, his fourth choice for a camp, nonetheless the most sheltered and beautiful of the three hut locations on Ross Island. Shackleton set off in late October 1908 for the geographical pole and returned 128 days later, having made it to within less than a hundred miles of his goal before being turned back by the conditions. At the same time, a party headed east from Cape Royds, crossing McMurdo Sound and the Transantarctics to reach the South Magnetic Pole on January 15, 1909. By the spring of 1909 all that was left to complete the drawing together of the earth's field were the two geographical poles. That April Peary and Cook separately reached the northern one, or so they claimed. Now all that remained was the South Pole.

The next year, while Shackleton was still on the ice, both Amundsen and Scott sailed south. Amundsen reached the South Pole first, on December 17, 1911, with Scott and his four men finding the flag Amundsen had left for them precisely one month later, on January 17. Scott's last journal entry, made while pinned down in a tent during a blizzard, was on March 29.

There are many factors explaining why the feats of Scott and Shackleton are so much better known than Amundsen's. Beyond the mythological status conferred by tragedy on Scott's journey is the fact that Norway was a relatively small economic, political, and military presence compared with England, which was still ruling over an empire. Norway just didn't command as much press as did London. Another reason Amundsen's achievement received less attention than Scott's failure is that he went about his business with meticulous preparation and a certain undramatic solidity, which some people translated into a disdain for Scott's errors in judgment. This did not exactly endear Amundsen to the English-speaking press, which even in the early twentieth century had more than a little influence over international opinion. It also helped the newspapers that Scott was an excellent diarist, his literary skills far more developed than Amundsen's.

But even more than the literary reasons for the disparity in attention is the difference between the visual documentation. The English had already long prioritized images in their Antarctic explorations, from Hodges through Ross to Wilson. And following the *Belgica* expedition, so well documented by Cook's spectacular photographs, the Frenchman Jean-Baptiste Charcot's two southern journeys in 1903–1905 and 1908–1910 brought additional visual pleasure to an expectant public. During the first expedition alone, Charcot's photographer, Paul Pleneau, made several thousand images; the twenty-eight volumes of reports from the second were illustrated with some of the three thousand photographs taken. Expeditions now had less factual credibility, not to mention media potential, without numerous, diverse, and high-quality images, created by a photographer dedicated solely to the task. Just as the role of science had graduated from being an afterthought to exploration to a partner in discovery, so the role of the photographer grew in importance.

Although Amundsen took a few photographs of his journey, the Norwegian expedition had no dedicated imagemaker, and the visual record of his feat is very thin. Scott, in contrast, took with him a full-time photographer, Herbert Ponting (1870–1935). Self-taught, Ponting was one of the world's most famous traveling photographers in 1909 when Scott asked him to accompany the expedition. He had worked in the Himalaya and the Alps and was accustomed to traveling light in the field. Nonetheless, by using small apertures and long exposures with a 7×5-inch reflex camera, he was able to attain the greatest possible depth of field in his landscape work, and was considered successful both artistically and topographically. While on Ross Island, he made black-and-white images and color autochromes, although the latter turned out spotted and unsatisfactory to the perfectionist Ponting.

Scott asked Ponting to take a panorama of the Transantarctics, a photographic sequel to Wilson's earlier coastal profile. After numerous attempts defeated by mirages and thermal distortions, Ponting had a January day with just enough wind to disperse the thermal layers, but not enough to disturb the camera on its tripod. Climbing up one of the moraines at the foot of Erebus, thus eliminating the foreshortening of the foreground (his lens, magnifying at six power, would have made the mountains seventy miles away appear almost as close as the icebergs just offshore), he obtained two sets of lapping negatives, twelve in all.

Ponting was also able to take excellent photographs of Mt. Erebus and the nearby Barne Glacier, of an iceberg lit by flash at night, the *Terra Nova* in the sea ice, and portraits of both men and animals. He was, however, unable to capture the nighttime aurora. Although photographs had by that time been made of the northern aurora borealis, even his exposures as long as five minutes failed to reveal more than a faint glow from the aurora australis.

Ponting also shot the first Antarctic film, a classic in exploration cinematography, *With Captain Scott to the South Pole* (1913). He had no knowledge of movie cameras before being asked to join, but thought a motion picture could place the expedition in the public eye better than any book and so undertook a fierce course of study under a professional cinematographer. In all, Ponting took two movie cameras, several still ones (including a model for photomicrography), and telephoto lenses, all packed in watertight cases. During the Austral summer months of 1911, he constructed his darkroom and spent every waking hour working around both Cape Evans and Cape Royds. His camera gear weighed in at two hundred pounds, and when sledging away from the ship for more than a mile or two, he was forced to take another two hundred pounds of food and survival gear with him. During the winter he worked outside in temperatures of twenty below zero and colder, then spent hundreds of hours indoors washing and developing thousands of feet of movie film in fifty-foot segments—no small feat with a small glacier growing on the back wall of the darkroom, which he chipped out with an ice axe every few days.

Ponting took what has become one of the most reproduced images in Antarctic art, *A Grotto in an Iceberg*. He set up his large-format camera several yards inside a deep hollow in the ice and had two men stand at the entrance in sunlight, thus giving scale to the ship, which was anchored a mile away at the foot of the ice. He took numerous photographs from within this icy frame, a right-leaning ovoid with icicles hanging from the top, managing to capture both the sublime and the picturesque of the Antarctic. Here was Claude Lorrain's classical composition, a conceal-and-reveal scheme, set in the severe isotropy of the sound. Your eye is held in balance, allowing for slow contemplation of the scene—yet the ship is appallingly small in the distance.

Ponting did not accompany Scott's polar party, Wilson being a-ccorded priority as a physician and naturalist as well as an imagemaker.

The photographer sailed back to England in the spring of 1912, where he made preparations to have a joint exhibition with Wilson on the doctor's return. He was devastated when he learned in February 1913 of the tragedy. The remainder of his life oddly echoes that of Hodges. The Antarctic turned out to have been the high point of Ponting's work, and although his film and a book, *The Great White South*, were both critical and popular successes, they never earned him what he expected. Contractual confusions between Scott and Ponting were part of the problem, and Ponting died almost penniless in 1935, having spent much of his financial resources in putting out a second film, *90 Degrees South*.

While Scott was hunkered down at Cape Evans, the Australian geologist Douglas Mawson (1882–1958) was conducting the Australasian Expedition on another part of the continent. He sailed the *Aurora* into what has since been called the windiest place on earth, an inlet where the polar plateau simply falls off the continent, bearing with it almost constant katabatic winds. With him was the second great photographer to work on the continent, Frank Hurley (1887–1962). Another self-taught artist, Hurley had run away from home when he was fourteen and become a dockworker in Sydney. He purchased a Kodak Brownie box camera when he was seventeen, and by his early twenties he was running a postcard business. When twenty-five years old he heard that Mawson was on a train traveling across Australia to meet his ship. Hurley bought a railway ticket himself, cornered the explorer in his compartment, and talked nonstop throughout the journey. The scientist hired him to be the expedition photographer.

Hurley took another of the Antarctic's signature images during his first experience on the continent, of two men fighting their way across the ice in a blizzard, an all-too-frequent occurrence at their base. Hurley determined that he should make storms themselves the subject of a film, and would crawl about on hands and knees during blizzards to shoot them. The result, *Home of the Blizzard* (1913), is another classic in the genre. Mawson's massive account of the expedition by the same title contained more than 250 black-and-white photographs, most of which were by Hurley, including six fold-out landscape panoramas.

Hurley's film was so successful that Shackleton hired him to be the photographer for his next Antarctic expedition—much to Hurley's delight, who found civilization claustrophobic. Shackleton, in quest of another geographical first, was planning to make an 1,800-mile-long transcontinental traverse with six men and dogsleds. They sailed south aboard the *Endurance* in August 1914 and six months later found themselves frozen tight in one of the most featureless environments on earth, the million-square-mile ice pack of the Weddell Sea. Hurley, who had been hanging from the bowsprit to document the breaking of the ice by the ship's passage, now turned his attention to documenting the ice-bound ship. Not only was the vessel the literal and powerful symbol of civilization, but its masts were the only strong vertical elements within sight, and thus the focal point around which to document their presence.

Although Hurley's photographs of South Georgia Island, both at the beginning of the expedition and then on a return trip, are stunning landscape works, it is these photographs of the *Endurance* beset in the ice that earned him a place in the art history of exploration, and helped elevate Shackleton to his status as an international hero. Using a large-format glass-plate still camera as well as a movie camera, Hurley made images of the ship during both day and night. One black-and-white still photo taken in the dark is the most haunting picture of a vessel in ice since Gustave Doré illustrated Coleridge's *Rime of the Ancient Mariner* in 1878. Illuminated by a series of photo flares, the spars and rigging glow in their sheaths of ice, while the hull looms darkly over us, pushed upward by slabs of frozen ocean. Venerated for both technical achievement and aesthetic quality, it remains the greatest romantic image made on the ice, a marriage of science and the sublime.

Shackleton, who had returned from his first expedition to a mountain of debt, was determined to avoid that predicament this time around and had sold the film rights as part of his underwriting scheme. Even as the *Endurance* began to sink, Hurley, filming the slow implosion of its hull, remained well aware of this responsibility: he dove into the icy hold of the foundering ship to rescue his negatives.

The subsequent trials of the expedition are well known. They drifted helplessly in the sea ice for months, then escaped in two small boats to bleak Elephant Island, only to be forced to launch one of them into a gathering storm in hopes of reaching the whaling station at South Georgia. That feat of navigation, and the subsequent crossing of mountains and glaciers on the unexplored island, became the premiere true adventure yarn of the twentieth century. Partly this is due to Shackleton's not losing a single man despite incredible privation and dangers—not to mention Frank Worsley's navigational tenacity—but Hurley's images were critical in the mythmaking as well. The movie he made afterward, *South,* is another milestone in exploration cinematography.

In 1999 the American Museum of Natural History opened *Endurance: Shackleton's Legendary Expedition*, an exhibition of Hurley's work made during the trip. Published to accompany the show, Caroline Alexander's book of the same title set off a wave of cultural adulation that is still going strong. Church had painted the aftermath of the Franklin expedition in *The Icebergs*, and Bradford had haunted us with images of ships beset in the Arctic. But it was Frank Hurley's film of the sinking *Endurance* that gave the public a true understanding of what it means to see your only recognizable landmark be swallowed by a sea of ice.

The Heroic Age began to wind down with the return of the *Endurance* members in 1917; with the Great War raging, the attention of the world would be diverted for a few years. Now that the poles had been reached, the basic geographical inventory of the world had been completed—just in time for a revolution in both science and art that would forever sweep aside the notion not only of a fixed universe, but of one that operated independently of human consciousness.

The alchemists had called it *solve et coagula*—the dissolution of a substance that was then reconstituted through a process that transmuted it into another, lead to gold being the most famous example. Humans want to take apart the watch of the world, then put it back together again, not as the same watch, not even as a better watch, but as an entirely different machine. Apply the analogy with alchemy to information and you have what is called a paradigm shift.

Science had sought to put the world in an encyclopedia that built up in hierarchies from inanimate minerals to animate plants and animals, to humans and upward toward theological realms. When too many anomalies accumulated, new systems of organization were required that could include them in a larger framework. While science was busy parsing its collections into finer and finer distinctions between types of rocks, insects, birds, and astronomical entities, it was by necessity simultaneously looking for unities, many of which would lead scientists to the Antarctic for answers.

Faraday and Gauss had been concerned during the nineteenth century to understand how the earth acted as an electromagnet, and showed how you could picture a force field surrounding the earth (Faraday was the scientist who gave us that favorite demonstration of schoolchildren, where you bring a magnet up under a piece of paper holding iron filings and watch the pieces organize into a coherent field with a north and south pole). It would be necessary to field observers at both poles to assess the shape of the earth's magnetic field. In 1905 a patent clerk in Switzerland published a paper proposing that observers in differing motions relative to one another will have differing measurements of time—and the hunt for a universal field theory was launched. The nature of that field will not be determined, if ever, until the messages carried by neutrinos collected at the South Pole and the CMBR are decoded. In the same year, the 1903 Nobel laureate in chemistry, the Swedish physicist Svante August Arrhenius (1859–1927), expressed concern about global warming from fossil fuels, an early analysis of how human beings might be altering the entire planet. In 1907 he proposed "panspermia" as a theory for the interstellar distribution of microorganisms carried by meteorites. The ice shelves of the Antarctic are indicator environments for global warming, and the off-planet existence of microorganisms a debate fueled by the Martian meteorites found on the blue ice. And in 1912 Alfred Wegener (1880–1930) conceived his theory of continental drift, a prime example of how, eventually, accumulating data turns up enough anomalies to require a profound shift in thinking. All of these theories, attempts by scientists in the northern hemisphere to create larger frameworks for our understanding of the world, would find proof in the Antarctic.

As the nineteenth century progressed, geologists kept finding more and more fossils in common between land masses, yet they continued to assume that the continents had been distributed throughout the ages as they are today. By the turn of the century, however, some scientists were propounding the theory of "isostasy," which stated that the crust of the earth floated on a molten mantle. This could account for a geological anomaly: the obvious upward rebound of regions, such as Scandinavia, that had been buried under glaciers during the Ice Age. Wegener, a German meteorologist, had been watching ice floes break up and drift apart, which helped him visualize a theory of floating continents after reading a paleontology paper that used land bridges to explain the dispersal of species. He then looked at the coasts of Africa and South America (an "overview" provided by cartography) and, like Humboldt before him, came to the obvious conclusion that they had once been joined. Marshaling evidence from geodesy and geophysics, paleontology and paleoclimatology, and living biology, he proposed the existence in former times of a supercontinent, which he named Pangaea, that had split into separate pieces. The continents had then borne the animals apart as they floated away from one another.

Wegener died in Greenland in 1930, his theory dismissed and ignored by the majority of the geologic community until the early 1960s, when seafloor spreading along an upwelling of magma that formed the midocean ridges was discovered, along with the subsuming of material in the deep trenches. This was evidence of a convection mechanism capable of recycling the crust of the planet and moving continents. By the end of that decade the dynamics of plate tectonics had been described. When earthquake data for the decade were collated on a worldwide basis, the boundaries of the plates themselves were clearly outlined.

While Wegener was pondering continents as floating islands and

Einstein—now out of the patent office—was defending his theory of general relativity, the profile of yet another kind of island was being traced. Harlow Shapley (1885–1972), working in 1918 with the huge telescopes on Mt. Wilson above Los Angeles, was measuring the dimensions of the Milky Way and able to place Earth on an outer arm—yet another step in removing us from the center of the universe. In 1924 Edwin Hubble, working at the same observatory, measured the distance to the Andromeda Galaxy as 2 million light years. By 1934 he had determined with photographs that there are at least as many galaxies in the universe as there are stars in the Milky Way.

Discoveries of such magnitude produced a need to understand how we know what we know. The year that Shapley measured the Milky Way, Ludwig Wittgenstein (1889–1951) published his *Tractatus Logico-Philosophicus*, stating that all we can know is what we can say. All that is ineffable is unknowable. In 1927 such epistemological conundrums were complicated further by the physicist Werner Heisenberg with his principle of uncertainty: the more you know about the position of a particle, the less you know about its velocity, and vice versa—an idea that is taken as much as a metaphor as an equation, and was given widespread currency in many disciplines. It was the same year that Buckminster Fuller began investigating geodesics as "the most economical relationship between two events."

All of this looking outward into the universe and inward to atomic particles was paralleled by aesthetic movements in the arts. During the 1880s the heroic visual encyclopedia exemplified in the United States by the landscape paintings of Church and Moran was supplanted by Impressionism, which was breaking down the visual field of the picture plane into its spectral components. Cubism, Surrealism, Dadaism—all these aesthetic movements were in step with advances in other fields of study. Cubism wanted to see everything all at once, to represent things without simply picturing them, a goal that has often been identified with the shift from Newtonian to quantum physics. Surrealism looked for a larger reality by attempting to connect the dream life with the waking life in a new kind of lucidity, a movement having strong associations with the new field of psychoanalysis. Dadaism's random acts of theater acknowledged that indeterminacy was a prime operating principle in a universe that was not at all concerned with the fate of human beings.

The artists who came after the Impressionists were increasingly interested not so much in representing external reality as in understanding art itself, its materials and techniques and methods, as a cognitive activity. They were, in essence, enlarging the frame of their perceptions to keep up with accumulating knowledge about the world—just as the scientists and philosophers were doing.

Despite all these advances, however, the Antarctic was still mostly a *terra incognita:* not just an unexplored space, but one unimaginable to most people. It thus demanded not only continued cataloging, but continued representation in topographical terms.

Following the Heroic Age, Antarctic exploration, formerly that man-hauling, dogsledding, and pony-riding foot servant to science, sought a higher orbit of observation. Indeed, given that the unseen parts of the continent totaled more than all the remaining unknown territory in the world, it was quickly recognized that the only way to catalog it all would be by means of airborne cameras. Elevation of view had always been critical to measuring the earth, whether it was Humboldt tracing zones of climate or John Charles Frémont and Charles Preuss, his cartographer, climbing up in the mountains of Utah and Nevada to determine the boundaries of the Great Basin in 1843. The use of aerial photographs in science had been discussed as early as 1839 by the French geodesist Dominique Arago, and it was his fellow countryman, the artist Nadar, who initiated balloon-borne aerial photography in 1858. Balloons were considered indispensable to understanding the extent of Antarctica during the Heroic Age as well, and once the Wright brothers flew their heavier-than-air, gasoline-powered craft in 1903, it was obvious that aviation would be the most advantageous means of viewing the continent.

Mawson brought an airplane to the ice in 1911. Although it had crashed during a trial flight in Adelaide, he nonetheless took the fuselage and engine with him and used it briefly as a tractor to pull loads until the engine seized. The first successful flight over the ice was not made until November 1928 by Sir Hubert Wilkins, an Australian aviator who had served as a World War I combat photographer with Frank Hurley. That short flight, made from an airstrip carved out of volcanic tuff on Deception Island, was just a test run. The next month he undertook a 1,300-mile-long flight southward from Deception Island over the Antarctic Peninsula and the Larsen Ice Shelf. It was the first Antarctic mapping and aerial photography flight, and he dropped a territorial proclamation from the plane on behalf of the British government.

At the same time, Richard Byrd (1888–1957), a brash young pilot in the U.S. Navy, was making his first flights over the continent from the Bay of Whales on the Ross Ice Shelf, some 375 miles east of Ross Island. Byrd claimed to have flown over the North Pole in 1926, and he successfully repeated Lindbergh's nonstop crossing of the Atlantic the following year. Before returning to the United States after that flight, he announced that he would try next for the South Pole. In an issue of *Popular Mechanics*, he speculated publicly about the possibility of finding new forms of life in Antarctica, perhaps with links to prehistoric times. Sir Arthur Conan Doyle's *The Lost World*, published in serial form in 1912 with doctored photographs showing supposedly live dinosaurs on a high plateau in the Amazon, had been released in 1925 as a wildly popular silent film. Its premise was considered entirely plausible by a public just then reading about the opening of King Tut's tomb and the discovery of "dragons" on Komodo Island. This same public received Byrd's speculations avidly.

Byrd made his first Antarctic flight in January 1929 over Marie Byrd Land, naming a mountain range he discovered for the Rockefeller family, important patrons of his expedition. He overwintered at his base on the Ross Ice Shelf, Little America, and in November 1930 flew with his crew across the shelf toward the South Pole. The Ford tri-motor, not able to climb over the 15,000-foot Transantarctics, followed a glacier up and over a pass near Amundsen's route to the plateau. Four men, including the photographer Ashley McKinley, flew over what they believed was the South Pole just after midnight; they dropped an American flag and sent a radio message to base camp announcing their feat. A photograph by McKinley, one of 1,600 taken during the nineteen-hour journey, showed a limitless plane of sastrugi with a faint horizon in the distance. In all, McKinley captured 150,000 square miles on film. There was no ground control, so the work had only limited application for cartography, but it was at least a document of what the route and its surroundings looked like. Afterward, McKinley would spend months analyzing shadows cast by sastrugi, ice hummocks, and mountains, influenced as well by altitude, time, and camera angle, in order to place the images in correct sequence.

Byrd didn't find prehistoric life, but his expedition inspired science fiction writer John W. Campbell to write a classic genre short story, "Who Goes There," about the discovery of an alien that crash-landed in the Antarctic 20 million years ago and, when thawed out, is able to absorb humans and imitate them perfectly. If Byrd couldn't find a Lost World of dinosaurs, imaginary aliens would have to fulfill the need of the public for a definitive "Other" in the last place on Earth. Subsequent film versions in 1951 and again in 1982, now going by the title *The Thing,* show how stubborn a need that is, a conception kept very much alive today by sci-fi movies such as *The X-Files,* which features a huge flying saucer embedded in the East Antarctic ice cap. The trouble McKinley experienced in assembling his aerial photographs came from having no familiar landscape with which to work—exactly the reason the Antarctic attracts science fiction writers and moviemakers. As in all deserts, its landscape fails to provide an objective correlative to the audience; nothing is there to visually contradict the reality constructed by the writer or director—or to guide the aerial photographer.

Byrd's radio message to Little America that he was flying over the South Pole was picked up by radio operators in New York, and the news was broadcast from loudspeaker in Times Square. The *New York Times* commissioned David I. Paige (1901–1979), a muralist and portrait artist with a studio on Fifth Avenue, to design and supervise the painting of the country's largest cyclorama—a panorama with three-dimensional figures inserted in the foreground—depicting the expedition, to be installed at Luna Park, a popular amusement center. Thirty artists worked on the 350-foot-diameter, 50-foot-high painting, which featured in the foreground a seal, several penguins, and mannequins sawing ice blocks. Although the birth of cinema in 1895 had supplanted panoramas as mass entertainment, Byrd himself was famous enough that it proved to be a popular attraction: the ice formations were gothic, the mood somber, the humans properly heroic. As various expedition members viewed the cyclorama, Paige made friends with them and was soon working up a series of Antarctic paintings based on their recollections, works that depict the Antarctic as a gothic icescape.

Byrd, now a rear admiral in the U.S. Navy, returned to Antarctica on another privately financed trip in 1933. Although at first reluctant, he agreed to bring Paige with him as expedition artist, part of a fifty-six-man party that would reoccupy and expand Little America. Continuing in the tradition of using film as a fundraising opportunity, he also hosted two cameramen from the Paramount movie studio, and he capitalized on the airwaves as well, sending the first direct broadcasts from the ice beginning in February 1934, weekly reports that were carried to the nation on CBS. Byrd's men, including McKinley, surveyed 450,000 square miles from the air using cameras positioned on both the vertical and the oblique, which allowed them to document huge stretches of the continent to both sides of the plane. Paige busied himself sketching pastels of life at the base and color studies of the skies, at one point during the winter making more than 300 drawings of a thirty-six-hour-long display of the aurora australis, thus capturing what Ponting had failed to photograph.

On returning home in 1935, Paige busied himself with lectures and editing a film from expedition footage, wrangling unsuccessfully for years with Byrd over various copyright issues, a process reminiscent of Ponting's contract struggles. In 1938 he was living in Pasadena and trying—with continued lack of success—to convince Admiral Byrd and others that the Smithsonian should purchase the hundred pastels he had made on the ice for $250,000 and put them on permanent display (a number of the surviving works are now held with the Byrd Archives in the library at Ohio State University). He was extremely proud of being the first professional American artist to document the Antarctic and to winter-over, but he eventually gave up painting as a career and went to work for Hollywood, first as a scene painter and then as a respected cinematographer.

(NASA has long used the Antarctic as an analog environment for Mars, a connection in which Paige inadvertently participated. In 1956 he fathered a son who as a high school student would go with his astronomy club to Mt. Wilson and eventually build his own telescope for planetary observations, in particular those of Mars. The son, also named David Paige, went on to become a planetary scientist. In 1999 he built a ninety-degree panorama from photos of his trip to Antarctica's Dry Valleys earlier that year, which was used as a backdrop to a full-scale model of a Mars Polar Lander and used in a *Newsweek* article. The craft carried an instrument package designed by Paige that included cameras, weather sensors, and a gas analyzer to test soils near the Martian South Pole for water.)

After the Byrd Antarctic Expedition II, and as the British and Americans were jostling with the Norwegians and Australians for sovereign rights over parts of the continent, the Germans joined the competition in a somewhat more methodical and aggressive fashion. The 1938–1939 German Expedition catapulted aircraft from its oceangoing "aeroplane mothership," the *Schwabenland,* each plane reputedly carrying 400 pounds of steel-tipped javelins engraved with swastikas. Tests in the Alps had showed that, if dropped from 1,800 feet, they would drive about a foot into the ice, and the crews had instructions from Hermann Goering to deploy them every eighteen miles over the Antarctic. Not content to convert terrain into territory by symbolically spearing the continent, they also introduced photogrammetry to the ice. Photogrammetry—the cartographic measuring of land surfaces through photography—was first used during World War I, and cameras made especially for aerial photography were being manufactured by the 1920s, when the U.S. Army devoted an entire mapping unit to what it considered to be this strategic activity. The German pilots flew in rectangles, using the coastline as a baseline, and mapped 350,000 square miles with 11,600 pictures. Without any control points on the ground to verify and correct results, however, the consequent cartography was sometimes off by as much as sixty to a hundred miles.

In response, the Navy sent Byrd back to the ice in 1939–1941, this time to command the United States Antarctic Services Expedition, the first official expedition to the Antarctic since Wilkes. This trip saw the making of the first color aerial photographs; in addition, a distinguished commercial artist, Leland Curtis (1897–1989), was along for what would eventually total three visits with Byrd. Curtis, who lived in California and was skilled at painting the Sierra Nevada peaks and highly isotropic desert of the Great Basin, was well prepared to address the ice. His paintings of icebergs, mountains, and the Ross Ice Shelf are topographically accurate, but much more overtly emotional than Wilson's work. The canvases tend to be dark and brooding, and the wind is a palpable presence.

After World War II, the Americans continued to send Byrd south. Operation Highjump in 1946–1947 was essentially a military mission, allowing the United States, nervous about the Soviet presence in the Arctic, to secretly practice maneuvering in a polar environment; this exercise marked the first use of icebreakers and helicopters in the Antarctic. As goes the military, so goes mapping, and the expedition also saw the USGS on the ice, there for the first time to begin establishing ground control points for aerial mapping missions. Trimetrogon photography was introduced, which deployed five cameras taking simultaneous pictures—one pointed downward, two pointed out at thirty degrees from the horizontal (capturing the horizon), and one each pointed at a clock and at an altimeter. Two planes flew parallel with each other making overlapping photos in order to check results against one another. A single six-hour flight could map 50,000 square miles using the system, and 70,000 aerial images were captured. Serious photogrammetry had come to the continent. Byrd claimed that the expedition documented a third of the continent—more than had been seen during the previous one hundred years put together. Furthermore, what remained as the longest unexplored coast in the world was mapped, roughly equal in distance to the West Coast of the United States. The military explorers discovered twenty-two previously unknown mountain ranges, twenty-six islands, and twenty glaciers.

As stunning a cartographic accomplishment as this was, involving thirteen vessels (including a submarine) and 4,700 personnel, it was the International Geophysical Year in 1957–1958 that at last established a permanent human presence on the ice. Following World War II, rockets had evolved quickly from their narrow status as a weapon into strategic tools capable of exploring the outer atmosphere. A new high ground had thus been defined that would offer not only military advantage but, for the scientists, a much larger panoramic view of the planet as well. The scientific community urged politicians to set aside Cold War hostilities to mount the IGY during a cycle of maximum sunspot activity, when they could launch rockets from the poles to study the effects on geomagnetism. Three months after the IGY kicked off in July 1957, Russia launched *Sputnik I,* the first satellite to orbit Earth, and the Space Age was born.

The IGY saw approximately sixty thousand scientists from sixty-six countries measuring everything imaginable at the time on, under, and over the earth. Although the Antarctic work involved only sixty of the four thousand primary stations reporting data, the military-industrial resources brought to bear opened up the entire continent. Twelve countries participated in Antarctica during the IGY, with more than forty new stations established, including permanent ones by the Russians at Vostok near the geomagnetic pole, some 1,300 miles inland from the coast, and American bases at McMurdo and the South Pole. Prior to IGY, only ten people had ever stood at the Pole. During the 1957 winter eighteen men lived there, and the station has been occupied continuously since.

During that amazing year, the British completed a bit of business left unfinished by Shackleton and traversed the continent on motorized vehicles. Glaciers were surveyed, weather balloons were launched, geo-magnetic studies were conducted, and the aurora australis was pho-tographed simultaneously from end to end over thousands of miles. So many maps and charts and aerial photographs were made that people lost count. The Americans alone shipped home twenty-seven tons of scientific records from the continent. And for the first time, scientists began to look under the ice, using seismic listening devices and radar to probe how thick it was. The results forced them to revise upward their estimates of the total Antarctic ice mass by 40 percent. Gauss had pre-dicted early in the previous century that fluctuations in terrestrial mag-netism might be caused by electrical currents in the sky, and during the IGY and the following year the Russians launched 175 research rockets and the United States nearly 300 to study this phenomenon. The exper-iments in and above the earth's atmosphere proved him correct, as well as linking the behavior of the auroras and telecommunications recep-tion to sunspot activity.

Various artists worked in the Antarctic in association with the IGY. The U.S. Navy brought in Leland Curtis for his second visit in 1955–1956, together with two more artists, the civilian Robert Charles Haun (1903–1975) and Commander Standish Backus (1910–1989). Their watercolors documented military life, science projects, and natural history subjects such as seals and penguins. Curtis returned for the third time in 1957, which made him the dean of Ice Art. New Zealand sent Peter McIntyre (1910–1995), another war artist and the most renowned postwar painter in his country. Arthur Beaumont (1890–1978), a distinguished painter of military and historical subjects, was brought down by the U.S. Navy in 1959, and the next year he returned to visit the South Pole station, where he made the first plein air painting on that spot. The work of these artists was much the same as that of Jackson and Moran for Wheeler when he was exploring Yellowstone. They made images that documented expeditions in a place so exotic it was almost otherworldly, images that captured the imagination of the public and thus provided the political fuel necessary to keep congressional appropriations flowing to support the effort, which as always had a mix of scientific and strategic motives.

Maps and topographical art, whether drawings, paintings, or photographs, can help us travel mentally from "here," where we live, to "there," a place we cannot directly see for ourselves. In that sense they are more utilitarian navigational devices than art, and as in centuries past, the ones created in the 1950s continued to serve military and political needs. But artists can also manipulate the scene to reveal how we think about space and place, terrain and territory, and how we place ourselves within them. Just as Turner opened the way for landscape art to perform these cognitive and cultural functions in the modern world generally, so Emil Schulthess (1913–1996), a Swiss photographer, brought modernist art to the ice. Schulthess was a famous commercial artist who at various points in his career worked for *Life* magazine, was the art director for Swissair, and published photo-essay books on regions from Africa to the Amazon. He claimed, however, that the four months he spent on the ice during the IGY were the highlight of his life—a feeling that seems to have marked every one of his predecessors from Hodges to Hurley. *Antarctica,* the photo essay he produced, was published in a long horizontal format. Although it is not known widely to the public anymore, it remains one of the most influential visions of the continent for other artists.

Schulthess took five handheld Leica cameras and nine lenses with which to work, as well as a homemade fish-eye camera. He took panoramic shots of sastrugi on the polar plateau, the crenellations of the Ross Ice Shelf, and various atmospheric phenomena, and telephoto pictures of the Transantarctics. He dangled out of helicopters to take aerial shots of seals and penguin rookeries (and would later go on to become the most prominent aerial panoramic photographer of his day). Mounting his fish-eye camera flat on a tripod, he took twenty-four-hour exposures of the sun circling in the sky, then superimposed a clock around the perimeter of the one made at Pole. In another Pole picture showing three people, he mounted the camera so it was look-ing downward, then overlaid meridian lines labeled with the interna-tional cities the lines would ultimately reach. The long horizontal for-mat of his work was ideally suited to the isotropic space of the Antarctic (as well as an allusion to coastal profiles and the panoramic tradition in exploration), and his superposition of graphic devices foregrounded the anthropocentrism we display when faced with such a large space. His work imposed a visual formalism on the ice, in the process making that formalism visible—a thoroughly modern artistic convention.

Phillip Law, the Australian scientist who would later head up his coun-try's Antarctic Division, estimated the total cost of Antarctic operations during the IGY to participating nations at $280 million. Walter Sullivan, the science reporter for the *New York Times,* reported approximately $1 million spent just for each of the eighteen men overwintering at Pole. Sullivan also noted in his fine book on the epic effort, *Assault on the Unknown,* that the needs of the IGY for rocket-borne instrumentation forced the United States to establish in 1958 its first permanent and large-scale government exploring agency: the National Aeronautics and Space Administration. This marked the beginning of what histo-rian Stephen Pyne calls the Third Age of Discovery, a logical extension of what his former mentor, William Goetzmann, described as the Second Age that was initiated by James Cook.

The technology of the Second Age consisted of sailing ships and an increasing precision in optics. Both allowed explorers to travel afar, whether around the globe, down into microscopic realms, or out to the planets and nearest galaxies. Third Age technology allows us to deploy remote-sensing instruments that send back the information they collect, once again extending the range of our senses. Examples of what that means in the Antarctic include the monitoring of seismic events in Wright Valley by the air force and watching eruptions of Mt. Erebus with remote cameras that send images to New Mexico via satellite, even during the winter. The expense of maintaining people would be ameliorated while, at the same time, the data flow could be increased.

The IGY also laid the groundwork for the Antarctic to become the only continent governed by an international treaty, which took effect in 1961—versus allowing it to be carved up de facto into wedges of sovereignty defined by flags and, yes, javelins dropped from airplanes. The American agency given the authority to fund and coordinate national IGY activities, many of which centered on the Antarctic, was the National Science Foundation. It was only logical that the agency then administer the country's subsequent scientific interest on the continent. The NSF had been chartered in 1950, an offspring of the government's wartime Office of Scientific Research and Development, and its first director was a physicist, Alan Waterman, who was then chief scientist at the Office of Naval Research (ONR). He would serve until 1963, filling his top administrative posts with colleagues from the ONR. In turn the Navy would provide all the logistical and operational support for the United States on the continent until the early 1990s.

Given the fundamental connections between the Navy and the NSF, it is not surprising that Leland Curtis was the first artist to receive NSF support to visit the Antarctic. The next person they sponsored was the poet Donald Finkel in 1968, then in 1975 photographer Eliot Porter and the painter Daniel Lang, both of whom advanced landscape art on the ice to a level not seen before. Although they did not travel together, sending both a photographer and a painter to the ice strongly echoed Jackson and Moran being sent to Yellowstone. By the mid-1970s artists from Great Britain, Australia, and New Zealand were also being sponsored by their national programs to work in the Antarctic; like Porter and Lang, they were chosen not from among the ranks of military illustrators, but from the larger pool of artists and writers at large in the culture. The topographical tradition would continue for decades to be NSF's primary aesthetic criterion for the American artists, but the other countries, having had a longer history of Antarctic images brought before their citizens, began to select artists less concerned with documenting the exterior landscape and interested instead in the interior responses of people living and working in a place that merely bordered the possible. They would, as always, seek to work where science had not yet reached, beginning to pendulum this time away from imaging and back into imagining.

11   ON THE MOUNTAIN
OF MYTH

WHEN PEOPLE AT MCMURDO plot their activities around an Antarctic landmark, it's not the South Pole to which they anchor their thoughts, but Mt. Erebus. The Pole is a real place—the earth does revolve around it—but it is not a visible landmark. It's more a geographical abstraction into which all cartographic lines bend, which severely compromises your ability to navigate. Once you've been at McMurdo for more than a week you have north and south sorted out— the Pole lies in the direction of Minna Bluff, and north is up along the shoreline of the town toward Cape Evans—but the cardinal points of east and west remain suspect, hostage to the circular path the sun describes every twenty-four hours. The South Pole fulfills the symmetry of terrestrial mapping, but the fact that it is a singular point versus the continual horizon of north confuses people. Anecdotal evidence suggests that the better you are at orienting yourself in the middle latitudes where most of us live, the greater the difficulty you will have on the ice. Our internal compasses are set to cues that at home appear linear, but here tend to be circular, whether it's the path of the sun or the cyclonic behavior of storms.

Erebus is not only the nearest verticality of monumental proportions; it also offers what we instinctively seek when faced with navigational confusion: the highest vantage point within sight. And within an icescape that has little perceptible movement in it, its plume is always changing shape, volume, and direction according to the amount of activity in the crater, the humidity in the air, and the wind. If you're in town, it's just out of sight over the hills, but go a few hundred yards in almost any direction—out onto the sea ice or up Ob Hill—and its steaming summit is the most alive part of the landscape (Plate 25). If you ask a resident here where they would most like to go on the continent, almost always their first answer is "Up Erebus," though this wish is seldom granted, helo time on the mountain being reserved primarily for researchers studying the eruptions. The mountain has, however, attracted a deep layer of literary, artistic, and scientific images, and I'd been scratching my head ever since arriving trying to figure out how to finagle my way up there.

The camp on Erebus is run by Philip Kyle, the renowned volcanologist from the New Mexico Institute of Mining and Technology who's been studying the mountain since 1969, and the answer to my quest arrives unexpectedly from the legendary Sarah Krall. I'd been told before coming to the ice that I should talk to Sarah, who over the course of twenty years on the ice has had many jobs here and truly loves the land. She has, indeed, been a font of information and inspiration about places I should seek out—and this year she's the head helo tech, the person in charge of the crew that rigs loads for the helicopters. Sarah is an old hand on Erebus and a friend of Phil's, and he's given permission for both myself and Henry Kaiser, a visiting musician, to come up the mountain if she accompanies us as our safety person.

For many people, experiencing Erebus involves the ascent not so much of a summit, but of a myth. At 12,447 feet, it is the southernmost active volcano in the world and one of possibly only three on the planet with a lava lake burbling away in its crater. The molten lakes that form in the Hawaiian volcanoes, for example, are different, formed when magma from depth rises to the surface, fills a crater, and then either slowly cools or feeds into tubes to reappear downslope as a lava flow. Erebus, however, holds in its crater a constantly convecting pool of magma that connects to a chamber deep inside the mountain. Looking into Erebus is to be granted a rare view into the circulatory system of the planet.

Volcanoes are often taken to represent the unpredictable power of nature, and in the first known visual representation of a volcano, on the maplike mural from Catal Hayuk, Turkey, from 6,200 B.C., the eruption is clearly posited as a threat to the rationality of human endeavor, as represented by the carefully gridded town. On arriving in the Antarctic, the effect is similar. Look the right way at an aerial image of Ross Island taken from the plane as it lands and you have a sister image to the ancient Turkish mural: McMurdo is laid out before you, with Erebus steaming away in the background. You can't help but wonder if the Antarctic volcano will swallow the town, even though you've been told that that is extremely unlikely.

When the Greeks witnessed the eruption of Mt. Etna in 734 B.C., they explained it as the struggle of gods beneath the earth. Two hundred years later Pythagoras took a different tack, arguing that the center of the earth was a giant fire, and volcanoes were places where air escaping through cracks heated the rocks. When Pliny the Elder (A.D. 23–79), the Roman author of the world's first encyclopedia of natural history, died of asphyxiation while investigating the eruption that buried Pompeii, he knew of only ten active volcanoes in the world. During the Dark Ages volcanoes were considered to be the chimneys of hell. It wasn't until the late seventeenth century that a Sicilian natural philosopher, Francesco d'Arezzo, observed that volcanic rock appeared to be created through a process of fusion similar to that employed in glass blowing. By the mid–nineteenth century, most of the 1,511 volcanoes active in the world during the last ten thousand years were in the process of being cataloged, and although volcanoes were known to exist in the sub-Antarctic islands, none were known to exist on the continent itself.

Sailing into what is now the Ross Sea in January 1841, Sir James Ross and his crew sighted the smoking Mt. Erebus from fifty miles away, his captain's log noting that the mountain was "emitting flame and smoke in great profusion." He recorded a plume two to three hundred feet in diameter that rose up to two thousand feet above the crater, and stated that his officers "believed they could see streams of lava pouring down its sides until lost beneath the snow." Hooker could have been speaking for much of the crew when he wrote in his journal that the sight gave him "an indescribable feeling of the greatness of the Creator in the works of His Hand."

A lithograph of that sight, based on a watercolor by J. E. Davis, second master of the *Terror,* appeared in Ross's published account of the expedition. It shows the *Erebus* and *Terror* in the calm waters of Ross Sound, a few growlers—bits of partially submerged ice—floating nearby, with Mt. Erebus and the much smaller Mt. Bird in the background (Plate 26). To the left a shore party in a launch hunts seals with a rifle. The view is radically foreshortened, the height of Erebus dramatically increased by the perspective and the inclusion of a layer of stratocumulus clouds floating in front of the summit cone, aesthetic decisions that represent the impression the volcano made on the collective imagination of the expedition.

Ross named the volcano after his ship, the bomb vessels in the Royal Navy usually bearing names of volcanoes and related hellacious matters: Vesuvius, Aetna, Sulfur, Beelzebub. The name Erebus derives from Greek mythology, which held that "in the beginning there was chaos," and it is directly from this void that Erebus appeared, an entity that was both a place and a personification. Erebus was not a god, but something much older and larger. He was Darkness and the father of Day. His mists wrapped the edges of the world where sky met earth, mists that also filled the hollow center of the earth. He was where death and night dwelt, and his name was also Hades. Ross declared that the discovery of Erebus could not help but further our understanding of the nature of the globe.

When Ross sailed into McMurdo Sound, the leading theory of volcanism was one proposed in 1808 by the English chemist Humphry Davy (1778–1829). It held that volcanoes were the result of chemical combustions in the crust of the planet, and that Earth's temperature actually grew cooler as you descended into its depths—that, indeed, the planet was cooling as it grew older, part of the Great Chain of Being paradigm. The idea that volcanism was the result of exothermic reactions had its roots in experiments by medieval alchemists with sulfur, and remained essentially unchallenged until Descartes proposed in 1644 that the earth had been formed out of a vortex of matter and contained a still-molten core capable of fueling eruptions. Lyell, ever the uniformitarian, disagreed with Davy and followed Descartes, suggesting in his 1830 *Principles of Geology* that the core of the earth was molten under enormous pressure and of a relatively constant temperature.

Although the British astronomer Edmund Halley had proposed late in the seventeenth century that the earth was hollow and that the aurora borealis was caused by gas escaping out of the North Pole, it wasn't until after Davy's theory was published that John Symmes (d. 1829), an eccentric former U.S. Infantry captain, could propose in 1818 with any credibility that the earth could be entered through holes at the North and South Poles. Symmes begat a slew of science fiction and fantasy novels that feature explorers clambering down inside volcanoes to find lost worlds, a narrative tradition that continues to this day. One of Symmes's followers was Jeremiah Reynolds (the author of "Mocha Dick," the short story that in part inspired Herman Melville to write *Moby Dick*); Reynolds successfully lobbied Congress to fund the Wilkes expedition in 1838 to look for the South Pole entrance. Just prior to its departure, Edgar Allan Poe (1808–1849) published "The Narrative of Arthur Gordon Pym of Nantucket," in which the hero disappears into a mystical whirlpool only to reappear mysteriously in the United States. Poe's tale perhaps owes its impetus to *Symzonia: A Voyage of Discovery,* the supposedly true account published in 1820 of a journey into the earth by one "Captain Adam Seaborn," in all likelihood a pseudonym of Symmes.

Ross, by discovering a live volcano in the Antarctic, fueled the imaginations of still other authors. Jules Verne (1828–1905) was inspired equally by accounts of polar expeditions and the newly available translations in France of Poe's works. He accepted Davy's hypothesis and subsequently wrote *Journey to the Center of the Earth*, published in 1864 and often considered to be the first science fiction novel. Verne took Alexander von Humboldt as a model for his hero and had been reading Elisha Kane as well; he gave his characters entrance into the planet via a dormant Icelandic volcano. He also penned *The Sphinx of the Ice Fields* (1897), an Antarctic sequel to Poe's narrative. The American inheritor of Poe's mantle, H. P. Lovecraft (1890–1937), was likewise fascinated by accounts of polar exploration, and created Antarctica's fictional Mountains of Madness, which his heroes would attempt to breach after honing their mountaineering skills on Mt. Erebus. Beneath the Antarctic they would find the city of an ancient alien civilization. Just as geologists were reading downward into the earth's strata to reconstruct the history of the planet, so the writers were using fiction in order to plumb human imagination.

The mountain was actually first ascended during Shackleton's *Nimrod* expedition of 1907–1909, which was based at Cape Royds approximately fifteen miles away. The team—a party of six that included Douglas Mawson, who would become Australia's premier Antarctic explorer of the Heroic Age—made the ascent in six days, basically following a beeline straight up to the summit. Leaving Royds on March 5, the men endured temperatures of –28°F and a blizzard, and at times were forced to climb blue-ice gullies on their hands and knees while pulling a six-hundred-pound sledge. On March 9 they reached the caldera rim, the edge of the large plateau created when Erebus blew off its upper portion 37,000 years ago, and the team was spotted from the Royds Hut through a telescope. On the tenth, minus one member left below to nurse his frostbitten toes, they reached the summit and looked down into the "vast abyss" of the active crater. Two days later they were back at the hut, having made the first mountaineering ascent in the history of the continent.

During the following winter, the crew produced ninety copies of the first book to be printed in the Antarctic, and the southernmost book to be printed in the world, *Aurora Australis*. The London printing firm of

Sir J. Causton & Sons, Ltd. had donated paper, ink, type, and the press, as well as having given Frank Wild and Ernest Joyce a three-week course in printing. The pride that Wild and Joyce took in the production is evident in the carefully even impressions of the pages, although they modestly noted that the ink wasn't laid on perfectly, as they had been forced to warm the inking plate with a candle, and the printing was done in the six-by-seven-foot space they shared with the large expedition sewing machine and bunks for two men. The whereabouts of only seventy-five copies of *Aurora Australis* are known currently, making it the rarest and most desirable of all Antarctic books. The pages were hand sewn and bound in packing-crate boards, which today tend to be worn smooth into a soft patina from years of reverential handling.

Erebus is the dominant theme of the book. The first piece in the book is an essay, "The Ascent of Mt. Erebus," by a member of the summit party, T. W. Edgeworth David, illustrated with a woodcut by expedition artist George Marston. Shackleton himself contributed a poem about the mountain, calling it the "Keeper of the Southern Gateway" and describing it as a "grim, rugged, gloomy and grand" place "seared by the inner fires" through "untold aeons." He portrays his men as clinging to its "iron sides" during the blizzard, the "weird gloom made darker still dim seen perilous places." He signed this gothic set piece Nemo, Latin for "no one" and not coincidentally the name of the captain of that infamous submarine the *Nautilus* from Jules Verne's 1870 *20,000 Leagues Under the Sea*, which featured a voyage under the "Antarctic ice cap."

The most substantial creative writing in the book, however, was the story "Bathybia" by Mawson, which recounts a fictional expedition over the Victoria Land Plateau during which a volcanic crater 30,000 feet deep is discovered. The explorers descend four miles below sea level, and at the bottom find an undulating plain where the temperature is 70°F and giant foot-long ticks wander about. They're forced to build a raft, as the jungle becomes too thick after a few days to proceed on land, and float down a river with the foliage eventually arching so thickly overhead that the only source of illumination is a phosphorescent fungus. Giant water spiders and rotifers (also known as "water bears") attack them, fictional enlargements of the creatures actually examined through microscopes during the expedition. It rains, there's a flood, and they're carried onto a giant salt lake, which they cross. They find a 17,000-foot high volcano, which they ascend. Finding an ancient and giant frozen rotifer, they take it into camp, where it thaws out and attacks—whereupon the author wakes up.

The tales by Poe, Verne, and all of the mythology of the Antarctic as a lost world are nowhere evoked more by reality than in the lava lake and ice caves found high on Erebus, and it is with a sense of elation and wonder that at five o'clock on a clear December evening Sarah, Henry Kaiser, and I board our helicopter to fly to Fang Camp at the 9,000-foot level on Mt. Erebus. We will be there to acclimatize for the requisite two days prior to moving up another thousand feet and spending the rest of the week at Lower Erebus Hut, the research field camp run by Kyle. Because Erebus rises so steeply within a short distance from McMurdo, the helo pilots are forced to gain altitude as quickly as possible on takeoff, making the flight a bit of an elevator ride. The *whump-whump* of the chopper blades echoes back at us from the ice-clad flanks of the mountain; it's as if we're accompanied by drum beats on a journey into a primordial realm.

Fang Camp is put in each year on an icy saddle no more than a quarter mile wide that extends out from the northeast side of the mountain and is flanked on either side by glaciers. The back of the saddle is formed by the slope that goes up to the 100,000-year-old caldera, its rocky plateau a remnant of the original, million-year-old mountaintop prior to its massive eruption. In front of the two tents, put up by Melissa and a small crew several weeks ago, the saddle is defined by Fang Ridge, a jagged cliff rising from a few yards in height to 500 feet that is a remnant of an old volcanic vent. On the other side of the ridge the mountainside drops off thousands of feet toward the ocean.

Once we're on the ground with our gear heaped around us, we realize that we can see only the bottom few hundred feet of the volcanic cone itself; clouds are building up quickly on top and merging with the thick plume of steam from the crater, threatening to obscure everything above us. It's much colder than down at McMurdo, and as soon as the helicopter lifts off, Henry and I busily sort and stow our supplies while Sarah gets a stove going both for warmth and to start the constant flow of liquids we'll need to avoid dehydration, which with our rapid ascent to this altitude could cause serious medical problems.

Henry is a slightly-built forty-nine-year-old guitarist from Oakland who is also here in the NSF Visiting Artists and Writers Program. He's recorded 180 CDs, most of which are avant-garde guitar work, but some of which are world music recordings in which he is playing with people from places as foreign to American listeners as Madagascar. His best work in that genre blends in the ambient sounds of his surroundings, making audible the relationships between sounds in the natural world and music created by the local culture. Henry proposed to NSF that he record sound and music in the Antarctic—not recording music that native residents have made in league with their environment, but creating the first such music himself. Only in the Antarctic would this be possible, on a continent with no previous indigenous culture.

Sarah, who is forty-eight this year, is a strong-boned woman of immense and patient humor, and most often wears her dark blonde hair in a thick ponytail that almost reaches her waist. She is an accomplished folk guitarist who also plays the mandolin and all manner of keyboards, and in addition to her duties as the chief helo tech, has been a field and safety mountaineer for the program. She and her husband have been working together in the Antarctic for more than a decade and a half, and she's spending this week as our guide. She has brought one of her guitars, too. One reason Phil invited Henry and Sarah to come up the mountain is because they've promised to play for the research team.

Although it's still clear at our level, by the time the helicopter struggles up an additional thousand feet to make a cargo drop at the hut above, which is invisible beyond the rocky rim of the caldera, the summit of Erebus is draped in a lenticular cloud that means the atmosphere is loaded with moisture. As the pilot circles the plateau, the rotors leave a slow thick contrail, something that we usually see emanating from a jet airplane at 25,000 feet or higher, where the contrast between the hot engines and the frigid atmosphere produces condensation. It is already foggy at the rim, and the helo contrail just makes it worse, so the pilot is forced to leave, unable to drop the supplies.

Sarah has water boiling within minutes inside the larger of the two Scott tents, where she will cook and sleep. The temperature outside is near zero, with a wind chill of about minus fifty; Henry and I are infinitely grateful for the warmth when we crawl in through the bulky tube that serves as the tent's entrance. One of the virtues of the old-fashioned, yellow, double-walled canvas pyramids that work so well here is that it is perfectly all right to crank up a Coleman stove inside one. I know from unhappy experience that modern nylon mountaineering tents have a nasty tendency to melt if you try to cook in them. Her tent is soon sixty-five degrees at head level when we stand up, though still a degree or two below freezing at ground level, and we spend a comfortable evening cooking and swapping stories until we're sleepy. The sun goes behind the mountain around 11 P.M., so there's a semblance of actual night when Henry and I go to our tent. The mountain is mostly invisible above us, its steam mixing with the clouds, the size and shape of Erebus beyond our comprehension. During the night we're awakened by loud pops that sound like gunshots—the ice contracting as it cools in the shadow of the mountain.

The next morning we're up at 7:30; conditions are calm in the saddle and the peak of the mountain is free of clouds. After breakfast I take an ice axe and stroll across the wind-slabbed snow to the ridge, scrambling up for a view down the other side. Seemingly at my feet are more than a hundred icebergs frozen into the sea ice. The smallest are the size of mansions. The largest is B-15, that Delaware-sized monster that's been stopping the currents and wave action that at this time of year would normally have broken up the sea ice halfway down to McMurdo. The ice front is visible—the first time I've seen open water since reaching the continent—but it's sixty miles out from where it usually is. And the tabletop expanse of B-15 extends northward farther than I can see, more than a hundred miles.

Henry and Sarah join me, and we contemplate below us the site of the infamous 1979 Air New Zealand crash. Air tourism to the Antarctic has been going on since the 1950s, and it used to include overflights of the continent. They were discontinued after the accident, when a commercial jet found itself off course in a whiteout due to a programming correction in the navigation computer that the pilots didn't know had been made. The plane slammed into the mountainside below us, killing all 237 people on board, the worst accident of any kind in the Antarctic and at the time the fourth worst aviation disaster in the world. There's no evidence of the crash from up here, but I've been reading the transcripts of the pilots' last words. They had only just realized that they were turned around in the clouds when the alarm warning them of approaching ground went off, giving them six seconds to react, an impossibly short time in which to gain altitude. Since then the alarms have been recalibrated in jets to provide up to two minutes of warning.

I turn and look behind us at the cone of Erebus, which has been assembled during the last thirty-seven millennia out of alternating layers of snow and lava bombs coursed by lava flows. The volcano sends up a plume of steam that drifts gently away from us to the south. Looking to my left, I note that the ridge cuts off a view of Krall Crags, part of the mountain named by the USGS in official acknowledgment of Sarah's service in the Antarctic. By the time we walk back to our tents for lunch, which look to be only yards away but are at least a ten-minute trudge, I note that clouds are forming over the 10,700-foot summit of Mt. Terror to the west. It looks as if weather shows up first on the smaller of the two peaks, which to me is a clear warning.

We spend the rest of our first acclimatization day reading and talking, Sarah at times working on an elaborate piece of beadwork, all of us enjoying the quiet after the relative frenzy of McMurdo. I ask Sarah about her experiences with previous visiting artists and writers. One writer she met is Henry's and my friend Kim Stanley Robinson, who she says got a great deal of life on the ice just right. Henry observes that Stan liked being in the Antarctic immensely—so much that he wants to return—because he was, for the first time, actually "living in a science fiction novel."

Anywhere we travel, our perceptions of the place tend to be preconditioned by images other people have made, especially at sites of historical or scenic significance. Think, for example, of scenic viewpoints in national parks, established by the park service to look out over panoramas captured visually by artists such as the photographer William Henry Jackson or the painter Thomas Moran. In the case of Antarctica, a disproportionately large number of cultural images are provided to the visitor by science fiction literature and movies. Partly that's because speculative culture loves a desert—there's no objective correlative to contradict the fantasy. But it also stems from the fact that science fiction is a way of bringing an alien landscape within our cognitive grasp by setting familiar stories within it. The narratives can range from the heroic, as in the space operas of *Star Wars,* to political and social commentaries, such as the *Dune* novels by Frank Herbert and Stan's Mars trilogy, which begins with astronauts training at McMurdo and in the Dry Valleys. Sarah and I nod in agreement with Henry's assessment.

When Henry and I leave Sarah's tent to go to bed the wind has picked up, and there's no loitering outside for a view. We warm our smaller tent quickly with the stove, which makes it cozy enough to take notes without wearing gloves. I fall asleep while Henry is still reading.

During the night the winds increase, and when I poke my head outside the tent at eight the next morning visibility is less than a hundred yards. I can see Sarah's tent through the blowing snow, but we're definitely in a Condition Two—not as bad as the snowmobile ride out to Cape Evans, but still something to be careful in. Henry and I leave the tent together as a safety precaution and crawl into breakfast. Sarah is sitting calmly in a corner doing her beadwork, completely unconcerned about the storm.

We spend the second day of our acclimatization doing much the same things as the day before, knowing that the planned afternoon helicopter ride up to the hut is out of the question. Phil Kyle calls at six that evening, asking if they should send a snowmobile team to retrieve us, but we reply that the snow gully down which they would have to travel is still completely whited out. Although we're anxious to get higher on the mountain and chafe at the delay, it's not yet safe.

On the third morning the winds have calmed to a whisper and the sun is shining, but once again Mt. Terror is buried in a lenticular cloud being whipped over its summit by high winds. To the east and west are nothing but low clouds, the mass of Erebus parting the weather so that we're in the protected lee of the peak. My personal forecast, which I voice only to Sarah, is that a major storm is due. I am, however, an utter novice at anything Antarctican, so I don't press it—but she frowns at the possibility.

At 10:30 that morning, three of the seven members of Phil's team ride down on snowmobiles to collect us. The window of clear weather on this side of the volcano may not last long, and they're anxious to have everyone on the mountain together if a storm closes in. The trip up the gully to the plateau of the caldera is genuinely surreal, the windblown crust of frozen snow atop twisted volcanic rocks making the landscape so unfamiliar that my mind automatically tries to create an analog. It's only with difficulty that I shake off the illusion of riding through giant sagebrush after a Nevada snowstorm.

Once on the plateau we see that the entire summit cone is cloaked in swirling cloud, though down where we are there's only a light breeze. The Lower Erebus Hut camp consists of two small but securely anchored flat-topped wooden structures, ten mountaineering tents, and one Scott tent, which means everyone has his or her own domicile. (The Upper Hut, a few hundred feet higher on the mountain, was abandoned in 1984 after an eruption lobbed huge lava bombs all around it.) Antennae for telemetering seismic and GPS data down to McMurdo are scattered about, along with fuel drums, a wind generator, a half dozen snowmobiles, and shovels and ice axes stuck into the ground for each of us.

It's a relief to enter the larger living hut and stretch our legs out while sitting in folding chairs. At roughly twenty-four by sixteen feet, the space is luxurious after being shoehorned into a small Scott tent for two days; it holds two long folding tables for community dining, a well-stocked kitchen, and a small workspace crammed with remote-sensing equipment in various stages of disarray. Phil and his longtime associate Bill McIntosh are sitting at the tables with four students who range in age and experience from a senior at New Mexico Institute of Mining and Technology deploying GPS stations around the mountain to measure deformation of the ground, to a postdoctoral researcher monitoring infrasound sensors in conjunction with the seismometers. Our company is rounded out by a science teacher visiting from upstate New York and a lab tech. Jeff Johnston, the postdoc, is a tall mountain climber from Seattle who wears his hair in a ponytail. Jessie Crain, a master's candidate monitoring emissions in the plume for the last three years, is a petite brunette. Soon after we arrive the two of them suit up in full gear and head out on snowmobiles, despite what are obviously deteriorating conditions above. They'll be able to ride to within 650 vertical feet of the crater rim, and the quarter-mile hike up from there will take them only twenty minutes or so, even in the gathering cloud and wind.

In the afternoon Henry goes off to scout the nearby ice towers and caves. (Volcanic steam exiting fumaroles beneath the snow freezes into the hollow white pillars; the caves, which are entered through the towers, are created by the warm rocks underneath.) Meanwhile, Sarah and I stay behind to build snow walls around the tents, cutting out snow blocks with a saw and stacking them up three and four high almost all the way around. The most severe threat you face on the ice is loss of shelter, and what most often collapses tents here is wind and drifting snow. The walls are meant to hold them back as much as possible.

After dinner we have a concert by Henry and Sarah, ninety minutes that veer from Sarah's traditional blues and Irish street music to one of Henry's set pieces, a music and spoken word performance recreating the childhood trauma he suffered when he discovered that *The Flint-*

stones was an animated cartoon, not a documentary featuring real dino-saurs. Afterward, before going to my tent at bedtime, I check the weather station on the wall. Winds are at 34 mph and the wind chill at minus thirty-five—not that cold. Perfect conditions for a storm.

I've learned to wear both earplugs and a sleeping mask during the night to block out wind noise and light, but I wake up at three in the morning. The wind gusts are strong enough to concuss my sleeping bag even inside the tent. The poles of the tent are bending and snow is slithering through the cracks between zipper pulls. I go back to sleep, knowing the tents are designed to take moderate winds and snow loads, but wonder how close we'll get to testing their limits.

The next morning, I poke my head out in preparation for walking the two hundred feet to the hut and breakfast. I can just make out Henry's tent ten feet away, but nothing else. People at McMurdo would call this a full-on Condition One; in the field it's simply a day to spend in the hut. Getting there, however, isn't that simple. The first task is to reach Henry's tent next door, which I do by keeping my back to the wind and shuffling sideways, thus keeping my tent in view until I reach his. I repeat the process to the next tent. And then—then I have to make a decision, since I can't see anything in front of me. But I know which way the wind is blowing, and that there are piles of equipment nearby, so I shuffle forward, keeping that last tent in view—and just before it disappears, I make out some dark shapes a few paces away.

It turns out I'm face to face with a rock wall. I believe that if I turn left I should encounter two other tents, then the hut, so I grope my way cautiously forward. For a few seconds nothing is visible, not even my own feet. I don't stop, fearing to lose my trajectory, and to both my amazement and relief I end up at the hut itself. The two tents, though only a few feet away, are lost in the whiteout. I had the right general idea, but hadn't made a careful enough mental map of the site the day before. I'm lucky.

Inside I find Henry and Sarah, one of the grad students, Tina

Calvin, and Rich Esser, the camp technician. Rich, who also happens to have a master's degree in geology, is the person who determined the true age of Mt. Erebus by identifying excess argon trapped in rock samples. The anemometer has frozen, so Rich goes out through the double freezer doors, clambers up the drift that leads to the roof, and frees it temporarily. The wind is blowing at about 50 knots in minus twenty-nine degrees centigrade. I do the math on a scrap of paper. Call it a wind chill of −70°F.

After he returns and warms up, Rich suggests that he and I string a safety line out to the farthest tents, which sit on the other side of the rock wall I'd stumbled into. We go out and collect ice axes to string as pickets, stagger into the lab hut to coil a rope for feeding, then go back out into the storm. It only takes fifteen minutes to set the axes and string the 165-foot rope from tent to tent to wall, but we're pretty blasted when we return to the hut, and my left cheek is in the first stage of frostbite where my face mask had slipped.

When Phil stomps in a few minutes later, he calls Mac Ops to report that the phone repeater is out, one radio antennae is gone, and all that's left is the VHF (very high frequency) radio, which bounces its signal off the single stationary repeater that's still up. Tina's tent is down with wind-broken poles. Sarah goes to work making cinnamon rolls, knowing the value of comfort food, as the rest of the crew trickles in. By noon the winds are clocked at 77 mph (the first level of hurricane designation starts with winds of 70 mph), and bits of volcanic grit are pelting the double-paned windows. Storms such as this one, which is still climbing, are known to last three to five days.

During the afternoon the anemometer, though losing accuracy from the buildup of rime, shows the wind climbing past 85 mph. Henry's tent is now down, and at this point the wind has exceeded the structural limit of the mountaineering domes. Even the tents angled just right into the wind and with adequate snow walls will eventually fail as the accumulation of wind-driven spindrift between tent and fly, in combination with the buffeting, collapses the poles. It is now too dangerous for most of us to risk getting to and from the tents, so we'll sleep in the huts.

We stay up until one, until we're as sleepy as possible, then split into two groups, one for each of the two huts. Only experienced people with the strongest tents—Phil, Bill, and Jeff—will sleep out. With earplugs, I have my best sleep in weeks. Unbeknownst to us, the winds at Crater Hill above McMurdo have hit 107 mph. The town itself, somewhat protected, is under only a Condition Two, but everywhere else in the Ross Sea Area is experiencing a strong Condition One. Planes haven't flown since Wednesday, and researchers who had planned to be home by Christmas are starting to fret.

We sleep until after eight on Saturday morning. Three of the tents are now down, including Phil's, and a fourth is on the verge of collapse. Lava gravel the size of marbles blasts the side of the hut. We whittle away the hours by reading, playing cards, talking, taking notes. In midafternoon Bill and I grab a couple of ice axes and crab our way sideways over to the other hut, where the stove has gone out. It needs to be relit, the pretext for our excursion, but really we're just looking for a quiet place to talk, and we alternately fuss with stoking it and chatting. It's cold enough inside that even with glove liners on I have to warm my hands over the heat every few minutes in order to write.

Bill tells me that there are more than a hundred extinct volcanoes in the Antarctic, many of them under the ice or underwater. Some volcanoes in the Antarctic stand out clearly, appearing relatively young even at five million years old—like Mt. Discovery across McMurdo Sound. That's in comparison with the Cascades in North America, where after only a million years in a much wetter climate they're eroding into shapeless lumps. Other Antarctic volcanoes, however, such as Mt. Hartigan in Marie Byrd Land, are nothing but circular rims filled with ice and barely breaking the surface of the continental ice sheet, which is up to fourteen thousand feet deep in places.

Bill, who first came to the Antarctic in 1977 to work in Marie Byrd Land, says, "Volcanoes act like dipsticks," referring to their usefulness as a glaciological tool. "If the lava is pillow-like, then it erupted under the ice. If it was within six hundred or so feet of the surface, water would get into the vents and create steam explosions, so you'd have tuff, or smashed rocks. And then, if it erupted above the ice, you'd have just plain lava. You can date the volcanic material, thus tell the depth of the ice at a certain time."

At the end of that season, back in McMurdo, Bill was killing time before his flight home when the young Phil Kyle approached him and said he was looking for someone to accompany him up Erebus. Bill said he'd think about it, but then realized, "Here was a smoking one!"—in contrast to the extinct volcanoes he'd been studying. In those days Erebus was throwing thousands of lava bombs a year over the rim, and when he picked up his first one hot out of the lava lake, he was hooked. He's hardly missed a season on the mountain since then. When he returned for his second stint, the year they put in the Upper Hut, it felt like he was coming back to a summer home. In 1983 he met Nelia Dunbar on Erebus, a graduate student whom he later married, and who has since done work on melt inclusions in Erebus feldspar crystals and on volcanic ashes in the ice sheets in West and East Antarctica. This is the first year since they've been married that he's been on Erebus without her.

Like many volcanologists, Bill is never happier than when rocks are falling out the sky around him. The largest eruption he's witnessed on Erebus was the one in 1984, when bombs the size of small cars came thumping down all around Upper Hut—which was promptly abandoned. He describes how, when he put his ice axe into a hot bomb and then pulled it out, volcanic glass stretched from the molten center like taffy.

When I ask him about the crater itself, he replies that scale is the first problem in being able really to see it. It's not just the typical Antarctic lack of features, or huge size, but the fact that the landscape itself is so alien. "It's even more foreign up there than in the Dry Valleys." He pauses, searching for an analogy. "You can go to the Grand Canyon, and it's huge—but you grew up with a gully in your backyard, so you at least know what it is you're looking at. How many people grow up with a crater? There's no comparison, and the geology is moving, which is very apparent with the lava lake.

"And then there's direction, which is a problem I've noticed on other volcanoes. You wouldn't think it'd be a problem on a high point, but on a crater you just keep walking around and around in a circle. I must have walked around Erebus eight times before I could tell where I was on it. Plus, you're often in cloud." He lifts the lid on the oil stove to make sure the fuel is feeding in, then continues. "Here you're in a place where you have all the compass points right in front of you, and you think you've walked most of the way around—but you're only halfway. Or you think you're almost back to where you started and you're only a third of the way. There's such an excess of symmetry that you have a hard time turning that circle into a protractor and telling where you are.

"Sometimes when you're up on the rim, you think you see motion out of the corner of your eye, some small animal like you'd see on peaks at home. But you look and there's nothing there."

That's a story I've heard before down here, the mind expecting to see life, as if we were in a familiar place. Melissa has told me how, the first year she came down, she kept seeing mice in the buildings at McMurdo.

By Sunday morning the wind is slowly dying down, but still gusting strongly. At one point we look at the record of seismic and infrasound data from the crater for the last twenty-four hours, which shows there was a pretty big event in the volcano at 10:45 the previous night. It was completely obscured by the storm. In midafternoon the wind abates enough that Bill, Sarah, and I decide to wander out to Helicopter Cave, a short walk from the hut. We grab ice axes and head out over the frozen lava and wind-packed snow.

On the way we pass a dramatically smashed helicopter made famous by its passenger, the writer Charles Neider. The "crash" itself occurred when the helicopter landed unevenly, damaging the under-carriage; most of the destruction now visible is from storms over the years and scavenging. Although Neider claimed that he and the pilot were in danger of starving to death, in fact the aircraft was bearing an entire crate of citrus fruit. Five years later Phil was still salvaging edible oranges from the wreckage. Neider, of course, was merely trying to increase the heroic mythology of the mountain as an unpredictable and dangerous place, a literary strategy of which I am acutely aware as I take my notes. People who have worked in the Antarctic for a long time, however, take a dim view of such exaggeration; the reality is quite vivid enough.

Neider also claimed that they could easily have frozen to death. Although there was no hut nearby at the time, all he and the pilot had to do was descend a short ways into one of the ice caves—multiple entrances to which we find this afternoon within fifty feet of the incapacitated helicopter—and they would have been relatively warm. The lava beds here, which are only twenty-five to thirty thousand years old, are still warm enough to melt tunnels in the ice and maintain them at or near the freezing point. Indeed, it's so comfortable inside that when we enter we unzip most of our clothing. We then corkscrew on our backs down a short tunnel to the main room. Bill says that the cave has shrunk quite a bit in the last year; there's only one medium-size cavern left, a calm and subdued chapel made of white ice and blue light. The wind is inaudible, our voices too loud for the space. Looking up at the radiant blue ice is calming; I can feel my eyes relax. At the same time, I'm aware that in the far corner of the room there's a small gap that leads under the ice and into deeper caverns within the warm and gritty lava. "Monsters be there," I think to myself.

Clambering back out with the help of our axes, we reenter the wind and cold and proceed over to the larger Hut Cave, where we expect to find Henry playing guitar, recording the acoustics of the ice. Once we descend the fixed aluminum entry ladder and slither through another tunnel, we find blue roofs of smooth ice vaulting over huge lava boulders, a warren of rooms filled with ice crystals, ice flows and ripples, stalactites and pillars—everything you'd find in a limestone cave, only in a different palette. Several feet of snow has drifted onto the floor, and we probe our path cautiously with the axes. Huge hidden holes drop away to lower levels, and it would be easy to break a leg.

We climb, slide, and crawl on our hands and knees from one chamber to another. Snow stalactites sway eerily in eddies created as the wind sucks at the entrance outside, though once again the silence is broken only by the sound of our clothes rasping on ice and rock and our voices as we keep track of each other. Bill leads off down a passage several hundred yards long that brings us back to the entrance, where we puzzle over a set of footprints that came ten feet into the cave, then stopped . . . and no Henry giving us a concert. We shrug and return to the camp—with Sarah a few steps ahead, since she's anxious about the dinner she's left in the oven, a concern that I find absurdly domestic. When we arrive, we find Henry and the others, who had decided the cave was too risky to enter, a decision we understand given the inability to see a safe path inside.

What Sarah and a couple of the guys are dishing up is either a late Thanksgiving or early Christmas dinner: turkey with oyster stuffing, gravy and mashed potatoes (prepared using a partly full vodka bottle for a masher), cranberry sauce, yams, peas and onions in a cream sauce, and two bottles of white wine. It's a spectacular meal, very much in the English tradition of "When the going gets rough, the tough *eat*."

On Monday the wind continues to drop slowly but steadily, now down to 35 mph. This is the day we're supposed to be extracted, and the helos make an attempt in the morning but are thwarted by a continuing cloudbank stuck on the caldera and unpredictable wind gusts. Bill and Henry and I take a short hike out to the edge of the caldera, where, during a prolonged break in the clouds, we can see the open ocean. B-15, which contains enough water to supply both domestic and agricultural needs in the United States for four years—two years' worth of Mississippi River outflow—has been shoved sideways to the left and is now grounded on the sea bottom. The amount of wind energy it took to move something so massive is calculable, but hardly comprehensible.

In the early afternoon we receive a message from Helo Ops that there will be no more attempts to get aircraft up the mountain today. That frees us up to move away from the camp if the weather clears a bit more. By midafternoon the wind is below 25 mph, with visibility extending to more than a quarter mile. Bill and a couple of others go up on snowmobiles to a seismic site on the older and smaller crater to the side of the main one. He radios down to report that the cables tethering the wind generator mast have sawed through in the wind and the mast has toppled. It's too late to replace all the cables around the mountain this year, but the record storm has left the team no doubts that they will have to do so next year at the latest. When he returns with digital photos, Tim, the teacher, comments that "it looks like a tornado" hit there.

By 8 P.M. the air is dead calm and there's not a cloud in the sky, though the volcanic plume 1,500 feet above is blowing to the west. Bill decides that it's safe enough for Henry and me to accompany him, Sarah, and Rich to the summit. The storm has signaled the end of the field season on Mt. Erebus, and we can help them carry down some of the monitoring equipment from the rim. The covers of some of the snowmobiles have been torn to pieces in the wind, and the engines are packed with spindrift. Ice can easily get into the carburetors and fuel lines, so everything first has to be thoroughly cleaned, which takes an hour. Even so, one machine has obviously ingested some snow and will need constant manual attention to the primer pump and throttle before it runs smoothly.

The drive up from the hut to Nausea Knob (named for the effect the altitude has on many people who ascend from sea level too quickly) is fun but tricky, a winding course in between the snow-covered lava flows, up a steep hill topped by bare windblown gravel, then out onto a moderately angled slope of icy snow, where we're forced by rocks to stop. From here on up we'll be walking on a deep layer of mixed snow and gravel strewn with Erebus crystals, one of the most prized of Antarctic mementos.

Feldspar is common to volcanoes worldwide, but large anorthoclase crystals are found on only three in the world, Mts. Kenya and Kiliman-jaro in Africa and here. The African volcanoes are extinct, so the two-inch elongated minerals on Erebus are the only new feldspar crystals being created. Bill explained to Sarah and me one night in McMurdo over a glass of wine how they start out as small nuggets and add layers each time they circulate upward within the lava lake. Eventually a gas bubble in the lake will explode with enough force to throw out lava bombs that range in size from baseballs to Dodge vans. The lava bombs are hot, hollow, and soft, squashing as they land. Take an ice axe to a cold one, and the black glass crumbles. The bombs weather quickly in the harsh Antarctic weather, leaving the ground strewn with the rough rhomboidal crystals.

We shoulder our packs and start up the last six hundred feet, planting our feet carefully in the steep, loose volcanic rubble. Old bombs of all sizes surround us, and we rest every few steps staring at the dark gray crystals underfoot. At ten o'clock that night we're standing on the rim, the sun at our backs. Enormous clouds of steam rise from the lava lake six hundred feet below us, a red open wound roughly thirty feet in diameter partly covered by a thin and cracked scab of cooler rock. Across from us the wall of the crater glows an unexpectedly vivid yellow, the rocks coated with salts that have precipitated out of the rising billows of gas rich in sulfur and hydrochloric acid. This is the most color I've seen on rocks anywhere on the continent, and along with the circular dissonance of the crater, that super-symmetry that destroys scale, it disorients me so much that I have to take off my glacier glasses with their heavily tinted lenses to confirm what I am seeing.

I've stood before on active volcanoes in Hawaii and Mexico, but this is the most toxic and unearthly place I've ever been. Glass lenses on the cameras that are rigged on the crater's edge were replaced by plastic ones after the gasses corroded the original set, and the various metal fittings have darkened from the acids. The fumes aren't going to hurt us for the short time we're up here, but I wonder how Jessie's lungs are faring after several years of repeated exposure while monitoring the gases.

The steam turns to cloud in front of us, rising over our heads as a white and blue column that the wind blows fifty miles out over the frozen sea. At the bottom of the crater, a black mark on the side of the lava lake indicates a "splat" where new material has been thrown out, probably the event recorded two nights before. Bill and Rich work on the cameras to clear the lenses and cables of rime ice, while Bill urges the volcano to act up. Nothing would please him more than to have it toss a few lava bombs our way (Plate 27).

I spin slowly in a circle trying to take it all in, and Henry snaps dozens of digital pictures for posting on his Web site. Sarah stands by herself on the rim. Erebus is a place with which she has cultivated a deep personal relationship, a locus not of alienation but of memories layered year upon year. Steam coalesces into cloud around and between us, and I tilt my head as far back as I can to watch the plume build towering castles above us. From the dungeons of the ice caves to the ramparts of the sky within hours.

Bill and Rich finish cleaning the two video cameras mounted in their bomb-proof casings. Pointed at the lava lake and nearby steam and ash vents, they transmit images back to the hut and on to McMurdo, then out over the Web to the rest of the world. Once it's clear the cameras are back in working order, we traverse around the rim to Jessie's gas-sampling rig. Underfoot are hundreds of fragile "Pele hairs," or strands of fused ash that have fallen out of the plume. They're scattered on top of the snow, one or two per square yard, which means there was an eruptive event here within the last few hours. Pele is the Hawaiian goddess representing yet another volcano. A traditional belief has it that if you remove lava from a Hawaiian flow, misfortune will follow you until you return it to its proper place. I find myself considering that as I pick up an Erebus crystal. Into a pocket it goes.

The batteries, pumps, and sampling rack at the next knob along the rim are all fine, but Jessie's solar panel is nowhere to be found, just the ragged end of an electrical cord from which it sailed away. Last year it was the cord that was damaged, burned through by a bomb that landed on it. We pick up everything else and stuff it into packs, twenty-five- to thirty-pound loads for most of us, then hoof it back down to the snowmobiles. We'd like to stay longer, but we're tired and cold, ready for a night's sleep. Along the way we find a section of old wire, part of an immense figure-eight draped around both the active crater and a slumped section of the young cone, a pioneering attempt to measure electrical fluxes during eruptions. On a topo map in the hut, surveyed by a Kiwi crew on foot during 1981, the loop appears as an elegant piece of human geometry, outlining the natural terrain as if science were its own contour line.

We get back around midnight. Jeff, who has been waiting for us to come back with the snow machines, immediately sets off to install an infrasound rig. He'll be up all night, trying to get as many of his sites up and running before we're pulled out in the morning. Phil, before going to bed, brings me a shrunken orange from the Neider helicopter crash. Now, thirty years later, the fruit is no good to eat, but it's proof of what was in the cargo.

In the morning the helos are able to get in, and over the next thirty-six hours we're extracted from the camp piece by piece, person by person. Back at McMurdo we eat prodigiously, scratch at our frost-damaged, peeling skin, sleep profoundly, and marvel at the fact that a large Christmas tree has been installed and decorated in the galley during our absence.

12 FROM ART TO CHART

THE DAY AFTER CHRISTMAS finds me searching through the Crary shelves for a book edited by Phil Kyle on the continent's volcanoes. When I find it, it opens to a lithograph based on the J. E. Davis painting of the *Erebus* and *Terror* at anchor in McMurdo Sound, the mountain rising steeply behind them—the signature image accompanying Phil's introduction. A few essays in, however, I stumble across a much more recent picture, a Landsat image made in late January 1985. Within the mass of cobalt and indigo blues, the circular shape of the volcano and its ancient caldera is clearly visible. At the top is Fang Ridge and the saddle, the gully we rode up to the hut, and Nausea Knob. To the right a great arc of blue-gray cloud bands envelops one side of the mountain, a large cyclonic storm like the one we'd just sat through. In the center is an orange-red dot—the lava lake, a mysterious anomaly in coldest, deepest Antarctica (Plate 28).

Erebus is one of the larger volcanic masses in the world, rising to its height of 12,444 feet straight out of the ocean. To have a view that captures its enormity—a view 9.3 miles across—and that puts the peak into battle with an immense storm under such dramatic lighting is utterly romantic. I sit stunned by it, then take it over to show Kelly Brunt, who is as wowed as I. Even so, as magnificent an example of high-tech scientific imaging as it is, I realize it's just as foreshortened a view as the one Davis made in 1841.

To make his striking picture, Davis collapsed the distance-to-height ratio of the view to put the ships close to Erebus and increase the vertical relief of the mountain. In a photograph of the same scene, by contrast, the mountain would appear smaller to the viewer than it does in "real life"—not because our eyes see differently than a camera lens, but because our minds do. The mind takes in information gathered by the eye in a series of saccades that not only range across the scene but also, in longer glances, go deeply into it. When looking at a photograph, the eye is limited to traversing a flat, two-dimensional picture plane. Everything is in a fixed relationship of relative size; that is, the scale is fixed. Even in a photo made with a telephoto lens, you're limited to a flat scan of the image. Look at the world, though, and your mind moves through multiple planes, emphasizing some shapes while ignoring others. The scale of things changes depending on the importance accorded them by our mind.

In a normal snapshot of Erebus—neither a wide-angle nor a telescopic view—things are neither reduced nor enlarged optically. Erebus is tiny. Examine the nineteenth-century picture, however, and you see as the mind sees: the mountain is large because it is the most significant vertical landmark in view. Although you are still limited to a two-dimensional experience, the artist has reproportioned the scale to account for the dynamic relationship between the viewer and the world. Both camera and lithograph have it "right," but they are different truths.

And the Landsat image? In late January, when the image was made, the sun is still fully up. There is no deep blue twilight; what we should be seeing is mostly whites. As for the lava lake, it isn't a red-hot glowing coal visible from 438 miles above the earth. All you'd see from the satellite, even with a powerful telescope, would be steam rising from the crater. Instead, the Landsat image gives us pixels of temperature, thermal imaging that resolves details down to only 100 square feet (30 square meters) in the infrared part of the electromagnetic spectrum, which the human eye cannot capture. The thermal scan is converted into digital information and transmitted by radio down to earth, where computer programs smooth out random noise. The colors are selected by computer and enhanced for your viewing pleasure. And yet, undeniably, that's the mountain and the storm and the lava; if I had to pick the most "real" image to represent my experience on the mountain, this would be it.

What "is" is not exactly what we see, while what we see is not exactly what we represent, and neither of these two images, one a piece of "representational art" and the other a "scientific graphic," is necessarily more accurate or complete a view than the other. Aesthetic choices have been made in both cases; indeed, they are as rampant in scientific imagery as in fine art. When David Paige made his mock-up of *Pathfinder* on Mars, he used photos he had taken in the Dry Valleys; these he enlarged and tinted a red he thought looked "realistic," then mounted them on boards to make his ten-by-forty-foot panorama. He placed a model of the lander in front of it, *et voilà:* a spacecraft on Mars. The photos appeared in national newsmagazines.

The point in dissecting such images is not to expose a falsehood, but merely to point out that all images are constructed internally by our cognition as much as externally by technology. The scientific and journalistic pictures of the Antarctic and Mars may or may not have higher degrees of veracity than paintings and photographs representing the same landscapes. And in fact, the pointillist technique of assembling maps from satellite data is often enhanced at NASA and the USGS by artists, who deploy airbrushes and erasers to massage the final printed appearance closer to the reality we perceive through telescopes and cameras. This makes the maps more useful to astronauts, as well as more meaningful to the buying public. (NASA computer artists, in fact, go so far as to completely colorize images from the Hubble Space Telescope as if the human eye could see in the infrared and ultraviolet. Their intent is not to provide more information that is scientifically useful, but to pump up public support for NASA funding. Now, objects that appear only as fuzzy gray patches of dust in the visible spectrum through even the largest instruments glow incandescently in the galactic dark.)

The mapping of the Antarctic became an ever greater priority for the scientific and military communities after the International Geophysical Year. Scientists wanted to complete their task of measuring the earth, and American strategists wanted to own the high ground of the southern polar region, which, unlike its northern counterpart, was not adjacent to the USSR. Three factors frustrated everyone: the size of the continent, the bad weather, and the fact that its icy surface was constantly on the move, in some places pushing forward only inches a year, but in others traveling thousands of feet.

Human beings, even while standing at the highest point on Earth, cannot capture within their vision more than about 15,000 square miles of the planet's 197-million-square-mile surface. Nevertheless, they have thought of the earth as a globe since at least the time of the Greeks. When Ptolemy envisioned a graticule of 360 lines of longitude stretching from pole to pole and two sets of 180 lines of latitude running parallel with the equator, he provided a bounded framework within which an infinite number of points could be plotted. It was a geometry that compelled the user to imagine the earth from above, and a scope of vision that, as the cartographic historian and theorist Denis Cosgrove points out, would be achieved in reality only with the Apollo space missions. Cosgrove has written a fine book that traces the development through maps of the "Apollonian gaze," that tendency of humans to seek a high enough vantage point—either in imagination or reality—that will provide a single point of view, or perspective, allowing all the diverse facts of natural history to be unified. During the eighteenth and nineteenth centuries in particular, every explorer seemed to be climbing a ladder of visualization: Humboldt and Bonpland on the slopes of the Andes, Frémont and Preuss in the peaks enclosing the Great Basin, Clarence King and Timothy O'Sullivan along the fortieth parallel of the American West.

The Space Age was an extension of that ever-accelerating process. It took millennia to map most of the earth; even the Great Basin required two centuries to become fixed more or less accurately on paper. It took only from 1966 through 1977 for five Lunar Orbiters to circle the moon and send back 1,950 photographs, covering a body in space the size of North and South America combined. Within a single year, the Apollo astronauts had maps to carry with them for their first walk on the moon. Percival Lowell labored over the eyepiece of his telescope in Flagstaff, Arizona, from 1894 through 1916 to make his maps of Mars. In late 1972, within a single month, USGS cartographers in Flagstaff produced the first comprehensive map of an entire extraterrestrial planet, using 7,000 television images sent back the preceding year by the orbiter *Mariner 9*.

It is a testament to the difficulties presented by the Antarctic environment that Mars was mapped in 1972, but as late as 1997 Antarctica had yet to be thoroughly charted. Indeed, it would take the NSF, USGS, NASA, and the Canadian Space Agency working together over several decades to provide both the spatial and temporal technology to map the ice, a job that would not be completed until the advent of satellite-borne technology that had been honed in space, as well as on other parts of the earth.

Within days of the Russians launching *Sputnik I* in 1957, American scientists realized that they could determine its orbit by observing the Doppler shift in the frequency of its radio signals—how the wavelengths shortened as it approached and lengthened as it drew farther away. By the early 1960s, they were using satellites of their own to do the reverse, to act as navigational points from which to triangulate the shape of the earth where no such points were otherwise available—that is, out of sight of land and over the vast isotropy of the oceans, which covered the majority of the planet. As during the days of the search for the Northwest Passage, the driving force to do so was still strategic geodesy—in this case, to accurately target the intercontinental ballistic missiles of the Cold War. The eventual outcome within the Department of Defense was the GPS system, its 24 satellites costing $12 billion from the launching of the first one in 1978 through the last in 1993.

It was also during the 1960s that scientists realized they could listen to satellite signals with more than one antennae at a time and, using atomic clocks, record the tiny differences in time it took to receive them. If you repeated those measurements periodically with stations placed around the world—an idea of which Humboldt would have approved—you could measure movements in the earth's crust. During the next decade they began to bounce laser signals off satellites, an even more precise way to measure time and distance. By the end of the 1970s they were able to make geodesic measurements so accurate that they could pinpoint continental drift, which turned out to be a surprisingly fast few centimeters a year. The earth was no longer a static entity, but a body with a continuous circulatory system that could be monitored.

The first Landsat satellite was put up by NASA in 1972. Taking photos of Earth from space before then had been the sole province of the military, but as astronauts began to take more and more images, it became evident that the extent of everything from mineral resources to crop diseases to earthquake faults could be deciphered from these small-scale virtual maps. NASA was authorized to start a civilian program, and the results were revolutionary. Within two years 80 percent of the planet's landmass was covered and maps worldwide were being revised—everywhere but in the Antarctic.

The problem in Antarctica was cloud cover, which prevented conventional optical sensors from seeing all of the continent at the same time—essential for accurate mapping of a surface that constantly moves. Without reliable maps, moreover, it was impossible to tell if the ice was growing or shrinking, an issue that by the early 1970s was of major concern as the extent of global warming became known. Nearly 70 percent of all the freshwater on Earth is locked up on the continent. A collapse of the West Antarctic ice sheet would raise sea levels about twenty feet, putting major coastal metropolises such as New York and Tokyo underwater. The question of whether the West Antarctic ice sheet is stable or not remains open to question, although the East sheet seems secure. But the dynamics continue to be unclear, and the suddenly accelerating breakup of the Larsen Ice Shelf on the Antarctic Peninsula is a reminder that such events have occurred in the past:

14,200 years ago a partial collapse of Antarctic ice shelves caused sea levels to rise seventy feet.

The solution for mapping Antarctica was finally provided by Radarsat, a Canadian satellite using "synthetic aperture radar," which was launched by NASA in 1995. Normally used to collect data from the northern polar regions, its instruments can record the surface of the ice regardless of weather conditions. In 1997 it was rotated in order to take 5,500 images of the Antarctic during thirty-seven hours over an eighteen-day period. Assembling the data took two years, but in 1999 the first accurate, detailed map of the entire continent was finally published. In 2001 the radar imaging of the ice was done again at an even more detailed level, and the motion rates of individual ice streams, which carry 90 percent of the continent's ice oceanward, became known.

As always, the amassing of such large quantities of new data (a typical USGS topo map alone contains roughly 100 million bits of data) required new technologies to process the results. During the 1980s the USGS began to scan its maps and digitize the information. Until that time, maps had always been pictures that contained data, whether they were the encyclopedic T-O charts of the Middle Ages or the topographic series carried by backpackers. Now the two functions were separated, which meant the data were freed for manipulation. Using Geographical Information System (GIS) software, you could now plot one map atop another to measure changes. Applying GIS to Antarctic mapping data meant that you could now track annual changes in the flow of ice, which turned out to be an incredibly complicated affair. The Antarctic is inscribed with a dense network of interrelated ice streams that react to surface temperatures and other weather variables much more quickly than thought before, increasing the chances that global warming could trigger a collapse of the ice shelves.

A map of Taylor Valley made by the USGS in 2001 brought home to me just how good the agency had gotten at turning digital data into maps. At a casual glance, satellite image maps of the Dry Valleys look almost like color aerial photos taken straight down from a jetliner. In fact they are mosaics of data sets collected by various satellites at different times; the "Matterhorn" sheet for Taylor Valley, for instance, which covers the hike Joe and I took from Lake Bonney to Lake Hoare, used one data set from the French SPOT satellite collected in 1987 and a second one from the American Landsat in 1993. Electromagnetic radiation recorded in visible, near-infrared, and infrared bands of the spectrum are recorded, collated, and tones visible to the naked eye assigned to digital values. The tones are balanced, filtered, resampled, balanced again, and corrected to ground truth.

The primary image is printed on the sheet in color. In the righthand margin keys indicate what satellite took images when and how low the sun was at the time. An oblique black-and-white aerial photo is also printed so you can mentally correlate the views into three dimensions. On the Taylor Valley sheet I can see individual sand dunes that Joe and I walked around—but this isn't a photograph. It's a constructed picture.

Posted on a hallway in Crary Lab late this January is a large printout made by a USGS representative that portrays the LIDAR (Light Detection and Ranging, or laser altimeter) mapping flights now being made through the Dry Valleys. A series of colored pathways, it bears a distinct resemblance to a new bathymetric chart of Pine Island Bay in the Amundsen Sea (near the base of the Antarctic Peninsula), produced by a scientist at the University of Maine who has been experimenting with how to best present his data.

Measurements made by satellites hundreds of miles up, if they are to have geodesic veracity, must be correlated with very precise control points on the ground. Twin Otter aircraft flown by the USGS have been passing over the Dry Valleys this month, bouncing foot-long green laser pulses off the ground. By correlating the bounce-back time to the position of the airplane using GPS measurements, cartographers will obtain a precise baseline—the "ground truth"—from which to calibrate the altitude of the satellite, thus allowing them over time to measure how much ice is melting, evaporating, or otherwise being abducted by global warming and other factors.

Visually, however, the bathymetry and the LIDAR paths resemble Jackson Pollack more than the isotherms drawn by Humboldt or the contour lines on standard topographic quadrangles. These particular maps, instead of illustrating the shape of the land, display data. They have become as abstracted and difficult for a layperson to read as a piece of contemporary art—versus most Antarctic art, which holds no interest for the art critic but is easily accessed by the public. The two systems of representation have, in a sense, crossed paths and switched positions.

The NSF has been sending creative writers and artists to the ice since the poet Donald Finkel went in 1968, and its Antarctic Visiting Artists and Writers program has been in operation since the late 1980s. New Zealand has had Antarctic Arts Fellows since 1997, and the British Antarctic Survey began formally sponsoring artists during the 2001–2002 season; both programs are modeled somewhat after the American one. The Australian Antarctic Division runs what they label a "humanities" program, a rubric that allows them to be more candid than the other countries about including both artists and journalists.

The imagemakers who have most often been chosen by national programs to visit the ice are photographers, who are sent as both artists and journalists to create work for exhibition and to illustrate books and articles. Photography is often touted as being the predominant Antarctic art form, both because of timing—photography arose as the dominant visual medium during the Heroic Age of Antarctic exploration—and because of its acceptance by the public as the best way to represent exotic environments. As stated bluntly to me by a New Zealand appointee to their program's governing board, the purpose is to ensure continued public support for government funding of the science programs. As a result, the emphasis placed on scenic value, charismatic wildlife, and dramatic pictures of ice-encrusted scientists has been slow to change from the days of the IGY—but change it has.

American landscape photography in the mid–twentieth century was dominated by the model of Ansel Adams (1902–1984), whose dramatic pictures of mountains and unpeopled wilderness were popularized by the Sierra Club. This was an aesthetic rooted in the preceding century, when John Ruskin declared mountains in general and the Alps in particular to be the cathedrals in which the Sublime was to be worshiped, and the Romantic poets were declaiming the alpine peaks as sites where one's emotions ran almost to madness, so close was one to Nature. The pictorial apotheosis of this attitude was embodied by the Italian mountaineer and photographer Vittorio Sella (1859–1943), whose alpine views made with large-format equipment extended from the panoramic to the telephotographic, from the Alps to the Himalaya. The popularity of his work at the end of the nineteenth and beginning of the twentieth centuries declined precipitously just in time for Adams to come on the scene.

Eliot Porter (1901–1990), one of America's preeminent nature photographers, first trained as a biochemist and then, during the 1950s, pioneered the use of color film in picturing landscape, a radical departure from the reigning aesthetic of the time, which demanded that serious landscape work be done only in black and white. His images were also published frequently by the Sierra Club, and if the art world at first considered him somewhat suspicious because of his flagrant use of color, in the public eye he was a worthy inheritor from Ansel Adams of the photographer-as-supreme-conservationist mantle. It was therefore only logical that the United States Antarctic Program, which cared more about connecting with broader public sentiment than with art critics and curators, would want him in the Antarctic, and he went twice in 1975. He had been to Iceland three years previously, which prepared him to work with ice and the high-latitude light. Although Schulthess's *Antarctica* is one major inspiration to artists working on the ice, Porter's coffee-table photo essay book of the same title is also cited by artists as a decisive factor in their desire to work on the ice.

Following determinedly in the tradition of taking a large-format camera into the wilderness, Jody Forster (b. 1948) first went to the ice with his 8×10-inch camera in 1992, the only artist in the program to bring such a large camera onto the continent in contemporary times. Forster, formerly a high school wrestler, had put his physical strength to work previously as the photographer on a Himalayan climbing expedition, where he'd carried his fifty-five pounds of equipment up over

19,000 feet, making black-and-white views comparable to those by Sella. Although he admired Adams for his technique, he cites the painters Bierstadt, Moran, and Church as his real inspirations. Like Sella, Forster sometimes included the human presence on the ice, but he is known for capturing the utter stillness of a pristine wilderness, an attitude routine for American nature photographers such as Philip Hyde, who only reluctantly in the 1990s noted the diminishing availability of such unadulterated subject matter in North America. Forster's large prints of Antarctic ice- and landscapes manage to capture the iridescence of glacial ice, which speaks well of his technical abilities and patient familiarity with the subject, the twin hallmarks of large-format photographers in the wilderness (Plate 29).

Another American photographer, Neelon Crawford (b. 1946), son of the precisionist painter Ralston Crawford, went to the ice five times from 1989 through 1994; he worked from a standpoint that admitted human presence on the ice. Some of his most interesting images come from a visit when he wintered-over at McMurdo, in which artificial light provides the only illumination. A perfectionist who works with a 4 × 5 camera, he captured floodlit landscapes and town scenes in both color and black and white.

The American who has photographed most prolifically around the Antarctic is Stuart Klipper (b. 1941), having been there six times, starting, like Crawford, in 1989. The Minnesotan works with more portable cameras than Forster and Crawford and has voyaged twice aboard ships in the archipelago of the Antarctic Peninsula, as well working extensively on the continent. Many of his more than ten thousand images were taken with a Linhof Technorama panoramic camera, which places him squarely in the topographical tradition of exploration artists from previous centuries (Plates 3, 14, 20, and 21). The panoramic format imitates the incessant horizontal sweeping that the eye makes in the Antarctic as it seeks visual anchors in the void, a mimesis to which curators, critics, and the public have responded avidly. His Antarctic work has appeared in national advertising campaigns for corporations such as IBM and been featured in an exhibition at the Museum of Modern Art in New York.

Klipper has photographed in Greenland, Israel's Negev Desert, and many other large isotropic areas where he feels that he is standing on the border between elemental spaces—seeking the spiritual, if you will, in that liminal zone of cognition. Klipper posts the latitude and longitude of his home on his business card and e-mails, locating himself as literally and authoritatively in his landscape as did his predecessor Walker Evans, the American photographer whom he lists as an important forefather. But beyond the topographical tradition in which his work is situated, he is also insistent that he is a Kabbalistic-like interrogator of the immanent, the transcendent in nature. Light hovers somewhere over the oceanic horizon and illuminates an array of tabular icebergs as if they were temples cast adrift from a holy city. Sastrugi on the polar plateau become a kind of braille you read on your hands and knees as you crawl toward the infinite.

Anne Noble (b. 1949), who made her first visit to the ice in 2002, is a New Zealand photographer based at a university in Wellington who works across many genres within her medium. Sharing Klipper's investigative temperament, she tends to be more interested in formal inquiry through her art than in capturing decisive moments of beauty or action, and in addition to landscapes, she has published and exhibited work on nuns, her family members, and other subjects. While at Scott Base, the New Zealand station just on the other side of Ob Hill from McMurdo, she photographed in whiteouts and took pictures straight into white snow and white skies (Plate 30). She pushed the lack of definition in the landscape so far that, when she turned in her films for processing, the photo lab called her up to alert her that there was "nothing" on the film. That's exactly right, as what she was investigating was the cognitive ambivalence of isotropy.

The relationship of members of the former British Empire with the ice is very different from that of Americans. Whereas Americans tend to display a touristic fascination with the continent, Australians and particularly New Zealanders have a much more intimate view of the place. Britain's relationship to the ice goes back to Cook, of course, and in 1923 it claimed the Ross Dependency—encompassing the Ross Ice Shelf and Dry Valleys—as its territory; this it put in the care of New Zealand, which established its first base, on Ross Island, in 1957. Scott Base was the jumping-off point for the British Commonwealth Trans-Antarctic Expedition during the IGY. The co-leader with Sir Vivian Fuchs of that expedition was Sir Edmund Hillary, who together with Sherpa Tenzing Norgay had been the first to climb Everest a mere four years earlier, in the process becoming the most celebrated Kiwi of the twentieth century. Not only was New Zealand given a serious charge in overlooking the southernmost portion of the British Empire, but its favorite son also triumphantly helped to complete Shackleton's dream of crossing the ice, the last great transcontinental expedition of the twentieth century. Images of Antarctica have ever since been common in New Zealand, and most especially in Christchurch, which for years has been the staging area for everyone flying into the Ross Sea region.

The major role that such a small country has played on the ice—New Zealand has a population of less than 4 million, compared with 293 million in the United States—is a cause of national pride, and helps explain why Antarctic art is routinely exhibited in its major museums. There are other reasons, too, for the Antarctic is woven into the Kiwi psyche at several levels. For one thing, as Felicity Milburn, a curator in Christchurch, pointed out to me, no part of New Zealand is very far from the ocean or the mountains. A necessarily close and self-reliant relationship with the land is therefore foundational to the country's artistic heritage. Landscape, moreover, is a three-dimensional affair that includes weather, as was drummed into Hodges by his crewmates when surveying the Pacific, and the cyclonic storms generated by the Antarctic directly shape the weather of New Zealand. In addition, Antarctic support businesses are a small but important part of the economy (as are the ice people who every year settle in New Zealand for several months as they reintegrate into the outside world). Finally, there was the Air New Zealand crash on Erebus, which many people still annually commemorate.

Precisely because New Zealand has such close ties to the ice, its Antarctic art has expanded beyond the topographical tradition. Milburn also pointed out that the Kiwi arts program tends to pick important artists and send them to the ice without an agenda, letting them figure out how to respond to the place in their own way. That's in contrast to the American program, which has tended to select artists based less on their achievements in the art world and more on how their work fits the science community's vision of what Antarctic art should look like; as a result, the American emphasis is for the most part on representational imagery. Because, in a sense, New Zealanders already know what the ice looks like, they've moved on to investigating what it means. Many Americans, however, still think polar bears live there, making the need for realism as the governing aesthetic much stronger.

The difference between American artists and those from other countries becomes even more pronounced in the traditional media of oil and watercolors, which are more overtly subjective than photography. American painters who have visited the ice include Daniel Lang, Alan Campbell, and Peter Nisbet. Lang's landscape work from the Antarctic could be labeled as romantic, yet it is more topographically rooted than not (Plate 31). Alan Campbell has worked with several scientific organizations in places as various as the Costa Rican rainforest, the Galápagos Islands, and Antarctica. Pellucid moments of great clarity characterize his style, one well suited to long vistas in the Dry Valleys or across ocean waters to icebergs. His paintings often include notes about place and context written on the border, a practice familiar to Cook, Humboldt, and Wilson (Plate 40; see also Plate 5).

Peter Nisbet, a Santa Fe painter whose role model is Turner, specializes in views of the desert Southwest, and in particular the Grand Canyon. He accompanied Forster in 1995, and they worked together on a ridge overlooking the Airdevronsix ("VXE-6") Icefalls, which they dubbed "Artists' Point" in homage to the Yellowstone pictures of Moran and Jackson (Plates 32 and 33, respectively). They also spent three weeks in a portable hut by the Barne Glacier, working mostly from ten in the evening until five in the morning when the sun is lowest. At the same time and only fifteen miles away, the painter Lucia deLeiris and the writer Sara Wheeler were working, also sharing a hut on the sea ice. Although Lang's and Nisbet's brushwork is liberated enough at times to be called expressionistic, and the watercolors of Campbell and deLeiris are relatively free on the paper, all of their Antarctic landscape work remains strongly anchored within a representational tradition.

The painter David Rosenthal, an Alaskan who worked for several seasons in the Antarctic as a field assistant, later returned as a participant in the NSF program. As a result, he has been able to view more of the continent and during different times of the year than any other artist who has represented it. His technique is competent and self-assured, capturing immensely deep fields of vision and the intense colors of ice under varied lighting conditions. When I give slide shows about the ice, I often use a mix of photographs and paintings, including oils by Rosenthal more than anyone else's. Not only are his paintings topographically accurate, but because my projected slides reduce the surface quality and his brushwork, people slip easily between the photographs and Rosenthal's work—which, indeed, they at first have trouble telling *isn't* photography. But once again, the painter can do what the photographer cannot. Photographs transmit more visual data than paintings, more exacting details; but paintings can select from among those details and subtly alter the relationship of background to foreground, thus reframing the view, all of which places us firmly in the dynamic relationship of eye vis-à-vis landscape (Plates 4, 22, and 41).

By contrast, consider the work of two Australian painters, Sidney Nolan (1917–1992) and Nel Isabel Law (1914–1990). Nolan, perhaps the most acclaimed Australian painter of the mid–twentieth century, had painted among other subjects aerial views of the deserts and mountains of Central Australia for decades when he was invited by the U.S. Navy to visit the ice in 1964. He stayed in McMurdo, flew through the Transantarctics, and subsequently produced thirty paintings. The landscapes are vivid and express the deep unease he experienced while there.

Nel Law was married to the prominent Antarctic physicist Phillip Law, who directed the Australian Antarctic Division for nineteen years, and accompanied him on board the *Magga Dan* in 1960–1961. She was the first Australian woman, and the first woman artist, to set foot on the continent. Her work progressed from a moderately expressionistic representation of landscape to much more abstract works, even when dealing with that perpetually cute subject, penguins (Plate 34). Her choice to geometricize the Antarctic icescape is akin to that of other landscape painters in other places, from Cézanne to Georgia O'Keeffe.

The London painter David Smith (1920–1998) first went to the ice aboard the RRS *Bransfield* with the British Antarctic Survey in 1975–1976. It was so cold he was forced to thin his oil paints with duty-free gin and shove the resulting sludge around with a palette knife. He returned to the Antarctic Peninsula in 1979, this time sticking to watercolors. As a result, he was able to complete more than five hundred works. His work was used by the physicist G. E. Fogg in a history of Antarctic science, a book that uses historical images as well as Smith's paintings to augment the narration. Smith's work can run from the serenely surreal to sketches that approach what Turner (who he speculates would have "reveled" in the violent weather) might have done. His watercolor *Low Sun and Icebergs*, which faces into a setting sun, uses the sea ice and bergs as if they were prisms reflecting the artmaking process itself. Nolan, Law, and Smith, more overtly expressionistic in technique than the American participants, display how cognition engages Antarctic spaces, making the perceptual, intellectual, and emotional struggle to organize the sea, land, and ice into apprehensible scenes visible to the viewer.

Among those artists who have been sent to the ice by New Zealand is Margaret Eliot (b. 1952), a Wellington painter (who also earned a degree in science) who first visited in 1999 and returned in 2001. Her earlier landscapes from alpine and coastal New Zealand, which often counterposed human structures to their severe surroundings, utilized a somber palette akin to that of Caspar David Friedrich, though her brushwork was much more palpable. She often worked in a panoramic format, and paid direct homage to her predecessors by labeling her landscape sketches "coastal profiles." The brooding romanticism of her work is well suited to portraying the collisions of ice and land surrounding Ross Island. Using successive applications of paint and adding actual soils to her pigments, she evokes the dark volcanic earth in contrast with steep glacial faces, the rucked-up pressure ridges of sea ice, and the fractal layering of both ice- and landforms (Plate 35). As with most painters on the ice, she uses notebooks for sketching and recording colors, then works up paintings afterward, a method she compares to that of scientists collecting information in the field which is later analyzed in the lab. As in the case of Nel Law, her paintings represent not so much specific places as parallel entities, as her use of abstracted titles, such as *Erosion I* and *Creeping Ice,* makes clear.

Only a few sculptors have been sent to the ice, among them Gabriel Warren, who lives in Rhode Island but summers in Nova Scotia, and Virginia King (b. 1946), who resides in Auckland. Warren works very slowly, but has produced pieces inspired specifically by his 2000 visit. His earlier work, based on his imaginative musings about the ice sheets of Greenland and the Antarctic, juxtaposes sheet metals such as stainless steel with weathering Cor-Ten steel to echo the way ice and rock meet beneath the ice. Warren cites Humboldt and Agassiz among the scientists who have inspired him, although the sculptural vocabulary of his work is clearly mid-twentieth-century modernist. King, who also visited in 2000, based her sculptures on electron micrographs of diatoms (Plate 11). Working on the ice at the same time was the Kiwi composer Chris Cree Brown, who composed a score to accompany King's 2001 sculpture and video installation *Antarctic Heart,* which showed in galleries throughout New Zealand.

Although artists are often paired to travel together for safety and logistical reasons, such as Nisbet and Forster, or Wheeler and deLeiris, formal collaborations are relatively rare. An eight-day trip made by Nigel Brown (b. 1949), Bill Manhire (b. 1946), and Chris Orsman

(b. 1955), all from New Zealand, in 1997 was part of one notable collaboration. Brown, a painter who uses a deliberately naive, almost cartoonish style to portray historical figures, adds words to his canvases to frame the scenes in an irony calculated to deflate historical pretension. *Warmth Is Something to Be Worked At* (Plate 36), for example, features flying penguins, a helicopter hovering over Blood Falls, various historical huts, Scott and dome tents, a mummified seal—all jumbled together under the phrase "I would have laid all this out carefully but these are fast shallow times." The poets Orsman and Manhire (the latter a poet laureate of his country who has edited an anthology of Antarctic poetry) wrote about both their direct experience and that of the Heroic Age explorers. The three produced a small book while there, *Homelight,* the first since *Aurora Australis* to be printed on the ice (later reprinted in New Zealand).

A decade earlier, the Australian artists John Caldwell (b. 1942), Bea Maddock (b. 1934), and Jan Senbergs (b. 1939) made a cruise to Heard Island and the continent, and the Australian government issued a fine small book, *Antarctic Journey,* to present their work to the public. Senbergs had produced a notable body of expressionist landscape paintings about mines in the outback, almost cubistic in their splaying out of architectural typology; in Antarctica, he used a similar technique to capture the industrial clutter of the Davis and Mawson stations. One painting, simply titled *Mawson,* uses a curved horizon line with a trio of nunataks peeking up out of the ice sheet to indicate both scale and the encroaching nature of the ice, against which the station seems to huddle.

Maddock, who injured her knee while disembarking from a landing craft and was severely constrained from moving about during the monthlong journey, nonetheless completed two panoramic works, one a series of paintings from Heard Island, and the other from Mawson, a set of forty etchings on twenty sheets. *We Live in the Meanings We Are Able to Discern* is the title of the former; at the bottom of the paintings run long chains of compounded phrases in which intelligible words are buried. Under them a poem asked, "What are we here for / Just for seeing?" Thus Maddock transforms the coastal profile into a sentence to be read, conflating text and map while commenting on the primacy and limitations of vision as our primary sensory mode.

Over and over again one finds a panoramic response to the Antarctic dilemma of attempting to construct meaning in an isotropic space with no vantage point, no "prospect" from which to leverage it. The panoramic view is closely related to the Apollonian gaze, both being attempts to distance oneself sufficiently to see a larger context. In the Antarctic, the coastal profiles of Wilson, the panoramas of Klipper, the aerial photography of Schulthess, and wide-angle IMAX films display a common heritage that extends back through the Leicester Square exhibitions to the ancient mural from Catal Hayuk. Perhaps this argues for a cognitive root in our neurophysiological response to large spaces, as if we are attempting to freeze a succession of saccades for a closer examination. In this sense, the panorama can be considered not only a map of the territory, but also a profile of the mind that surveys the terrain.

Of the hundred or so "official" artists who have visited the continent over time (included in the "Antarctic Image Chronology," www .antarctic-circle.org/fox.htm), fewer than thirty were there prior to the IGY in 1957, twenty-one visited between 1957 and 1985, and as of 2002 fifty-five more had come, following the launch of the national programs. Such a distribution might lead one to expect a growing emphasis on abstract painting, video, installations, and performance art. Although such is the case to some degree, the change, in the American program in particular, has been very slow. Stephen Pyne, in *The Ice,* posited that the ice is itself such a reductive and modernist environment that it doesn't inspire obvious types of expression, such as minimalism. In speaking to me about his own experience, he said: "I made a classic journey to the source, or the underworld—from the outside to the inside, except there was no revelation. The information got less and less, and it was like a modernist erasure. No modernist artists go to the

Antarctic because there's nothing for them to do there; nature's already done it." Pyne achieved an epiphany when he came across a nunatak projecting above the ice in North Victoria Land: "This rock had been carved into an abstract shape by nature, and this was a positive to balance the negative. I had to have an assertion to balance the erasure, so it was nature as modernist."

Yet when we see the work of contemporary artists working in the northern polar regions, we can gain an idea of what could be done in the southern. A ready example is the popular British sculptor Andy Goldsworthy, who constructs interventions in landscapes made from materials at hand—rocks, leaves, ice. The works are ephemeral, often fixed for exhibition only through film, so transitory that they are more performance piece than sculpture. Other artists who come to mind, and whose works in landscape are documented mostly through photography, are Richard Long and Hamish Fulton, who create traces on the land by walking through it, by repetitive movement and cartographic narratives, respectively. Both techniques are suited to working in isotropic environments, creating a cognitive frame not through reliance on trees and buildings, or even mountains and rocks, but by means of the marks and annotations that are left in the environments themselves.

In 1985, sponsored by the NSF, Chicago curator Rachel Weiss created an exhibition called *Imagining Antarctica* that featured contemporary artists' proposals and models for engaging the tabula rasa of the ice. Proposals included assembling frozen gothic architecture out of sea ice, placing time capsules in glaciers that would arrive at the edge of the continent centuries hence, designing electrical lightworks to shine during the long Antarctic night, and creating cryogenic capsules with DNA from every living creature in the Dry Valleys. The catalog presented these ideas alongside capsule summaries of, and images from, ongoing science projects. The list of ideas was extensive, highly conceptual, and mostly impossible logistically, but that was beside the point: evoking another tradition in art was what mattered. As Weiss put it, the exhibition demonstrated that Antarctic art could move "beyond simple description and declaration" and into an active engagement with the science and geopolitics of the continent.

None of these artists had visited Antarctica, a fact that did not stop an American photographer ten years later—who had likewise not been to the ice—from creating an exhibition and catalog using the same title as the Weiss show. Sandy Sorlien (b. 1954) applied to the NSF in 1995 to work in the visiting artists program but was not selected. She decided instead to photograph close-up landscape scenes in the Northeast, primarily in New Jersey during the winter, as analogs. By eliminating references to a horizon, buildings, people, and any foliage, she rejected the objective correlatives necessary for the viewer to establish scale; as a result, the photographs pass for ones of nunataks arising from the ice, or of glacier fronts. By coincidence, her geologist brother ended up aboard an icebreaker in 1996 doing subsurface mapping of the Ross Sea, and some of his e-mails are printed alongside the photographs in her catalog. This juxtaposition leads us to accept her photographs as documents of an exotic landscape, not as what they in fact are: close-ups of a four-foot-high rock on a New Jersey beach (Plate 37). By manipulating vantage point and scale, Sorlien balances an interrogation of how we cognitively frame geography with her desire to see the Antarctic, an emotional context seldom examined in a nonsentimental fashion.

John Jacobsen, a physicist who also studied painting and printmaking in graduate school, did neutrino research at Pole for three seasons. On his return from his most recent trip in 2000, he painted a typology of contemporary life and structures at the station on twelve expired credit cards. The scenes, based on photographs taken by the artist, are tiny, yet they manage to evoke Turner's spirit in their dense atmospherics. The fact that they are painted on a discarded, found material, a financial instrument that is essentially useless in the Antarctic, is a contemporary twist on the Romantics' rejection of materialism (Plate 38).

The Australian artist Stephen Eastaugh (b. 1960) has now been twice to the ice. Just as Nel Law's growing familiarity with the continent allowed her to abstract progressively from it, so Eastaugh has moved from cataloging the topology of structures around Australia's bases (Plate 39) to creating small totemic sculptures in a "garden" at the Davis Station. This progression from embedding images of the place within a gridlike pattern—a mapping format often used by artists traveling to unfamiliar places—to embedding art itself in the landscape creates a cognitive feedback loop: by placing cultural objects that enhance familiarity and memorialize our presence, we refashion the land physically into a landscape that we desire.

Even if tourism increases dramatically, the Antarctic of the foreseeable future will remain an exotic and unreachable destination for most people; as a result, said Dwight Fisher, the senior NSF representative at McMurdo, the need for representational images will remain high—much to the delight of calendar and coffee table book publishers. The art will not, however, simply confirm our larger historical notions about the continent; rather, it will expand them. Nor will it necessarily be executed from within the traditional frames of landscape painting and photography. In many ways an art that is performed or installed on the ice, but that disappears within a season or two, maintaining a trace in the culture only through printed or online images, better matches not only the brevity of our own presence there but also the increasingly temporal and abstracted state of cartographic representation. I suspect, moreover, that the ice people—those technicians and scientists who return to the continent year after year to perform their work—will have as much to do with shaping that part of its visual culture as the visiting artists and writers, if not more.

As the Antarctic becomes more familiar to us, more within our cognitive grasp, the art made about it, whether on the ice or elsewhere, will include more symbolic works. These will not displace the topographically based work, nor should they. Instead, as was the case with southern and northern European landscape art of the seventeenth century, the representational and symbolic art of the Antarctic—the cartographic and the theatrical, if you will—should and will overlap and inform each other. Pyne is certainly correct: the Antarctic appears to artists as an analog environment for modernism in the lexicon of art history, most of its landscape having been erased by ice. But what painter did not start with a blank white canvas? Meaning *will* be created there, if more slowly than elsewhere.

13 ON THE EDGE
OF TIME

IT'S DECEMBER 30TH and the pivot of the Antarctic summer is here. A Coast Guard icebreaker is within fifteen miles of the station, the diesel smoke from its stack a faint smudge on the horizon. The vessel heaves itself forward every few minutes up onto the ten-foot-thick sea ice, which is two years old and as hard as concrete, and just sits there until it falls through, creating a brashy trough. Then it backs up and launches itself forward again. Although the ship is within sight, it will take it another four or five days to reach us, and a second icebreaker has had to follow close behind to make a channel in the stubborn ice that can accommodate the annual supply ship.

It's ten o'clock at night and a couple dozen of us are sitting on a wooden deck behind McMurdo's oldest building, a former navy hut that's recently been remodeled into a community center. We're having a birthday party for a member of the Exploratorium media team from San Francisco, one of a number of small New Year's celebrations seeing out 2001. It's so warm and windless that I take off my shoes and socks and roll up the legs of my jeans. Karen Joyce comes out and announces that we've just broken the all-time temperature record for McMurdo: 51°F. It's warmer here than at home in California. Weather isn't climate, and the sea ice doesn't look like it's going to vanish anytime soon, so it's too early to say if the Antarctic overall is defrosting—but it's on everyone's minds.

Yesterday I went out to work with the crew pulling the ice flags from the Cape Royds route, a seasonal task as the ice softens in the summer heat and makes the going unsafe. Royds, where Shackleton built his hut in 1907, is twenty-two miles to the north and as far out as any snowmobile route is flagged from town; the bamboo poles with their cloth pennants had already been pulled from Royds as far as Cape Evans, so we were after just the remaining several hundred that lead back into McMurdo (the same part of the route I followed on the trip with Ted Dettmar during the storm more than two months ago). Before getting to work, we drove out to Royds for a look at the hut and penguin rookery. Of the three historic huts in the region from the Scott and Shackleton expeditions, this is the one people say they like the best, and I was curious to see why.

Eleven of us rode on six machines, all doubled up except the lead mountaineer, Ty Milford, who was in front. We buzzed out of town at 9:30, earplugs firmly in place. Halfway to the cape we stopped briefly, at Barne Crack, a large fissure in the sea ice that runs out from a prominent glacier flowing down Erebus and into the sea. Two dozen Weddell seals were lying peacefully on the ice, and the photographers among us got down on their stomachs to wriggle as close as possible without disturbing them.

The Barne Glacier flows out as a promontory almost two hundred feet high, very near where the artists Peter Nisbet and Jody Forster had their hut. Here, the glacial front is a wall of blue ice that, when the sea ice recedes, calves large icebergs. It is not a wall you walk up to casually. The crack, which I'd come out some weeks before with a crew to measure with augers, was then just an incipient seam. Now it's a two-foot-wide open gap. Ty and I sat with our feet dangling into it, and were quite startled when a bull seal poked his nose up fifteen feet away to breathe and take a look at us. Two Adélie penguins waddled over to see what we were doing, the larger one in front, the smaller and shier one looking over the shoulder of the first. This was as much wildlife as I'd seen in one place while here; it made me feel as if I were in a zoo, evidence of the deep conditioning we get through television. This was how the Antarctic was supposed to be, all towering cliffs of ice and charismatic animals.

We remounted our machines and drove carefully across the narrowest part of the crack, where it was less than a foot wide. The sea ice was still generally safe, the main danger being that we'd swamp ourselves in a melt pool. The ice around us veered from a hard blue surface to slush up to our knees, however, and it was easy to see why this would be one of the last snowmobile ventures out of town.

We reached the backside of Cape Royds a little after noon and took lunches up over the low ridge to the hut, a weathered structure sitting two hundred yards below the crest. In front of it was the world's southernmost penguin colony; usually comprising four thousand nesting pairs of Adélies, this year, because B-15 is keeping the ice edge out so far, the penguins haven't had ready access to their feeding grounds and the colony is down to only a thousand pairs. David Ainley, the lead researcher on the colony, is predicting that it will fail completely. Farther up the coast at Cape Crozier, the emperor penguins have failed to raise any chicks, likewise having to walk miles to their food source at the ice front instead of being able to jump into the water right at their nesting grounds. Despite the bleak outlook for penguins, however, I found the scenery at Royds breathtaking. Pony Pond in front of the hut had melted out, and Adélies were frolicking about on their bellies. On the far side of the pond other colony members sat on nests, while skuas skimmed overhead, looking for exposed eggs to snatch up.

The hut is a modest twenty-three by nineteen feet, prefabricated in England and insulated with cork and felt—essentially a single snug room, with sleeping quarters divided from the work area by canvas strung from the rafters. The fifteen officers and crew all shared the tidy space, unlike in Scott's huts where the two groups were divided. This was the headquarters for Shackleton's second trip to the ice, the one on which crew members were the first to reach the south magnetic pole and to ascend Mt. Erebus (the foothills of which begin to rise only a mile and a half to the east). They also pioneered the Beardmore Glacier route to the polar plateau and got to within ninety miles of Pole, the farthest southing yet done (Plate 40).

The hut, restored in 1960–1961 after having been filled with snow for years, sits in a protected bowl with a sunny exposure and within earshot of the penguin colony. It was about as close to an idyllic oasis as I'd seen in the Antarctic. The two arms of the cape embrace you and frame panoramic vistas, while securely at your backside sits the peacefully steaming volcano. This landscape is therefore not isotropic at all because your field of view, hence sense of space, is comfortably framed.

We began our return trip at 2:30, heading south to the Barne Crack, then veering left and up close to the glacier, following its entire face back to Cape Evans—an exhilarating ride as we skimmed along within yards of the vertical blue wall. I rode solo at the rear and stood while driving, pausing every few minutes to take it all in, then racing forward to catch up with the group. At the southern edge nearest the Cape Evans hut a narrow waterfall almost a hundred feet high plunged off the lip of the glacier and disappeared under the sea ice in the transition zone, far surpassing the glacial outflows I'd seen in the Dry Valleys three weeks previously. "How often in the Antarctic do you see a water-fall?" asked Ty, pleased to surprise us with such a wonder.

A little farther, just before Scott's hut, we parked the machines and carefully probed a route through the transition ice onto shore, flagging our steps across the tidal cracks as we went and sometimes sinking in softening snow up to our hips. As we pulled out our feet, seawater sloshed beneath us. Ty led us up and over a slope to a small lake, a body of freshwater completely unfrozen for the first time in living memory, in which several blissful skuas were paddling about. If ever you wanted evidence of how warm it is in the Ross Sea region this year, this was it. The outflow of the lake was so vigorous that it resembled a trout stream in the Sierra.

Back on the snowmobiles, it was time to go to work. With teams leapfrogging along the route, each driver would pull up to a flag just slowly enough that the passenger could yank it out and toss it into the sled they were towing. I dawdled behind, rounding up stragglers, sawing off the poles that refused to be pulled, and otherwise helping out as needed. Apart from keeping an eye on the tail end of the operation, I was left to my own devices, and I couldn't help but compare this trip in from Cape Evans with that first trip in the Herbie. Instead of being eradicated by a whiteout, my view extended clear across the sound. The first icebreaker was visible far out to my right, smoke from its stack drifting lazily toward the Royal Society Range. A bank of fog from open water far to the north slowly worked its way along the base of the mountains, a bright white line separating the white sound from the white peaks. Every now and then I'd let myself fall back a half mile or so, shut off the engine, take out the earplugs, and sit—listening to absolutely nothing.

I was then, as I am this evening sitting on the deck, acutely conscious that I have only a few weeks left on the ice. The view across the sound tonight is only more staggering in my gaze, now that I've been here a while and had a few chances to cross that body of ice and water and construct an accurate mental map of its scale.

The turning of the year means that everyone is beginning to think about redeployment, or "going back to the real world," a phrase first heard during the week following the party and uttered in a tone of weary dismissal. It is, after all, difficult to decide which is more real: a consensual condition created by the majority of the world's population operating within a network of intersecting media, or the overwhelming in-your-face nature of Antarctica.

The first week of January also means that it's time for MAAG—the McMurdo Alternative Art Gallery exhibition. This year Stacey is running the show, and at eight o'clock on that Saturday evening she appears, dressed in a long evening gown and orange wig, outside the door of her daytime domain, the mechanical shop (or MEC), and, raising her arms above her head, leads a crowd of several hundred people into the partly finished Science Support Center next door, the newest building at McMurdo. We pack into the space, with its raw concrete floor and exposed steel beams. Stacey stands in front and invokes the spirit of Rube Goldberg, the mid-twentieth-century artist and spirit incarnate for the station. Goldberg was known for collecting bits and pieces of life's daily machinery and wiring them together in what seemed to be a haphazard fashion, but that nonetheless was able to produce a long series of connected events from ringing bells to flashing lights. That's McMurdo.

The lights go out and we hear the sound of a large metal ball rolling through sheet-metal ducts above our heads. The ball passes through resonating boxes that amplify the sound, then into a giant funnel where it dopplers down into a metal trash can with a tremendous bang! The lights come back up and Stacey leads us back to the MEC, where everyone sardines inside. Waiters circulate with trays of sushi held above their heads, and people on a railed balcony pelt those below with a giant smoke-ring cannon—even yards away you can feel the gentle concussion of air as you're encircled by one of the rings. There's an oversized figure made of metal standing in a pool of shallow water, a painting machine, a conceptual language piece posted on a wall—and Risk Miller has constructed a very Goldberg-esque contraption, which sends billiard balls down via ducts from the balcony through a noisy maze to come to rest in one of three slots: yes, no, or maybe. At the far end of MEC are tables stacked with junk, an assortment of power tools, and MEC staff available to help people to cut, bend, weld, and otherwise mangle the stuff into an ad hoc collaborative machine that will become operational at midnight.

Every year before Christmas there's an arts and crafts show, with lots of penguin and landscape art for sale, but MAAG is the flip side, the Mad Max–Blade Runner version. People's attire runs from strapless gowns to duct tape, wood screws, and feather boas. The first MAAG was presented as a theme party making fun of art gallery openings, a genesis still apparent in the amount of black worn, but now it has its own momentum. Karen wanders around in a dominatrix outfit slapping people's butts with a riding crop, the victims documented with digital camera for posting on the McMurdo Web site the next day.

People work on these projects for weeks, some even planning their pieces a year in advance and bringing special materials with them to the ice. There's much less separation at McMurdo between the mundane and the exalted, between work and art—as when Jordan at the power plant pointed out the untrammeled connection of cause and effect in his job. One might think that the harsher the environment and the more remote the setting, the less time and caloric expenditure would be put into art. Here and at this communal scale, at least, that's not true, just as it's not true of many tribal peoples living in what we classify as "wilderness." Art is just as important, if not more so, part of making visible the process of turning space into place and making it available for inspection and emendation. If you can actually see what you think of a place, or how you make a place for yourself in both the space and the community, you can make fun of yourself and your fears, for instance, or pay them ritual respect, in both cases increasing your comfort level with the environment, if not the universe. The art at MAAG has transitioned fully from the representational to the symbolic, taking place not on the land but in the charged theater of mechanical operations, in itself a symbolic choice of venue.

MAAG is the terminus of my investigation into local aesthetics, and Beacon Valley, as it turns out, will be my chance to reach the end of the cartographic story.

I'd been transfixed by longing when peering up at the glowing sandstones of the Beacon Supergroup from the Dry Valleys earlier in the season, and Sarah suggested that I talk to Ron Sletten to see if I could join his camp for a closer look. Sletten is a geochemist from the University of Washington studying the processes that pattern ground in Beacon Valley, the last hundred-square-mile outpost of exposed land before the polar plateau. He was already hosting several visiting scientists at his remote camp, and was amenable to another guest.

In the second week of January, there, I find myself flying back over McMurdo Sound and through the Transantarctics with Cheryl Hallam of the USGS, who's going out to talk with Ron about their LIDAR project making very precise surface maps.

The sound is now a parquet of ice floes and blue-green meltwater channels. The sea itself is not visible except in a few cracks, and the ice is still thick enough to bear the weight of the helicopter should we be forced down. At the several open cracks that we see during our half-hour flight, however, Weddell seals bask by the dozens on both sides. Off in the distance the second Coast Guard icebreaker is widening the channel into McMurdo, and steaming in from out almost as far as B-15 is the Russian icebreaker *Kapitan Khlebnikov*, now converted into a polar tourist ship. It's easy to recognize, with its enormous cubical superstructure that, rising several stories off its main deck, holds fifty-four first-class cabins. People spend $15,000 to $25,000 to sail several weeks through the roughest waters in the world for a visit to the lower end of Taylor Valley, then the next day disembark at McMurdo, where they take pictures of anyone in a red parka, visit the station store to purchase T-shirts, and ask friends to snap photos of them using the Wells Fargo ATM.

As we bank into the mouth of Taylor Valley and approach the Canada Glacier, we see a dozen or so passengers milling around the base of the ice, a warming tent behind them set up by their guides. Part of Antonia Fairbanks's work is to look at the impacts of tourism on this side of the glacier as well as around Lake Hoare. One motivating factor is a proposal the NSF is considering to include in the LTER a small ecosystem that is watered by Green Creek, an intermittent stream flowing off the Canada Glacier immediately uphill from the tourists. Shore parties like this one will only increase in number, and balancing the desires of the tourists with those of the scientists requires international protocols. It's best to quantify as quickly as possible the effects such visits are having, while the consequences are still relatively benign.

As we fly over the glacier we see that water is streaming so heavily that it's pooling on top of the ice before finding paths down into Lake Hoare. The camp, when we arrive for a brief layover, is now an archipelago, and the moat around the lake ice, which should be an easy three-foot hop to cross, is now ten and twelve feet wide in places. Camp manager Rae Spain is walking around shaking her head over it. I hike up the side of the glacier for half an hour to look at the waterfalls. For years people have speculated that the cracks on top of the glacier weren't stress fractures but instead old water channels, but no one had ever seen proof until this year.

By late morning we're in the air again and flying over the trail down from Bonney that Joe and I had walked. We pass over Blood Falls and into territory new to me. Where the Taylor Glacier descends into the arid valley, it looks like your typical alpine ice tongue, a narrow white ribbon that terminates abruptly in a sheer face. As we pass through the Transantarctics on the way to the big banded peaks of the Beacon Supergroup, however, the glacier broadens and changes character completely—and you see it for what it truly is: a huge ice field with numerous distinct flows. All of a sudden I'm back on the edge of the big ice, barely able to comprehend it in a helicopter swooping along at 100 mph.

Before us is a massive collection of cliffs and ridges, the western ramparts of the Quartermain Mountains, an enclave of ancient aridity. The phrase that comes to mind is "the mountains at the end of the world": the uncompromisingly steep cliffs surrounded by icefalls look like they could illustrate a novel by H. Rider Haggard or Sir Arthur Conan Doyle. Beacon Valley is much higher, colder, windier, and drier than even the rest of the Dry Valleys, and the ice under its rubble-covered floor is among the oldest known on Earth. The concatenation of literary allusion and geology couched in superlatives is alive and well here at the beginning of the twenty-first century.

The helo bucks steep winds flowing off the plateau and enters the valley through a gap I'd not been able to see from Taylor Valley. Beneath us is deeply patterned ground, sorted into polygons by millions of years of sand-wedging. Unlike elsewhere on the planet where freeze-thaw wedging performs a similar function as water seeps into tiny expansion cracks in the ground and turns to ice, here it is the grains of eroded sandstone that do the job. The ground in the lower part of the valley may be raised as much as four-tenths of an inch per year, bearing with it boulders the size of small trucks (Plate 41).

Around us, as we make our descent, are tower peaks that have never been climbed and ridges that have never been walked. Beneath us is ice that may be as old as eight million years. The oldest ice drilled at Vostok, the deepest core taken in the Antarctic, is less than half a million years old; how ice can have existed here for so long is one of the mysteries of the continent. Sletten's group stands waiting among four polar and two mountaineering tents; we're now a party of ten people standing in a field of ventifacts. Every rock has been sculpted, and time seems to shimmer in the air like a mirage, as if we were looking through it.

The Beacon Valley camp is classified as borderline "deep field," meaning that we're at the limit of where the helicopters can fly; communications with the outside world are limited to a field radio and, in this case, an Iridium phone as well, the satellite network being used increasingly by the United States Antarctic Program. As soon as we land, Ron shakes my hand, then hops aboard the helo with another scientist, Birgit Hagedorn, a German geochemist specializing in weathering processes. They're going to be dropped at the head of the valley, and from there they'll hike back down to camp for a long afternoon of collecting soil samples.

In the meantime, Chuck Kurnik and I will hike up Farnell Valley, a higher side valley that ends in a tremendous cirque. Chuck, a young engineer who heads up services in the Antarctic for UNAVCO, a university consortium that develops and supports the scientific use of GPS worldwide, had read deeply in the literature of cognitive science, and we've been angling to get out in the field for a conversation all season. The afternoon is cool and breezy, but we're bundled up, well prepared for the four-hour walk toward the head of the valley and back.

As we walk, every few minutes we pause to try and see where we are. It's not easy, the landscape is so large and odd. Entire granite boulders have been reduced within a hundred thousand years to small pillars sticking up out of the ground like so many life-sized phallic symbols. The harder dolerite has been weathered into inch-high gray and rust-colored pyramids, an assemblage of desert pavement more extensive, continuous, and elaborate than I've seen anywhere else. And the edges of the polygons, which in most places might run up to a foot high, are here five and six feet high, the result of the landscape being undisturbed by glacial action, earthquakes, or erosion for millions of years—something outside our normal experience. The temperate zones where humans evolved (or migrated to, such as North America) have undergone constant, episodic land-altering processes during the life of our species. Even arid places such as the Great Basin of Nevada, which we perceive as being old because its sedimentary layers are exposed, have been pluvial within the last dozen millennia. Chuck and I instinctively know that this ground is different, hence the sense of timelessness that hovers over it.

One characteristic of the valley helps orient us roughly from south to north. Look up the valley and all the rocks are reddish brown; look down and they are silvery gray. That's the direction the wind blows down from the plateau, and it changes the color of the rocks. It's such an alien process that at first you think the difference in color is based on where the light's coming from. It isn't until Chuck picks up one of the rocks and shows it to me that I see how marked the contrast in fact is.

Our sense of location is jarred also by the fact that the topo map ends not far from here. Walk to the top of the ridge and less than fifteen miles away out on the ice is what's known as the "limit of completion," represented on the map by a dotted line. Beyond that boundary on the 1:250,000 USGS reconnaissance sheet it's just white paper, and so it will remain. Maps aren't made anymore out there. For one thing, the 3.8-million-square-mile East Antarctic Ice sheet is constantly on the move, and its contours change from year to year. For another, most of the plateau is unvisited except for the occasional traverse of a tractor train or adventurer. Their navigation requires only satellite photos and a GPS unit.

Our sense of isolation is heightened by the fact that for the first time in weeks we're back in a landscape with no running water. There is no wind and everything is preternaturally still in the cold. The average temperature in Beacon Valley is −35°F, and although it's nowhere that cold now, it feels not so much as if winter is getting ready to return, but like it never left. The cold and stillness contribute to a sense of temporal dislocation that's at least as profound as the spatial one. Without sound, and with a sun that causes shadows continually to rotate without an interval of nighttime, our sense of when we are breaks down. Shadows are an important navigational clue, as is tactility—such as feeling the wind on our skin, which tells us what direction it's coming from. The cold not only stops sound, but it also forces us to swaddle up in clothes and gloves that prevent us from touching the external world.

It's not that Chuck and I are uncomfortable with the sensory displacement, but it heightens our awareness of how very strange it is here. We return to camp slightly wide-eyed and settle in to cook dinner for everyone in one of the Scott tents, which affords us a chance to warm up. Ron and Birgit return around eight. Spending half their lives in the polar regions examining the processes that cause patterned ground, they seem less affected than the rest of us by the cold and silence. After dinner, with eight of us crammed into a polar tent, hunched in semicircle around the camp stove, I question them about their work.

Given the mechanical processes by which the polygons form, I know, the rocks they displace should be turning over every few tens of thousands of years—but the moraines out here are dated in the hundreds of thousands of years. The ice under the polygons in midvalley, that stuff that, based on the age of an upper layer of volcanic ash, an earlier team determined to be eight million years old—common sense dictates that it should have all sublimated away by now, even insulated as it is under rock and in such a cold place.

"But common sense isn't always right down here," says Ron, staring into a beer, a rather frigid choice of beverage for the setting. "We started looking just at polygons, but out of necessity we're looking at the ice, the debris-covered glaciers, the mountains. We're not so interested in the history, but in the processes that create the history. But there's a mosaic of ages on the surface here—you can see it in the oxidization and weathering—and we have to understand it."

"I'm skeptical of the eight million years. Isotope dating says maybe a few hundred thousand years to two million years old for the ice here. But it doesn't matter. It's all an interesting story either way. This is an old area, but dynamic. The surface is young and moving. We've only cored down to twenty meters, and ground-penetrating radar doesn't work here because the soils contain up to 2 percent salt."

"Yes," Birgit comments, "but we don't need to core right away."

Ron agrees; I perceive his eagerness to find the bottom of the ice is tempered by her sensitivity to the ecosystem. "We need to do seismic testing first, and then if it's necessary to drill a hole, we do it once and do it right."

By the time the dishes are done, the sun has gone behind the mountains. I'm thankful for the extrawarm sleeping bags we've been issued as part of the deep field kit.

The sleeping turns out to be warmer than I thought it would be, and when I get up at 3:15 to pee, I find out why. A storm has moved in from the north, the Ross Sea area, and it's lightly snowing, a relatively anomalous weather event here. Snow does pass through Beacon Valley, but it's usually just wind-blown ice from the plateau that promptly blows out, leaving behind almost no moisture. Even this morning's ocean-generated precipitation is the driest snow you can imagine. When it melts it will leave behind virtually no trace of dampness anywhere.

When we get up at 7:30 it's still snowing, a gray chill day. The cliffs are dusted, and clouds wreathe the peaks. It takes our breath away to see the valley like this. The scene reminds me of winter camping in southern Utah, and I momentarily mistake the dolerite cliffs for the dark piñon-juniper woodland that sits atop sandstone mesas in the southwest—a typical cognitive templating problem, caused by our visual system's attempt to fit the unfamiliar into something we've seen before.

We split into two groups. Chuck and Shad, his assistant, were supposed to be flown out today, but we're definitely weathered in. Instead they will spend the day trying to identify and log GPS points on the ground that appear on aerial photos taken by the USGS, made as an afterthought while they've been painting the valley with radar. That's part of the reason Cheryl is here: she delivered the photos, and then she and Ron talked about how the very precise elevations provided by the radar can help him measure patterns and changes in the valley floor.

"Ortho-rectification" of these test photos, taken with an off-the-shelf digital camera hastily mounted on the bottom of the plane, is hopeless. Matching photos to a specific patch of land won't be much easier. The patterned ground is profoundly isotropic, with few distinguishing characteristics to orient you—even the bidirectional coloration of the rocks is disguised now by the snow—and some of the photos are out of focus. All they can really do is try to identify individual boulders. Still, the exercise will give the USGS, UNAVCO, and Ron a chance to compare the aircraft-based mapping with GPS points on the ground.

I'm in the other group, which will go out into the middle of the valley to dig a trench down to the ice on one side of a polygon, the purpose being to collect soil and ice samples. We're on our way around ten, walking on a path that is being slowly obscured by the snow. It's not falling hard enough to impede us, and visibility at times extends clear down to the white ice of the Taylor Glacier about two miles away, though at other times it closes to within a few hundred yards. We stop by a semipermanent data station that has been collecting information about the environment around the polygons, including their movement relative to one another and the forces in the landscape that produce them. Carefully avoiding the sensors, we find a well-delineated polygon and spend the next several hours excavating a trench fourteen feet long, three feet wide, and about two feet deep. We take turns with the shovel, and in the meantime eat innumerable chocolate bars and do jumping jacks, all in the interests of staying warm. It's a losing battle, but we fight it long enough to get the work done.

When Ron first came here in 1996, he and his teammates were intimidated by the rock-strewn valley floor, thinking it would be very hard work to dig down to an ice sample. Instead they found that the rocks were floating on a layer of sand, which in turn rested atop, as he puts it, a "sea of ice." The digging is, indeed, not that difficult, mostly sandy soil containing rocks smaller than your fist. While we prepare the trench, Birgit wanders around with a trenching tool filling in old ice-sampling pits, part of the constant remediation she and Ron do while in the valley. To a newcomer walking through the maze of polygons, the trashcan-sized holes are scarcely noticeable. Once your eye becomes accustomed to the natural patterning, however, the pits become painfully obvious.

There are three main layers of soil. The grayish material directly above the ice has been expressed out of the glacier. The yellow material directly under the topmost rock-and-sand layer is predominantly sand from the eroding Beacon Supergroup. And in between there's a mixture. Two women scientists from New Zealand set to work, sterilizing stainless steel trowels with ethanol and then taking samples from each soil layer, ultimately hoping to parse out the diversity of microbes. Then Birgit takes her samples, which she will analyze for isotopes to better understand the weathering processes at work here. It's delicate and slow work, very quiet in the snow, the landscape reduced to essential elements; I am reminded of Japanese prints of mountains in winter.

Next, Ron carefully brushes sand from the ice surface with a whisk broom—then picks up a chainsaw and yanks the cord. It rips into life, and he pushes its hardened carborundum chain into the ice, cutting out large wedges. This completely disrupts the mood, the racket so intense that it creates the illusion of warmth. The ice that he pulls out looks like soapstone, it's so old and loaded with sand, up to about 10 percent. Gray-green brown in color, it is striated with vertical foliations that no one has deciphered yet. It is also very cold—at almost 0°F, much colder than typical North American glacial ice, which rests at just below freezing—and extremely hard. After every two or three cuts Ron has to stop and tighten the blade.

The puzzling nature of this ice is not all that unusual for the substance we normally think of as a variant of water. In fact, ice is far more abundant in the universe than liquid water, and in that sense it's more accurate to talk about the crystalline form of H_2O as a primal substance than its fluid counterpart. Water ice can form into eleven different crystalline matrices, more than any other known substance, though only one occurs on Earth under normal temperatures and pressures. You can live and die in ice—have your body preserved in it for millennia, or sleep in anything from igloos in Alaska to a luxury hotel created anew each winter in Finland. Sometimes it's as clear as air, sometimes as opaque as stone. Geologists consider glacial ice to be a metamorphic rock because it's compacted, recrystallized, and then deformed under pressure. This is the first time I've seen ice that actually fits that description.

Ron is excited: one wedge from more than a foot down has a crack in it that's filled with sand. He isn't sure what it means, but it's something he hasn't seen before.

One of the unusual things about the ice in the valley floor is that it has two distinct characters. The glacier in the upper to mid part of the valley comes from the cirques high above at the head of the valley; from there it flows under the debris that falls from the surrounding cliffs, extending down almost to a point across from our camp, where it looks like what you would expect—relatively clear ice. The ice down the valley, however, is the dirty stuff we've been sawing up—leftover ice from the Taylor Glacier when it extended this far up maybe. Looking at the valley and realizing that the glacier is receding not upward (as elsewhere in the world, where the glacial fronts follow the cold) but downward is discombobulating. Here it's not just temperature driving the dynamics, but gravity as well, as ice flows down from the plateau. Ron loads up two packs with the wedges, which Birgit and I stagger back to camp with while the rest of the group finishes up.

The Kiwis are also collecting small samples of the ice, hoping to find microbial evidence, alive or dead. Two Russians who were out here previously coring the ice for Ron were able later to culture bacteria from their samples, but in general the soils and ice here are sterile. The only nematodes that have been found at this site, for example, are dead ones. Some cyanobacteria that are highly resistant to both cold and intense ultraviolet radiation can be expected, but only in low concentrations.

We spend a pleasurable evening over a dinner of sautéed shrimp and a bottle of wine. We may be in the deep field, but McMurdo has its priorities straight when it comes to keeping us well fed, thus warm and content. The snow has stopped, and by the time we're finished with dinner around eight the light has gone silver and gold on the peaks. The talus slopes of dark dolerite contrast sharply with the still-white valley. With low sun on the tents during the night and no wind, sleep is downright comfortable.

The next morning three helos arrive to extract not only us but also most of the camp. The field season here as elsewhere is almost over, the cold beginning to creep back toward the ocean. When we arrive in McMurdo the *Khlebnikov* and its passengers have already left, starting their return journey north before the sea starts to refreeze. Although there's still a bit of summer left in the marine belt around the sound, it hasn't been a favorable year for sea-based mammals and birds. One sure sign of summer, the plankton, only just arrived today, cutting underwater visibility from two hundred feet to less than fifteen within hours. The microscopic plants and animals that bloom in the ocean during the summer should have showed up much earlier, and what should have been a two-month-long time of feeding for whales and penguins is half that this year. Between the rookeries remaining icebound and the late arrival of the birds' major food source, only 8 percent of the eligible penguins in the Ross Sea region have bred this year.

A few days later, the temperatures are so high that Melissa decides it's time to check once more on the moss, and we hike along the familiar road to Hut Point—except that now shallow ponds of meltwater fill every depression, and a briskly flowing stream has cut across the road to create an unexpected chasm on the left. Stopping to peer into it, we find exposed multiple layers of frozen dirt and blue ice extending down ten feet. Even though I know the volcanic dirt of Ross Island is only a shallow layer lying atop the permafrost, it's still a shock to realize that the ice is everywhere so close at hand.

Instead of following the shoreline on the other side of the hut, which is now icy slush, we head up a steep ridgeline trail to the ponds higher in the hills. Every tiny basin we pass is filled with water containing algae; like the plankton in the ocean, the algae population explodes during the summer. Some of the smaller ponds are so bright with growth that the green looks radioactive. Even the tiny outflow rills, all of which contribute to the stream down below, are lined with algae. We find moss almost immediately, growing in the cracks of the patterned ground, and we're surprised to find it on both sides of the ridge. Most plant life in the Antarctic, especially that across the sound in the Dry Valleys, requires a specific microclimate and will grow only if it is precisely oriented to the right mixture of light, heat, and water. The moss here appears to be much hardier.

The next day Steve Alexander, a biologist who's been working as a diver this season, shows us the springtails he collected inadvertently in New Harbor, near the mouth of the Dry Valleys. He'd worked there before, but this time he chanced upon a meltwater stream that had just started to advance down the slope toward the ocean. He scooped up some of the foam at the front, thinking to filter it and burn off the remains to measure the carbon content entering the ecosystem in which they were diving. He stuck it into the refrigerator for a couple of weeks, then came back to start filtering. Lo and behold, there was movement: tiny, tiny black grains that when put under the microscope turned out to be springtails.

Much smaller than a flea, yet one of the most widely distributed insects in the world, the hardy springtail may have been on the continent 50 million years ago when Antarctica was a much warmer place joined with other continents near the equator. As the continents separated and the circumpolar currents developed, isolating Antarctica biologically from the rest of the planet—in essence, putting it into a deep freezer—pockets of life survived on mountaintops, the only land not covered by ice. During the last 30,000 years as the planet has warmed, these habitats have been spreading. Springtails that may have been living on only one side of McMurdo Sound are now found in the Dry Valleys by the Seuss Glacier. Like the fish that Art deVries studies, they produce antifreeze to survive the cold. Apart from a few species of wingless midges found on the peninsula, they are the only free-living insects in the Antarctic, feeding on algae and fungi and going dormant in winter.

On my next-to-last night on the ice, I return to the ridge to check on the moss we'd seen a few days earlier. This evening, however, I can find only a dozen or so patches. The moss is already desiccating into dormancy until next season—or some distant year when the temperatures once again warm to this year's levels. It may also be that life is more easily found by two pairs of eyes. Melissa and I have continually surprised each other this season with the things we've found in unlikely corners: the art critic trained to look for subtle differences in color, texture, shape; the scientist able to recognize likely habitats.

All during my time here I've tried to collate what I've seen with ways in which human sensory perceptions fail in large spaces and how we deploy cultural devices such as maps, artworks, scientific images, and architecture to compensate. Melissa and the other scientists have shown me that in the Antarctic life works hard to flourish under every conceivable circumstance. They have also made it clear that we can understand the continent better if we shift our sense of scale in both time and space. When we have trouble understanding a large and unfamiliar space, we often react by inflating our cultural response: commonplace effort becomes heroic struggle; the heroic becomes the mythic. We attempt to scale ourselves up to greatness, if for no other reason than to explain what we see. The heroic myth in which we've swaddled Scott and every subsequent explorer presents this continent as a sterile space almost beyond comprehension, when in fact it is permeated with life.

Scott wrote in the *Discovery* expedition journal that Taylor Valley was a dead place. That was not the case then, and is certainly less so now, but he was not trained to pry open rocks for evidence of endolithic bacteria. And he would be astounded by the extent and comfort of camps at Hoare and Bonney. Yet contemporary Antarctic literature still focuses more on the carcasses of mummified seals than on the live animals themselves; more on the ice than the flowing water. That's less than half the picture. The immense coexists with the microbial, the geological with the domestic. As E.O. Wilson reminds us, "The exact perception of wilderness is a matter of scale."

The American West was depicted in popular culture until recently as a limitless frontier subject to Manifest Destiny, a doctrine that stated that the earth is a resource to use at our will. This likewise incomplete view to this day sustains our extractive approach to the region. Because the Antarctic was opened to exploration a century later than the West, however, the heroic rhetoric that is applied to it is more open to revision by both scientists and artists. What scientists uncover about life here makes its way quickly into the literature and art of the continent, as nature is continually and promptly reassessed in culture. Although most books about Antarctica still dwell on the history of exploration, and most of the art is straightforward landscape work, that has begun to change. Stan Robinson wrote in his novel *Antarctica* about modern nomads living on the continent with a minimal use of external resources. His characters display a complex range of reactions to the place they inhabit, and the heroes are those learning to live with the ice, not attempting to rule over it. New Zealand sculptor Virginia King has focused our attention not on photogenic penguins but on plankton, unicellular Antarctic life on which so much other life depends.

I sit down on the ridge and look across the sound. One of the icebreakers churns slowly in a circle a few hundred yards offshore, keeping open a basin so the ships can turn around. The sun is noticeably lower now at midnight than during December, and the wind once again has a bite to it. I contemplate the moss, marveling at life wanting to live, but also at our own ability to overcome a genetically inherited narrowness of vision with cultural tactics, using optics and art to see those modest organisms that have found innumerable niches in which to survive. I ponder the complexity of microbial life breaking down the rocks and fixing carbon and nitrogen in the soil of the Dry Valleys, which is then utilized by larger organisms, such as nematodes. Eventually mosses and springtails will arrive there, and then, if the climate allows, larger insects and birds.

Parallels might be drawn with cultural colonization: first we are exterior to the land, but then, upon entering it, we begin to scale it to ourselves, and ourselves to it. We measure it, and sometimes it takes measure of us. We seek to represent what we see, and reshape what we see into what we need and want. At first this is a purely utilitarian project, but quickly it becomes also an aesthetic one. Once native materials come into play, we are inventing a local culture specific to a place.

As this process occurs in the Antarctic—a place that at first appears to us an open and blank slate on which to write our ambitions—we are presented with an opportunity to make the greatest leap in scale that is possible: from measuring geography to mapping our minds. We do this through optical and digital imaging, which extend our external vision in every direction, from the very close and minute to the very far and large. Yet it takes imagination to assign meaning to the images and assemble coherent versions of reality, of where we live physically. In a similar fashion, we have been making pictures of electrical activity in the brain through Magnetic Resonating Imaging, using science to assess the physical structure and functioning of the brain. Initial efforts are just now under way to interrogate artistic images about how that functioning, which we call mind, both shapes and is shaped by the process of turning external land into internal landscapes—a cartography of human imagination.

I've been asked by Melissa and Karen to write a poem for the bridge that crosses over the pipes between the lab and the galley, a signal honor for a visitor to the ice. Eleven steps up and eleven down, one word for each step to be burned into the wood, about people meeting and parting. The words will be a trope for the people who gather here every year to create a community and a culture, then, after a few short months, scatter to the winds. As people experience the words both visually through reading and physically by engaging in the acts of greeting and leavetaking themselves, on this very bridge, the poem will be transformed into an object that serves its function even while performing it. Neither the bridge nor the poem will last long; both will be weathered away by wind and cold. But by then someone else will have come along and, perhaps, written a new text, a poem not about the heroic unknown, but one of Terra Antarctica itself, a place that, precisely because it is so difficult to see it, allows us to examine more closely the nature not only of land but of ourselves.

BIBLIOGRAPHY

Scientific, historical, and artistic reports about the Antarctic are often so interwoven that it is difficult to separate them fully. In the first book listed, for instance, Caroline Alexander's account of Shackleton's travails, the photographs of Frank Hurley play as much a role in telling the story as does the author's historical description. I have therefore arranged sources by subject matter within a few general categories. The literature of the Antarctic is extensive, and this bibliography is focused on those sources used in the writing of this book. Readers interested in additional titles should consult the larger reference works for the field, such as Larry Conrad's *Bibliography of Antarctic Exploration: Expedition Accounts from 1768 to 1960* (Washougal, Wash.: L. J. Conrad, 1999).

ANTARCTICA AND ITS EXPLORATION

Alexander, Caroline. *The Endurance: Shackleton's Legendary Expedition.* New York: Alfred A. Knopf, 1998. Accounts of Shackleton's remarkable twenty-month expedition are numerous, but the 140 black-and-white photographs taken by Frank Hurley and reproduced in this book as duotones are remarkable. The book was published to accompany an exhibition at the American Museum of Natural History.

Antarctica: Great Stories form the Frozen Continent. Surrey Hills, N.S.W.,

Austr.: Reader's Digest Services, 1985. One of the two most comprehensive and useful general reference books about the continent.

Antarctica: The Extraordinary History of Man's Conquest of the Frozen Continent. Sydney: Reader's Digest, 1998. The single most useful book about the continent for the layperson, a large-format illustrated encyclopedia that is more comprehensive than the Greenpeace volume (see May, below).

Beaglehole, J. C. *The Life of Captain James Cook.* Stanford: Stanford University Press, 1974. The standard (and massive) biography.

Bellingshausen, Thaddeus T. *The Voyage of Captain Bellingshausen to the Antarctic Seas, 1819–1821.* Translated and edited by Frank Debenham. London: Hakluyt Society, 1945.

Borchgrevink, Carsten Egeberg. *First on the Antarctic Continent: Being an Account of the British Antarctic Continent, 1898–1900.* London: George Newnes, 1901.

Bowden, Tim. *The Silence Calling: Australians in Antarctica, 1974–97.* St. Leonards, N.S.W., Austr.: Allen & Unwin, 1999.

Burke, David. *Moments of Terror: The Story of Antarctic Aviation.* Kensington, N.S.W., Austr.: New South Wales University Press, 1994.

Byrd, Richard E. *Little America.* New York: G. P. Putnam, 1930. Byrd was a crossover explorer at the time of this, his first expedition to the continent, with one foot in the Heroic Age and the other in the subsequent "third age" of scientific exploration (as Pyne defines it, see below). Hence Byrd's hale and hearty tone as he dispenses scientific nomenclature.

———. *Discovery.* New York: G. P. Putnam, 1935. An account of Byrd's second expedition to Antarctica, on which he took the artist David Paige.

———. *Alone.* New York: Kodansha, 1995. A facsimile reprint of the 1938 classic, which, as David Campbell points out in the afterword, was probably ghostwritten by the reporter Charles Murphy.

Campbell, David G. *The Crystal Desert.* New York: Houghton Mifflin, 1992. The author, a Canadian biologist, relates his experiences on the Antarctic Peninsula and in the South Shetland Islands in one of the better books about the continent.

Chapman, Sydney. *IGY: Year of Discovery*. Ann Arbor: University of Michigan Press, 1959. A popular account of the International Geophysical Year activities.

Cherry-Garrard, Aspley. *The Worst Voyage in the World*. New York: Carroll & Graf, 1989. A firsthand account from 1922 of Scott's last voyage, acclaimed then as the *War and Peace* of Antarctic literature.

Cook, Frederic A. *Through the First Antarctic Night*. New York: Doubleday & McCune, 1900.

Crossley, Louise. *Explore Antarctica*. Cambridge: Cambridge University Press, 1995. A picture book from the Australian Antarctic Foundation with images not always seen north of the equator.

Desmarais, Emily. "Volcanoes and the Advance of Ancient Roman Science and Technology from the Classic Through the Renaissance Period," unpublished paper, New Mexico Institute of Technology, 2001. This and the next paper were both exceptionally useful for my chapter on Mt. Erebus.

———. "Monitoring Ground Deformation on Volcanoes with GPS," unpublished paper, New Mexico Institute of Technology, 2001.

Dumont d'Urville, Jules Sébastien César. *An Account in Two Volumes of Voyages to the South Seas*. Translated and edited by Helen Rosenman. Honolulu: University of Hawaii Press, 1988.

Fabian, Rainer, and Hans-Christian Adam. *Masters of Early Travel Photography*. New York: Vendome Press, 1983. This work reproduces some of the early Arctic photographs taken during William Bradford's 1869 trip to Greenland.

Fiennes, Ranulph. *Mind Over Matter*. New York: Dell Publishing, 1995.

Finney, Ben. *Voyage of Rediscovery*. Berkeley: University of California Press, 1994. Although Finney does not discuss the possibility that Polynesian navigators sailed clear to Antarctic waters, he documents contemporary roundtrip replica canoe voyages of up to 12,000 statute miles in length from Hawaii to Tahiti and beyond.

Fleming, Fergus. *Barrow's Boys*. New York: Grove Press, 1998. An excellent introduction to British exploration in the nineteenth century.

Fogg, G. E. *A History of Antarctic Science*. Cambridge: Cambridge University Press, 1992.

Green, Bill. *Water, Ice, and Stone*. New York: Harmony Books, 1995. Part memoir, part science book, this won the Burroughs Medal for its unusual combination of poetic and scientific language and metaphor. Ostensibly a book about the frozen lakes in the McMurdo Dry Valleys, it is also an extended meditation on water and its role in the world.

Gurney, Alan. *Below the Convergence: Voyages toward Antarctica, 1699–1839*. New York: W. W. Norton, 1997. A richly layered history of early exploration in the region.

———. *The Race to the White Continent: Voyages to the Antarctic*. New York: W. W. Norton, 2000. Sequel to *Below the Convergence*. To summarize Antarctic exploration as I have been forced to do feels like a crime against nature; I would urge readers to redeem me by reading Gurney's books.

Henry, Thomas R. *The White Continent: The Story of Antarctica*. New York: William Sloane Associates, 1950. Recommended not for accuracy but rather as a look at popular press attitudes toward Antarctica circa 1950, which remained enduringly sensationalistic.

Hurley, Frank. *Argonauts of the South*. New York: G. P. Putnam, 1925. Hurley was a charming writer, and his accounts of both the Mawson and Shackleton expeditions move swiftly and with humor. The contrast between the photolithographic prints of this 1925 volume and the crisp halftones of the Alexander book (see above) is instructive, the former appearing almost like paintings.

Gorman, James. *Ocean Enough and Time: Discovering the Waters around Antarctica*. New York: HarperCollins, 1995.

Imbert, Bertrand. *North Pole, South Pole: Journeys to the Ends of the Earth*. Translated by Alexandra Campbell. New York: Harry N. Abrams, 1992. This small but copiously illustrated book is by the

French naval officer in charge of his country's Antarctic expeditions during the International Geophysical Year. Among the illustrations are numerous rare examples of historical art depicting the polar regions.

Kyle, Philip R., editor. *Volcanological and Environmental Studies of Mount Erebus, Antarctica.* Washington, D.C.: American Geophysical Union, 1994. Volume 66 in the Antarctic Research Series. An earlier volume, #48, *Volcanoes of the Antarctic Plate and Southern Oceans,* edited by W. E. LeMasurier and J. W. Thomson (1989), also contains papers by Philip Kyle on Mt. Erebus.

Mawson, Douglas. *The Home of the Blizzard.* Philadelphia: J. B. Lippincott, 1915. The original two-volume publication is illustrated with almost two hundred photographs, sketches, and maps. The much-abridged 1998 reprint hardly mentions the work of either photographer Hurley or the other artist on the expedition, C. T. Harrisson.

Lopez, Barry. "Informed by Indifference." In *About This Life: Journeys on the Threshold of Memory.* New York: Alfred A. Knopf, 1998.

May, John. *The Greenpeace Book of Antarctica.* New York: Doubleday, 1989. A general encyclopedia of the continent with numerous scientific illustrations, this is an interesting second-generation example of the "exhibit books" pioneered by the Sierra Club to raise environmental awareness. Its political agenda is clear, and the information provided useful enough that one wishes the publication were updated regularly.

McKinley, Capt. Ashley. *The South Pole Picture Book.* New York: Samuel W. Miller, 1934. This inexpensive large-format paperback with forty-three black-and-white photographs by Byrd's number three on the Byrd Antarctic Expedition I provides instructive contrast to later photo books.

McCormick, Robert. *Voyages of Discovery in the Antarctic and the Arctic Seas.* London: Sampson Low, Marston, Searle & Rivington, 1884.

McGonigal, David, and Dr. Lynn Woodward. *Antarctica: The Complete Story.* Auckland: Random House New Zealand, 2001. A comprehensive encyclopedia.

Messner, Reinhold. *Antarctica: Both Heaven and Hell.* Translated by Jill Neate. Seattle: Mountaineers Books, 1991. An extreme mountaineer manhauls across the continent and meditates on the experience.

Murdoch, William Gordon Burn. *From Edinburgh to the Antarctic: An Artist's Notes and Sketches during the Dundee Antarctic Expedition of 1892–93.* Bungay, Suffolk, Eng.: Paradigm Press, 1984 (a facsimile reprint of the Longmans, Green edition of 1894). Purely out of curiosity, a Scottish commercial artist joined the Dundee Expedition, a whaling venture, and subsequently wrote this illustrated memoir, which is more an irreverent travelogue than an art book.

Murray, James, and George Marston. *Antarctic Days.* London: Andrew Melrose, 1913. Illustrated account of Shackleton's 1907 expedition by two artmaking members.

Neider, Charles. *Antarctica: Authentic Accounts of Life and Exploration in the World's Highest, Driest, Windiest, Coldest, and Most Remote Continent.* London: Allen & Unwin, 1973. A useful anthology of excerpts from books by major explorers.

O'Sullivan, Walter. *Assault on the Unknown: The International Geophysical Year.* New York: McGraw-Hill, 1961. The author, then the chief science writer for the *New York Times*, followed the IGY around the world.

Parfit, Michael. *South Light.* New York: Macmillan, 1985. An Antarctic travel book by an NSF-sponsored visiting writer.

Priscu, John C., editor. *Ecosystem Dynamics in a Polar Desert: The McMurdo Dry Valleys, Antarctica.* Washington, D.C.: American Geophysical Union, 1998. Volume 72 in the Antarctic Research Series.

Pyne, Stephen. *The Ice.* Iowa City: University of Iowa Press, 1986. An extended meditation on the geophysical nature and cultural meaning of Antarctica, this book does for the continent what Clarence Dutton did for the Grand Canyon in his *Tertiary Geology,* mixing science and aesthetics. Pyne, a MacArthur Fellowship recipient, provides us with an intricate, poetic, comprehensive guide to both the physical regimes of the Antarctic and its historical art.

Quartermain, L. B. *South to the Pole: The Early History of the Ross Sea Sector, Antarctica*. London: Oxford University Press, 1967.

Ross, Capt. Sir James. *A Voyage of Discovery and Research in the Southern and Antarctic Regions during the Years 1839–1843*, Vol. 1. London: John Murray, 1847. Also available in an excellent facsimile edition published by David & Chambers (London, 1969).

Ross, M. J. *Ross in the Antarctic: The Voyages of James Clark Ross in Her Majesty's Ships* Erebus and Terror, *1839–1843*. Whitby, Yorkshire, Eng.: Caedmon of Whitby, 1982. Written by the great-grandson of Sir James Ross, the book includes pencil sketches and paintings by John Edward Davis, as well as botanical illustrations by J. D. Hooker.

Rodgers, Eugene. *Beyond the Barrier: The Story of Byrd's First Expedition to Antarctica*. Annapolis: U.S. Naval Institute, 1990. A candid retelling of Byrd's Little America expedition, this book offers another view of the transition from Second to Third Age exploration on the continent by a former public information officer for the U.S. Antarctic Research Program

Rubin, Jeff. *Antarctica*. Hawthorn, Vic., Austr.: Lonely Planet, 2001. An indispensable collection of facts and travel tips.

Savours, Ann, editor. *Scott's Last Voyage through the Antarctic Camera of Herbert Ponting*. New York: Praeger, 1975. Elizabeth Arthur credits this book as a factor behind her writing *Antarctic Navigation* (see below).

Seaver, George. *Edward Wilson of the Antarctic*. London: John Murray, 1933. A highly appreciative biography.

Shackleton, Ernest. *South: Journals of his Last Expedition to Antarctica*. London: Heinemann, 1919.

Smith, S. Percy. *Hawaiki*. Wellington, New Zealand: Whitcombe & Tombs, 1898.

Solomon, Susan. *The Coldest March: Scott's Fatal Antarctic Expedition*. New Haven, Conn.: Yale University Press, 2002.

Spufford, Francis. *I May Be Some Time*. New York: St. Martins Press, 1999. An insightful intellectual history of the imaginative context in Victorian and Edwardian times for polar exploration.

Stewart, John. *Antarctica: An Encyclopedia*. Jefferson: McFarland, 1990. A quirky gazetteer and biographical dictionary.

Viola, Herman J., and Carolyn Margolis, editors. *Magnificent Voyagers: The U.S. Exploring Expedition, 1838–1842*. Washington, D.C.: Smithsonian Institution, 1985. A well-illustrated and comprehensive overview of the first American government-sponsored expedition below the Antarctic Circle.

Waterhouse, Emma J., editor. *Ross Sea Region: A State of the Environment Report for the Ross Sea Region of Antarctica*. Christchurch: New Zealand Antarctic Institute, 2001. A comprehensive overview with excellent bibliographic sources.

Weddell, James. *A Voyage towards the South Pole, Performed in the Years 1822–24, Containing an Examination of the Antarctic Sea. . . .* Newton Abbott, Devonshire, Eng.: David & Charles, 1970 (a reprint of the original published by Longman et al. in 1825).

Wheeler, Sara. *Terra Incognita*. New York: Random House, 1996. A popular account of the continent by an NSF-sponsored British writer.

Wilkes, Charles. *Narrative of the United States Exploring Expedition during the Years 1838,1839, 1840, 1841, 1842*. Philadelphia: Lea & Blanchard, 1845. The second volume, pages 281–365, contains the account of his journey to Antarctica.

Willis, Thayer. *The Frozen World*. London: Aldus Books, 1971. In the "Encyclopedia of Discovery and Exploration" series, this volume covers the exploration of both polar regions, complete with numerous examples of early art.

Wilson, Edward. *Diary of the* Discovery *Expedition*. Edited by Ann Savours. New York: Humanities Press, 1967. Containing material from the original manuscripts (housed at the Scott Polar Research Institute, Cambridge University), this volume and the next—both of which, unfortunately, are out of print—include exquisite reproductions of the artist's texts, notes, drawings, and paintings. The books were designed to evoke comparisons with the works of E. Seton Thompson, and they succeed admirably.

————. *Diary of the* Terra Nova *Expedition to the Antarctic, 1910–1912*. Edited by H. G. R. King. New York: Humanities Press, 1972.

————. *Birds of the Antarctic*. Edited by Brian Roberts. London: Blanford Press, 1967. Included in this volume are notes on Wilson's personal and professional life, as well as on his work as an artist.

ANTARCTIC ART

An annotated "Antarctic Image Chronology," compiled by the author, listing the artists significant to our visual perceptions of the continent can be found at Rob Stephenson's website "The Antarctic Circle": http://www.antarctic-circle.org/index.html.

Andrese, Stephen. *Arktis Antarktis*. Cologne, Ger.: DuMont, 1997. It is unfortunate that this German exhibition catalog was not translated into English, for it makes a valuable attempt to integrate the cultural assembling of the Antarctic within its history of exploration.

Arnold, H. J. P. *Photographer of the World: The Biography of Herbert Ponting*. Rutherford: Farleigh Dickinson University Press, 1971. Ponting was the first professional photographer to accompany an Antarctic expedition.

Boyer, Peter. *Antarctic Journey: Three Artists in Antarctica*. The Australian government sent three of the country's better-known non-photographic artists to the continent in early 1987 for a five-week trip. This is a small but handsome and informative catalog of the subsequent exhibition held in Hobart at the Tasmanian Museum and Art Gallery.

Brown, Nigel. *Inaugural Artists to Antarctica Scheme: Report and Related Material*. Auckland: photocopy publication copyrighted by the artist, 1997. Brown was part of a three-person team of writers and artists to be sponsored in the Antarctic by Australian National Antarctic Research Expeditions (ANARE); this is his report on his experiences there, as well as advice to other visiting artists.

Conly, Maurice. *Ice on My Palette*. Christchurch: Whitcoulls Publishers. 1977. A watercolor picture book by the New Zealand artist, with accompanying text by Neville Peat.

Crawford, Neelon. *Antarctica*. New York: Witkin Gallery, 1991. Exhibition catalog, with essay by Ben Lifson and the artist.

———. *Ramparts of Ice*. Washington, D.C.: National Academy of Sciences, 1994. Exhibition catalog, with essay by Robert Mahoney.

Dewey, Jennifer Owings. *Birds of Antarctica*. Boston: Little, Brown, 1989. An illustrated juvenile natural history by an NSF-sponsored artist/writer, this outreach product is typical of the Artists and Writers Program.

Dickenson, Victoria. *Drawn from Life: Science and Art in the Portrayal of the New World*. Toronto: University of Toronto Press, 1998. Concentrating on the representation of the Americas and the Arctic, Dickenson provides a well-illustrated history of the rise of scientific illustration as it relates to exploration from the fifteenth through nineteenth centuries.

Fagan, Jim, editor. *Captain Cook: His Artists, His Voyages*. Sydney: Daily Telegraph, 1970.

Ferguson, Richard G. *Images of the Great South Land: Fifty Years of Antarctic Vision and Endeavor by ANARE Artists, 1947 to 1997*. Melbourne: ANARE Club, 1997. This catalog, of an exhibition curated by Shelagh Robinson and shown in Melbourne and Geelong, lists 236 artworks by 49 artists ranging from professional painters to scrimshaw carvers.

Fogg, G. E., and David Smith. *The Exploration of Antarctica, the Last Unspoilt Continent*. London: Cassell, 1990. A general book about the continent and its culture of science, illustrated extensively by the British painter David Smith.

Easthaugh, Stephen. *Antarctica*. Self-published, 2000.

Joppien, Rudiger, and Bernard Smith. *The Art of Captain Cooks' Voyages*. Vol. 1: *Voyage of the* Endeavor, *1768–1771;* and vol. 2: *The Voyage of the* Resolution *and* Adventure, *1772–1775*. New Haven: Yale University Press, 1985. The definitive works.

Keneally, Thomas. *Victim of the Aurora*. New York: Harcourt Brace Jovanovich, 1978. Although the author, an Australian novelist best known for *Schindler's List*, has never been to the Antarctic, he drew extensively on firsthand accounts from the Heroic Age to create a modest mystery story that hews well to the reality of the place.

Kidd, Courtney. "The Unframed Eye: Perspectives on Antarctica." *Art and Australia* 33, no. 4 (winter 1996). An examination of how the artist Sidney Nolan connects the Australian desert and Antarctica visually.

King, H. G. R. "Heroic Painter of the Antarctic." *Geographical Magazine* 48, no. 4 (January 1976): 212–217. Article about Edward Wilson.

Klipper, Stuart. *Cardinal Points.* Iowa City: University of Iowa Museum of Art. 1998. Exhibition catalog, with statements by Stephen Prokoff, Martin Krieger, and the artist.

———. *Bearing South.* Colorado Springs: Press at Colorado College, 1991. Limited to fifty copies, this handsome collaboration with letterpress book printer and designer James Trissel includes twenty-eight black-and-white photos and running commentaries on a sailing voyage to the Antarctic by Klipper and shipmates Warren Brown and John Gore Grimes.

Legg, Frank, with Toni Hurley. *Once More on My Adventures.* Sydney: Ure Smith, 1966. Biography of Frank Hurley, with unusual examples from his entire photographic oeuvre.

Legler, Gretchen. "The Face of God." In this essay, a chapter from an unpublished book by a participant in NSF's Artists and Writers Program, Legler meditates on the work of Edward Wilson.

Lynch, Dennis. "Profile: Herbert G. Ponting." *Polar Record*, no. 26 (1990): 217–224.

Moss, Stanford, and Lucia deLeiris. *Natural History of the Antarctic.* New York: Columbia University Press, 1988. Another NSF-sponsored artist, deLeiris spent four months at Palmer Station producing the line drawings for this book.

Poesch, Jessie. *Titian Ramsey Peale, 1779–1885, and His Journals of the Wilkes Expedition.* Peale is a seminal crossover figure from science to art as well as from the American West to the Antarctic, having served as a naturalist-artist to both the 1819–1820 Long Expedition to the West and the Wilkes Expedition to the Antarctic in 1838–1842.

Porter, Eliot. *Antarctica*. New York: Dutton, 1978. Porter went to the Antarctic in 1974, when he was seventy-three years old, and made a second trip there the following year. The resulting large-format photo book has eighty color photos, two maps, and an account of travels by the artist.

Rosenthal, David. *The Antarctic: Views from the Bottom of the Earth*. Rancho Cucamonga, Calif.: Wignall Museum/Gallery, 1998. Exhibition catalog, with statement by Virginia Eaton and notes by the artist.

Robertson, Christian Clare. "Ice Edge: Excerpts from an Antarctic Journal, 1989." *Northern Perspective* 12, no. 2 (1989): 1–23 (a publication of Northern Territory University, Casuarina).

———. *Extreme Landforms*. Casuarina, N.T., Austr.: Museum and Art Gallery of the Northern Territory, 1998. Exhibition brochure, with statement by the artist.

Rowell, Galen. *Poles Apart*. Berkeley: University of California Press, 1995. Rowell, a participant in the NSF Artists and Writers Program, was typically classified as an adventure photographer. This interesting book, an intelligent mixture of wildlife and nature photography, documentary and art shots, and useful commentary, provides an unusual and valuable visual comparison of the two polar regions.

Schulthess, Emil. *Antarctica*. New York: Simon & Schuster, 1960. Printed in a panoramic format, this is a classic book of both Antarctic documentary and art.

Shackleton, Keith. *Wildlife and Wilderness: An Artist's World*. London: Clive Holloway Books, 1986. A picture book by a widely traveled naturalist/painter who has visited the Antarctic.

Simpson-Housley, Paul. *Antarctica: Exploration Perception and Metaphor*. London: Routledge, 1992. A slender academic volume tracing the imagery of the continent in art and literature through the Heroic Age of exploration; the author also describes cognitive difficulties experienced on the ice and provides a valuable analysis of Edward Wilson's paintings.

Sorlien, Sandy. *Imagining Antarctica*. Swarthmore, Penn.: List Gallery, Swarthmore College, 2000. Exhibition catalog.

Stuebe, Isabel Combs. *The Life and Works of William Hodges*. New York: Garland, 1979. In this informative doctoral dissertation, which that includes the complete catalog of the artist's works, Stuebe demonstrates how Hodges's Antarctic work anticipates Turner.

It should be noted that Edward Wilson's diaries (listed above with books on exploration) are among the most significant artistic accomplishments from the continent. Wilson was a great admirer of Ernest Thompson Seton, an early nature writer and one of the co-founders of the Boy Scout movement, and Wilson's books are designed in that spirit, with numerous color plates of his watercolors and drawings as marginal annotations.

ANTARCTIC LITERATURE

Although the literature about Antarctica or set there is slim compared with that of other places, numerous titles have been published. Most of the fiction written since 1605 can be found in the bibliography compiled by Fauno Cordes, *Tekeli-li* (www.antarctic-circle.org/fauno.htm). Pages about Antarctic poetry, music, and maps are also hosted at the Antarctic Circle website; for the full offering, see www.antarctic-circle.org/index.html. The books listed are ones that I found best illuminated the variety of ways in which people perceive the continent.

Anthony, Jason. *Albedo: Fragments of Antarctic Time*. Anthony has spent several seasons working on the ice, and these "reflections on aesthetics, geography, history, and experience" provide a wealth of physical and social observations, as well as extensive quotes from literature worldwide that, though not necessarily about the Antarctic, is immensely relevant. My thanks to Jason Anthony for sharing this work-in-progress with me.

Arthur, Elizabeth. *Antarctic Navigation*. New York: Alfred A. Knopf,
1995. Arthur was the first novelist to participate in the Antarctic
Artists and Writers Program.

Brown, Nigel, Bill Manhire, and Chris Orsman. *"Homelight."* Wellington, N.Z.: Pemmican Press, 1999. Facsimile edition of the chap-
book written and produced by these New Zealand authors in
Antarctica in January 1999.

Diski, Jenny. *Skating to Antarctica: A Journey to the End of the World*.
Hopewell, N.J.: Ecco Press, 1997. Alternating an account of a
cruise to South Georgia Island and the Antarctic Peninsula with
the painful reconstruction of her childhood with two abusive
parents, Diski uses the continent as a thoughtful, effective, and
evocative metaphor for alienation.

Fausett, David. *Writing the New World: Imaginary Voyages and Utopias
of the Great Southern Land*. Syracuse, N.Y.: Syracuse University
Press, 1993. A history of the literary tradition surrounding exploration of the southern hemisphere.

Finkel, Donald. *Adequate Earth*. New York: Atheneum, 1972. A long,
impressionistic poem built on a collage of quotes from Shackleton,
Cherry-Garrard, Cook, Byrd, and Peary.

———. *Endurance: An Antarctic Idyll*. New York: Atheneum, 1978.
Another long poem ruminating over Shackleton's expedition and
using the same technique as in *Adequate Earth,* but including quotes
from a wider arena. Finkel is the only poet to have been sponsored
by the NSF in the Antarctic. Sadly, both of these books are out of
print.

Freedman, Carl. *Critical Theory and Science Fiction*. Hanover, N.H.:
Wesleyan University Press, 2000. Freedman offers a useful discussion of "cognitive estrangement" as the basis for the genre.

Hoagland, Edward. "I Have Seen the Elephant." In *Tigers and Ice*. New
York: Lyons Press, 1999. Essay about a cruise to the Antarctic Peninsula by one of America's foremost nature writers.

Lenz, William A. *The Poetics of the Antarctic: A Study in Nineteenth-
Century American Cultural Perceptions*. New York: Garland, 1995.

A short, interesting academic study that plots the place of the continent within the context of American exploration and imagination.

Manhire Bill. *My Sunshine*. Wellington, N.Z.: Victoria University Press, 1996.

———. *What to Call Your Child*. Auckland: Random House New Zealand. 1999. Both these books contain Antarctic poems by the first poet laureate of New Zealand.

Mueller, Melinda. *What the Ice Gets: Shackleton's Antarctic Expedition, 1914–1916*. Seattle: Van West, 2000. An extended poetic meditation using extensive quotes from diaries and memoirs, somewhat in the manner of Finkel's work.

Neider, Charles. *Overflight*. Far Hills, N.J.: New Horizon Press, 1986. A novel based on the author's crash in a helicopter flight on Mt. Erebus.

Orsman, Chris. *South*. London: Faber & Faber, 1999. An account in verse of Herbert Ponting's experiences with Scott.

Robinson, Kim Stanley. *Antarctica*. New York: Bantam Books, 1998. A work of speculative fiction about eco-terrorism with numerous sly allusions to real participants in the NSF Artists and Writers Program.

The first book printed on the ice, *Aurora Australis*, was "published at the winter quarters of the British Antarctic Expedition, 1907, during the winter months of April, May, June, July, 1908" as part of the Shackleton expedition. Frank Wild and E. M. Joyce, with only three weeks' training in England by the firm of Sir J. Causton & Sons, Ltd., printed the book by hand letterpress, warming the inking plate over a candle. The book contains stories, poems, and essays, together with nine etchings and lithographs by George Marston. Only ninety copies were made, each hand sewn and bound between boards made from provisions crates, making it the rarest of all Antarctic books.

Examples of work from the annual McMurdo Alternative Art Gallery (MAAG) exhibition can be perused at: www.60south.com.

ART HISTORY (ESPECIALLY DUTCH, ENGLISH,
AND AMERICAN LANDSCAPE PAINTING)

Alpers, Svetlana. *The Art of Describing: Dutch Art in the Seventeenth Century*. Chicago: University of Chicago Press, 1983. Alpers distinguishes between the emblematic aspects of Italian Renaissance art and the more representational images of the Dutch; a key chapter for my purposes is "The Mapping Impulse in Dutch Art."

Andrews, Malcolm. *Landscape and Western Art*. New York: Oxford University Press, 1999.

Baetjer, Katharine. *Glorious Nature: British Landscape Painting, 1750–1850*. New York: Hudson Hills Press, 1993. The catalog of an exhibition of such works found in American collections, therefore doubly interesting, given the English influences in the development of American landscape painting.

Bell, Julian. *What Is Painting? Representation and Modern Art*. New York: Thames & Hudson, 1999.

Carr, Gerald. *The Icebergs*. Dallas: Dallas Museum of Fine Arts, 1980. An excellent review of the iceberg paintings and sketches done by Frederic Edwin Church, including influences on him and his subsequent influence on other artists depicting ice.

Casey, Edward C. *Representing Place: Landscape Painting and Maps*. Minneapolis: University of Minnesota Press, 2002. A philosopher's analysis of the relationships between the two modes of representation in both Western and Eastern traditions.

Farr, Dennis, and William Bradford. *The Northern Landscape*. New York: Hudson Hills Press, 1986. Covers Dutch and English landscape art and the extensive relationships between them.

Gage, John. *J. M. W. Turner: A Wonderful Range of Mind*. New Haven: Yale University Press, 1987. Perhaps the most interesting book on Turner because it covers not only his art but also his intellect and its context.

Jacobs, Michael. *The Painted Voyage: Art, Travel, and Exploration, 1564–1875*. London: British Museum Press, 1998. A readable and well-illustrated account of how art, science, and travel coincided during much of the first and second eras of exploration. It is particularly strong on William Hodges, and useful to read in combination with Daston and Park (see below).

Janssen, Paul Hays, and Peter C. Sutton. *The Hoogsteder Exhibition of Dutch Landscapes.* The Hague: Hoogsteder & Hoogsteder, 1991. The essays in this catalog on the history and the patronage and collecting of Dutch landscape paintings are of great value.

McGregor, Alasdair. *Mawson's Huts: An Antarctic Expedition Journal.* Alexandria, N.S.W., Austr.: Hale & Iremonger, 1998. This narrative by an Australian artist of the 1997–1998 expedition to restore Mawson's huts contains color reproductions of photographs and paintings of the historic location.

Slive, Seymour. *Dutch Painting, 1600–1800.* New Haven: Yale University Press, 1995. One of several major treatments of the subject, this splendid art history features a lucid text and excellent reproductions.

Townsend, Richard P. *J. M. W. Turner, "That Greatest of Landscape Painters."* Tulsa, Okla.: Philbrook Museum of Art, in association with University of Washington Press, 1998. Exhibition catalog that traces the influence Turner had on Thomas Moran, which encourages parallels to be drawn with the Antarctic work of Edward Wilson.

Walker, John. *Turner.* New York: Harry N. Abrams, 1983. A standard primer on the artist.

Westermann, Mariet. *A Worldly Art: The Dutch Republic, 1585–1718.* New York: Prentice-Hall, 1996. A compact overview of art and commerce during the Golden Age.

Wilford, John. *Jacob van Ruisdael and the Perception of Landscape.* New Haven: Yale University Press, 1991.

CARTOGRAPHY AND THE HISTORY OF EXPLORATION

Boorstin, Daniel J. *The Discoverers.* New York: Random House, 1983. Boorstin's book, though very much in the "great man" historiographical mode, remains the definitive popular account of worldwide exploration; an immensely informed and readable tome, it places exploration in the cultural context of information and feedback, which in turn helps explain where Stephen Pyne is standing.

Cosgrove, Denis. Ed. *Mappings*. London: Reaktion Books, 1999. This wide-ranging collection of essays on cartography is helpful in tracing how art and mapping have been linked in exploration. Of particular interest are Lucia Nuti's essay "Mapping Places," and "Mapping Tropical Waters" by Luciana de Lima Martins.

de Vries, Dirk. "Dutch Maritime Cartography in the Seventeenth Century: Chartmaking Is the Power and Glory of the Country." In *Mirror of Empire: Dutch Marine Art of the Seventeenth Century,* edited by George Keyes. Minneapolis: Minneapolis Institute of Arts; Cambridge: Cambridge University Press, 1990.

du Jourdin, Michel Mollat, and Monique de la Ronciere. *Sea Charts of the Early Explorers, 13th to 17th Century*. London: Thames & Hudson, 1984. No better way exists to grasp the intersections of science, art, and visual culture than by examining the portolan charts made during the Age of Exploration. This beautifully illustrated history is an easy way to begin.

Goetzmann, William H. *Army Exploration in the American West, 1803–1863.* New Haven: Yale University Press, 1959.

———. *Exploration and Empire: The Explorer and the Scientist in the Winning of the American West.* New York: Alfred A. Knopf, 1966.

———. *New Lands, New Men: America and the Second Great Age of Discovery.* New York: Viking Penguin, 1986. This now-classic trilogy of books on the history of American exploration slowly widens outward from a focused study on the U.S. Army Corps of Topographical Engineers to encompass the history of Western expansionism itself. Goetzmann, who was an important mentor to Stephen Pyne, always insisted on analyzing the works of the artists, as well as the scientists, accompanying the explorers.

Harley, J. B., and David Woodward, editors. *The History of Cartography*. Vol. 1, book 1. Chicago: University of Chicago Press, 1992. This ongoing multivolume series is the definitive history of cartography in English, starting with maplike markings in the Paleolithic and moving forward through Islamic mapmaking in the Mediterranean, among other topics.

Karrow, Robert W. *Mapmakers of the Sixteenth Century and Their Maps.* Winnetka, Ill.: Speculum Orbis Press, 1993.

Larsgaard, Mary Lynette. *Topographic Mapping of Africa, Antarctica, and Eurasia.* Provo, Utah: Western Association of Map Libraries, 1993. Contains a short history of cartography in Antarctica in the twentieth century.

Law, Phillip. *Antarctic Cartography.* Australia: Antarctic Division of the Department of External Affairs, 1958. Reprinted from the March 1957 issue of *Cartography,* the journal of the Australian Institute of Cartographers.

McIntosh, Gregory C. *The Piri Reis Map of 1513.* Athens: University of Georgia Press, 2000. This is the most current and sober evaluation of the map, a stunning achievement in Islamic and Renaissance cartography that may propose a coastline for a southern continent.

Ryan, Simon. "Inscribing the Emptiness: Cartography, Exploration, and the Construction of Australia." In *De-Scribing Empire: Post-Colonialism and Textuality,* edited by Chris Tiffin and Alan Lawson. New York: Routledge, 1994.

Silberman, Robert, editor. *World Views: Maps and Art.* Minneapolis: University of Minnesota Press, 2000. An exhibition catalog with an essay by Yi-Fu Tuan, "Maps and Art: Identify and Utopia," that is very worthwhile.

Smith, Bernard. *European Vision and the South Pacific.* 2d ed. New Haven: Yale University Press, 1988. A thorough account of how the exploration of the region helped shift scientific culture from creationism to natural selection, as manifested in the art and literature of exploration.

Thrower, Norman J. W. *Maps in Civilization: Cartography in Culture and Society.* Chicago: University of Chicago Press, 1996.

Wilford, John Noble. *The Mapmakers.* New York: Random House, 1981. This deservedly popular history of cartographers presents the complexities of its topic in admirably clear terms. It also contains a concise overview of cartography during the twentieth century, as well as a valuable chapter on mapping the Antarctic.

Woodward, David. *Art and Cartography: Six Historical Essays*. Chicago: University of Chicago Press, 1987.

COGNITION, VISUAL CULTURE, AND LANDSCAPE THEORY

Allman, John. *Evolving Brains*. New York: Scientific American Press, 2000. A notable book strong on systems of visual cognition.

Appleton, Jay. *The Experience of Landscape*. New York: John Wiley, 1975; rev. ed. 1996. An early author to propose a "habitat theory" for our preferences in landscape, Appleton catalogs a wide range of cognitive responses to land and art.

Barrow, John D. *The Artful Universe*. New York: Oxford University Press, 1995. Barrow tackles the relationships between evolution and our perceptual systems as they are manifested in art and science.

Clair, Jean. Editor. *Cosmos: From Romanticism to the Avant-Garde*. Munich: Prestel-Verlag, 1999. This superbly illustrated catalog of an exhibition traces the interrelationships between science and art in representing the world, from Humboldt to Hubble and the NASA missions.

Crosby, Alfred W. *The Measure of Reality: Quantification and Western Society, 1250–1600*. Cambridge: Cambridge University Press, 1997. An examination of how objective and systemized measurements enabled exploration and imperialism.

Daston, Lorraine and Katherine Park. *Wonders and the Order of Nature*. New York: Zone Books, 1998. A perceptive history of the changing identity of wonder, from fear through curiosity to experience of the sublime.

Dissanayake, Ellen. *Homo Aestheticus: Where Does Art Come From and Why?* Seattle: University of Washington Press, 1995. A seminal book in the anthropology of art.

Gee, Henry. *In Search of Deep Time*. New York: Free Press, 1999. A popular account of cladistics, a theory of biology that defends the unknowability of evolutionary particulars in the far past.

Haeckel, Ernst. *Art Forms in Nature*. Munich: Prestel-Verlag, 1998. The introductory essay by Irenäus Eibl-Eibesfeldt, "Ernst Haeckel—The Artist in the Scientist," discusses studies of genetic dispositions in the human preference for certain kinds of landscapes over others, and explains how the discoveries of the *Challenger* expedition influenced this nineteenth-century artist/naturalist.

Hoffman, Donald D. *Visual Intelligence*. New York: W. W. Norton, 1998. A primer on how we physically construct reality through vision.

Jakle, John A. *The Visual Elements of Landscape*. Amherst: University of Massachusetts Press, 1987. A somewhat dry compendium outlining how we perceive and build cognitive maps of landscapes.

Kinsey, Joni Louise. *Thomas Moran and the Surveying of the American West*. Washington, D.C.: Smithsonian Institution, 1992. A comprehensive analysis of how government, exploration, and economic interests intersect in art, using Moran's paintings of Yellowstone, the Grand Canyon, and the Mountain of the Holy Cross as evidence.

Klonk, Charlotte. *Science and the Perception of Nature: British Landscape Art in the Late Eighteenth and Early Nineteenth Centuries*. New Haven: Yale University Press, 1996. A discussion of the rise of phenomenalism in the art and science of the time.

Mithin, Steven. *The Prehistory of Mind: The Cognitive Origins of Art and Science*. London: Thames & Hudson, 1996. The author, an archeologist, uses physical evidence to provide a thorough and provocative overview of the evolution of human intelligence. He proposes that art, science, and religion developed out of our mind's modern ability to create analogy and metaphor.

Novak, Barbara. *Nature and Culture: American Landscape and Painting, 1852–1875*. Oxford: Oxford University Press, 1995. The definitive study of the concatenation in art of economics, politics, science, religion, and exploration in nineteenth-century America. It is essential reading for anyone wishing to understand how we define and represent nature, and why we send artists on expeditions.

Pinker, Steven. *How the Mind Works*. New York: W. W. Norton, 1997. Pinker describes how human evolution has shaped cognition in this large summary of his thinking to date.

Solso, Robert L. *Cognition and the Visual Arts*. Cambridge, Mass.: MIT Press, 1994. An exploration of the neurobiological basis for our perception of art.

Stafford, Barbara Maria. *Voyage into Substance: Art, Science, Nature, and the Illustrated Travel Account, 1760–1840*. Cambridge, Mass.: MIT Press, 1984. Crosscutting through its subtitled topics, this first book by one of America's preeminent visual theorists is exemplary in its thoroughness, though Stafford is never light reading.

———. *Good Looking: Essays on the Virtue of Images*. Cambridge, Mass.: MIT Press, 1996. Stafford urges that we redefine literacy to encompass not just reading but also seeing, arguing persuasively that we need more sophisticated ways to summarize and digest information in an increasingly computerized environment. Scientific visuals and the arts are key to her argument.

Tuan, Yi-Fu. *Topophilia: A Study of Environmental Perception, Attitudes, and Values*. New York: Columbia University Press, 1974. Tuan is the acknowledged authority on how human beings organize their minds and bodies within the physical world.

———. *Space and Place: The Perspective of Experience*. Minneapolis: University of Minnesota Press, 1977.

Wilson, Edward O. *Consilience: The Unity of Knowledge*. New York: Alfred A. Knopf, 1998. Wilson is the controversial progenitor of sociobiology, a multidisciplinary field that searches through all the sciences for keys to understanding our behavior. Reading Wilson with Barrow, Mithin, Pinker, and Solso will provide a general view of how our perceptions are related to the environment.

Wilson, Robert A., and Frank C. Keil, editors. *The MIT Encyclopedia of Cognitive Sciences*. Cambridge, Mass.: MIT Press, 1999.

Woodring, Carl. *Nature into Art: Cultural Transformations in Nineteenth-Century Britain*. Cambridge, Mass.: Harvard University Press, 1989.

Rich, dense, and interdisciplinary, this sometimes obtuse book traces the divorce of art and science during the nineteenth century, as art became more and more a subject of self-reflexive contemplation.

Information on the research and paintings of Komar & Melamid can be found on the Web at www.diacenter.org/km/, which contains information on both their original "People's Choice" project and "The Most Wanted Paintings on the Web," a piece commissioned by the host, Dia Art Foundation. The site provides the questions asked, tabulated responses, and the resulting most and least wanted pictures from fourteen countries.

THE ARCTIC

The two poles are, like exploration and art, linked inseparably in fact and imagination, a fact that is reflected in the literature about them. The following books about the northern high latitudes have influenced my writing about Antarctica.

Arms, Myron. *The Riddle of the Ice*. New York: Anchor Books, 1998. The author's quest to understand why his sailboat was blocked by unexpectedly heavy sea ice in the Labrador Sea becomes a splendid scientific voyage that illustrates how the polar regions are linked by ocean currents and climates.

Barrett, Andrea. *The Voyage of the Narwhal*. New York: W. W. Norton, 1998. As a sort of imaginative counterpart to the quest of Myron Arms, and one that sails through some of the same waters, Barrett's fictional account concerns a nineteenth-century expedition searching for the Franklin Expedition and a northwest passage. Crossover and contrast with Antarctic experiences are numerous.

Bolles, Edmund Blair. *The Ice Finders: How a Poet, a Professor, and a Politician Discovered the Ice Age*. New York: Counterpoint Press, 1999. A compact account of how glaciology arose as an accepted scientific discipline.

Houston, C. Stuart, editor. *Arctic Artist: The Journal and Paintings of*

George Back, Midshipman with Franklin, 1819–1822. Montreal: McGill-Queen's University Press, 1995. Back's pictures from Franklin's first arctic voyage were important in shaping the aesthetic responses to polar exploration during the nineteenth century.

Kane, Elisha Kent. *Arctic Explorations in the Years 1853, '54, '55.* Philadelphia: Childs & Peterson, 1856. A definitive example not only of nineteenth-century Arctic literature, but of exploration literature as a whole.

Kugler, Richard C. *William Bradford: Sailing Ships and Arctic Seas.* New Bedford, Mass.: New Bedford Whaling Museum, 2003. A well-illustrated catalog that documents how artistic imagery of the Arctic developed in the United States during the nineteenth century.

Lopez, Barry. *Arctic Dreams: Imagination and Desire in a Northern Landscape.* New York: Scribner, 1986. As Stephen Pyne's *The Ice* is my favorite book about Antarctica, so this is my favorite book about the Arctic. Lopez is eloquent and wide-ranging in his writing, covering the carvings of the Inuit, caribou migrations, and the intrepid, if sometimes foolish, forays of Arctic explorers.

Savours, Ann. *The Search for the North West Passage.* New York: St. Martin's Press, 1999. Ann Savours Shirley, a respected British authority on polar exploration, has gathered together with her typical thoroughness and sensitivity the artworks as well as the diaries of the key expeditions that shaped the nineteenth-century imagination about ice, be it north or south. Read it in combination with Barrett's novel mentioned above.

MISCELLANEOUS

Cockell, Charles. *Impossible Extinction: Natural Catastrophes and the Supremacy of the Microbial World.* Cambridge: Cambridge University Press, 2003. Cockell, who has worked with the British Antarctic Survey in the Antarctic and with NASA in the Arctic, examines the ubiquity of microbes in extreme environments.

Lambert, D. M., et al. "Rates of Evolution in Ancient DNA from
Adélie Penguins." *Science* 295 (March 22, 2002): 2270–2273.

Minnaert, M. G. J. *Light and Color in the Outdoors.* New York: Springer-
Verlag, 1993. A solar scientist working in Belgium, Marcel Minnaert
compiled this authoritative catalog of visual atmospheric phenomena over a lifetime. The book is essential to understanding why the
atmosphere appears as it does in polar regions.

Shepheard, Paul. *The Cultivated Wilderness; or, What Is Landscape?* Cambridge, Mass.: MIT Press, 1997. An illuminating series of medita-
tions on how we transform land into landscape; the section "Hope"
regards Antarctica through several lenses: history, economics, and
tourism.

Protection of the Antarctic environment is governed by a series of acts
and protocols that can be found in *Antarctic Conservation Act of 1978*
(Arlington, Va.: National Science Foundation, October 1995). The publication contains the complete text of public laws 95–541, as well as the
Protocol on Environmental Protection to the Antarctic Treaty, adopted
in Madrid, Spain, in 1991.

INDEX

Ablation, 37–38
Absolute Zero, 122
Académie Royale des Sciences, 59
Academies, establishment of scientific, 59
Adams, Ansel, 29, 240–41
Adventurers, problems with vision and, 19–20
Aethalometers, 162, 164–65
Agassiz, Louis, 140–42, 153
Agate, Alfred T., 146–47
Ainley, David, 257
Airdevronsix (VXE) Icefalls, 30–31, 245, plate 4
Air Force Technical Applications Center (AFTAC), 33–35
Airplanes, use of, during Heroic Age of exploration, 195–97
Air tourism, 217
Alexander, James, 154–55
Alexander, Steve, 272
Algae, 65–67, 272
Alpers, Svetlana, 95
American landscape photography, 240–42
Amundsen, Roald, 1, 181, 182; completion of Northwest Passage by, 58; documentation of expeditions of, 187; expedition to South Pole by, 186; race to South Pole by, 109–10
Amundsen-Scott South Pole Station, 110
Anaximander, 47, 60
Antarctic: administration of, 35; algae on, 65–67; American research facilities in,

69; describing, 36; discovery of first fossil on, 146; early American explorations of, 146; early mapmaking efforts of, 26–27, 52–53; early maps of, 55; first book printed on, 212–14; first sightings of, 145–46; geographical size of, 1; insects in, 272–73; lack of visual cues in, 19–22; lichens on, 66; *mappa mundi* and, 55; mapping of, 235–39; microbes in, 88; moss on, 63; mythology of, as lost world, 214; named as *Terra Incognita* by Ptolemy, 48; portolan charts and, 50; role of New Zealand in administration of, 243–44; sovereign rights over, 199; tarns on, 66–67; tourism in, 175–76, 217, 253; United Kingdom and, 243–44; volcanoes on, 223; weather reports in, 3; whalers and, 181. *See also* Explorations, Antarctic
Antarctic Arts Fellows, 240
Antarctic Muon and Neutrino Detector Array (AMANDA), 126–27
Antarctic Treaty, 5, 72, 131, 166, 176, 301
Antarctic Visiting Artists and Writers Program, 154, 240
Anthony, Jason, 180
Aquarium, in Crary Laboratory, 134
Arab cartographers, 49
Arago, Dominique, 195
Aristotle, 47
Arrhenius, Svante August, 192

Orsman, Chris, 248–49
Ortelius, Abraham, 54–55
O'Sullivan, Timothy, 153, 235
Our Lady of the Snows Shrine, 86–87, *plate 10*

Paige, David I., 197–99, 234
Painters: American *vs.* other countries, 245–48
Paintings, on McMurdo station, 80. *See also* Art; Landscape paintings
Palais, Julie, 121, 124
Palmer, Nathaniel, 145
Panoramas, 144–45
Parkinson, Sydney, 60, 100
Parmenides, 47
Parry, Edward, 143
Peale, Titian Ramsey, 146–47
Peary, Robert, 182
Penguins, 32, 166–67, 256–57
Perspective, 54; the Dutch and, 56–67
Photogammetry, 199
Photographers, 240–43; first deployment of, in explorations, 153
Photographs: of early expeditions, 187; use of, to depict landscapes, 153. *See also* Art
Photography: American landscape, 240–42; as dominant art medium, 240; importance of, for R. F. Scott, 8; for landscapes, 158; McMurdo station and, 84. *See also* Art
Pilots, cognitive dissonance and, 161–62
Pissarro, Camille, 157
Pleneau, Paul, 187
Pliny the Elder, 209
Poe, Edgar Allan, 211
Ponds, 66–67, 85, 272
Ponting, Herbert, 8, 18, 153, 187–89, *plate 2*
Porter, Eliot, 29, 205, 241; photographs of Bull Pass by, 36
Portolan charts, 49–50
Preuss, Charles, 195, 235
Priscu, John, 163–64, 172
Profiles, coastal, 51
Ptolemy, Claudius, 48, 49, 56, 59, 235

Pyne, Stephen, 10, 83, 250–51, 254
Pythagoras, 47

Radarsat, 238
Ray, Charles "Chas," 4, 11, 12
Raymond, James, 87
Raytheon, 35, 73
Reines, Frederick, 126
Re'is, Piri, 51–52, 52
Religion, on McMurdo station, 86–87
Reynolds, Jeremiah, 211
Reynolds, Sir Joshua, 105
Rhone Glacier, 170
Roberts, Henry, 93
Robinson, Kim Stanley, 174, 217–18, , *plate 15*
Robinson, Stan, 274
Rolland, Stacey, 79, 259–60
Rosenthal, David, 246, *plates 4, 22, and 40*
Ross, James Clark, 144, 149, 152, 180–81, 209–10; explorations of Antarctic by, 147–48
Ross, John, 143–45; discovery of magnetic North Pole by, 144–45
Ross Dependency, 244
Ross Ice Shelf, 180–81, 184, 185, 244, *plate 21*
Ross Island, 1, 5
Ross Sea, 144
Rowatt, Stephanie, *plate 18*
Rowell, Galen, 20, 84
Royal academies, establishment of, 59
Royal Society, 59, 93, 142
Royal Society Range, 15
Runways, at South Pool and McMurdo station, 128
Ruskin, John, 157, 241

Samach, Ralph, 81–83, 85
Sameshima, Haru, *plate 11*
Scaniello, Jeff, 4
Schimper, Karl, 141
Schulthess, Emil, 203, 241
Schweichart, Rusty, 84
Scientific academies, establishment of, 59
Score, Robbie, 36, 172
Scoresby, William, 143

Scott, Jim, 69–72, 76, 187
Scott, Robert Falcon, 1, 31, 62, 110, 140, 180,
    181, 273; bungalow of, 4–5; discovery of
    Dry Valleys by, 32; failed race to Pole by
    9; first expedition of, 184–85; history's
    changing views of, 13; importance of
    photography for, 8; race to South Pole
    by, 109; *Terra Nova* hut of, 6, 7–8, *plate 1*;
    1902 trip to, 7; 1911 trip to, 7
Scott Base, 244
Sculptors, 248–49
Sea atlases, 56
Seaver, George, 185
Second Age of Discovery, 204
Sella, Vittorio, 241
Senbergs, Jan, 249
Seuss Glacier, 173–74, *plate 23*
Sewage facilities, 73
Shackleton, Ernest, 1, 7, 180, 181, 182–83,
    190–91, 213, *plate 40*; investigation of
    Dry Valleys by, 32; race to South Pole
    by, 109; second expedition of, 185–86
Shapley, Harlo, 194
Shipley, William, 96
Sight. *See* Vision
Siple, Paul, 131
Sixth International Geographical
    Congress, 181
Skelton, Reginald, 185
Sleeping bags, 9
Sletten, Ron, 261, 264, 266–268, 270
Smith, Bernard, 97
Smith, David, 247
Smith, Isaac, 93
Smith, S. Percy, 99
Smith, William, 140
Snowstorm painting, 155
Society for the Encouragement of Arts,
    Manufactures, and Commerce, 96
Socrates, 47
Solomon, Susan, 13
Somerville, Mary, 156
Sorlien, Sandy, 252, *plate 37*
South Pole, 107–8, *plates 16 and 18*;
    Amundsen-Scott Station at, 110; Dark
    Sector at, 121–22; geodesic dome at,
    111–14, 119; greenhouse at, 117; halos

of, 128–29; mirror spheres at, 130–32;
    new station at, 118–20; panorama at,
    plate 3; race to reach, 108–10; runways
    at, 128; science projects at, 121–28;
    tunneling project at, 115–18
South Pole Clean Air Facility, 129
Spain, Rae, 175, 177, 263
Specimen collecting, 134–36
Sporing, Herman, 60
Sprawl, McMurdo station and, 83–84
Springtails, 272–73
Stokstad, Robert, *plate 16*
Storage yards, on McMurdo station,
    71–72
Stroud, Mike, 19
Sullivan, Walter, 204
Surrealism, 194–95
Survival, contour recognition and, 19–20
Sutton, William, *plates 1 7, 9, 22, and 25*
Symmes, John, 211

Tank farm, on McMurdo station, 71
Tarns, 66
Tasman, Abel, 58
Tasmania, 58; Dutch discovery of, 58
Taylor, Griffith, 32
Taylor Glacier, 167–70, 170
Taylor Valley, 162, 176, 238–39, *plate 24*
Te Aru-tanga-Nuku, 99
Telephone poles, 75–76
Terra Icognita, 50; Ptolemy's name for
    Antarctica, 48
Terra Nova hut (Scott's), 6, 7–8
Thales of Miletus, 46–47, 60
Thermal illusions, 17–18
Third Age of Discovery, 204
Thompson, Nainoa, 100
Thompson, Seton, 185
Tides, 65
Tierra del Fuego, 53, 58
Topographical art: development of, 95–
    96; as navigational devices, 197. *See also*
    Maps
Topography, 56; in landscape art, 104–6
T-O scheme, for maps, 49
Tourism, 253; air, 217; in Antarctic,
    175–76